RETURN of the BUFFALO

The willful slaughter by European immigrants of the Buffalo was intended to destroy the economy of America's indigenous population. Much of the killing had little to do with the animal's hide, meat or horns; it had a great deal to do with intentionally reducing the Native American population to a state of abject dependency.

One Native prophecy envisioned the return of the Buffalo. Metaphorically, the return of the Buffalo meant a return to economic independence. Many tribes today view Indian gaming, the operation of gambling casinos on formerly barren reservation lands, as their return of the Buffalo.

This is the story of the Cabazon Band of Mission Indians, the tribe whose U.S. Supreme Court victory in 1987 made Indian "Gaming" legal on reservations across the country, and whose former sand and rock reservation has bloomed in the California desert.

In little more than a dozen years this small tribe has moved from dependency to economic independence. This is also the story of their relationship with a revolutionary, socialist "radical" non-indian, John Philip Nichols, and his family—another "tribe" of sorts—and their successful and inspiring journey together through the minefields of bigotry, slander, yellow journalism and official sabotage, strewn by the philosophical descendants of those 19th century Buffalo killers.

RETURN of the BUFFALO

THE STORY BEHIND AMERICA'S INDIAN GAMING EXPLOSION

Ambrose I. Lane, Sr.

Forewords by Esteban E. Torres
and Terry L. Pechota

BERGIN & GARVEY
Westport, Connecticut • London

Every reasonable effort has been made to trace the owners of copyright materials in this book, but in some instances this has proven impossible. The author and publisher will be glad to receive information leading to more complete acknowledgments in subsequent printings of the book and in the meantime extend their apologies for any omissions.

Paperback cover photograph of Chief Hervasio Cabezon from the collection of the Smithsonian Institution, Washington, D.C.

Library of Congress Cataloging-in-Publication Data

Lane, Ambrose I.
Return of the buffalo : the story behind America's Indian gaming explosion / Ambrose I. Lane, Sr. ; forewords by Esteban E. Torres and Terry L. Pechota.
p. cm.
Includes bibliographical references and index.
ISBN 0–89789–432–4 (alk. paper). — ISBN 0–89789–433–2 (pbk. : alk. paper)
1. Cahuilla Indians—Government relations. 2. Cahuilla Indians—Finance. 3. Cabazon Indian Reservation (Calif.) 4. Gambling on Indian reservations. 5. Nichols, John P. (John Philip). 1924– .
I. Title.
E99.C155L35 1995
973'.04974—dc20 95–11677

British Library Cataloguing in Publication Data is available.

Library of Congress Catalog Card Number: 95–11677
ISBN: 0–89789–432–4
0–89789–433–2 (pbk.)

First published in 1995

Bergin & Garvey, 88 Post Road West, Westport, CT 06881
An imprint of Greenwood Publishing Group, Inc.

Printed in the United States of America

The paper used in this book complies with the Permanent Paper Standard issued by the National Information Standards Organization (Z39.48–1984).

10 9 8 7 6 5 4 3 2 1

Contents

Foreword

This important book impacts us on a number of levels and is in effect "a story within a story within a story."

The first story carefully documents a phase of the struggle by the Cabazon Band of Mission Indians to achieve economic self-sufficiency. This step-by-step chronology of the process serves as a textbook for those seeking similar goals. It is a remarkable chapter in the survival story of a Native American tribe that has confronted the pattern, unfortunately characteristic of the treatment of natives by invading cultures: deliberate de-culturation, hostility, disease, neglect and destruction.

The next story is about a remarkable, some would say controversial, family of strong individuals: the Nicholses, and about what happened when they began working with the Tribe.

The third story is an admitted effort to "tell the truth . . . and set the record straight" about the Tribe's climb out of poverty. This is an effort to counter what Mr. Lane characterizes as "savage attacks . . . sleazy innuendoes . . . and hatchet jobs" done on the Tribe by the media and by opponents of the progress that was achieved over this past decade.

Finally, there is the story about how "gaming" came onto the reservation and why this activity is important to the growth, survival and self-sufficiency of the Tribe.

The stories do not end here. In no way is it a final-chapter, ride-off-into-the-sunset kind of book, for there are gathering storm clouds of opposition building against the Tribe's newly won economic and cultural independence.

I have a feeling that the Cabazon Band of Mission Indians will overcome this current wave of opposition, because I sense the swing of the pendulum of history away from the destruction, exploitation, and death that has been their most recent legacy. Ambrose Lane said it best: "The Cabazon Band of Mission Indians has traversed the bridge that leads from nothingness to victory, from addiction to sobriety, and from hope to realization of dreams . . . the secret ingredient was unity at the core, the center, the moral center that demanded honor, and that always produced unity at the core . . . sufficient to be victorious."

I urge you to read this remarkable, albeit unfinished, American success saga.

Representative Esteban E. Torres (D-34th District CA)

Foreword

Terry L. Pechota is an enrolled member of the Rosebud Sioux Tribe and was raised on the Rosebud Indian Reservation. He graduated Cum Laude from Black Hills State College in 1969 and from the University of Iowa Law School in 1972. After becoming an attorney, he was director of Rosebud Legal Services on the Rosebud Indian Reservation, U.S. Attorney for South Dakota, and a staff attorney for the Native American Rights Fund. Mr. Pechota currently practices Indian law with the law firm of Viken, Viken, Pechota, Leach & Dewell in Rapid City, South Dakota.

Anyone with a general knowledge of the history of Indian tribes in the United States understands the adversity and struggles they have experienced since the arrival of the White man upon this continent long ago. The effort of Indian tribes to avoid the extinction and demise of their members has been stymied by a long history of fluctuating governmental policy, most notably that which envisioned the termination of tribes and the assimilation of their members, the destruction of culture and land base, and most recently the curtailment and erosion of tribal sovereignty in the courts and by legislation. The struggle for tribes continues. In this historical and captivating book by Ambrose Lane, we find the true story of a small tribe that has hurdled the often insurmountable obstacles placed in its way to become a showcase of economic development.

The Cabazon Band of Mission Indians, about which Lane writes, is a remarkable tribe that, as a result of various negotiations and treaties by the White man, was left with only a small fraction of land that it had originally owned. Lane tells the history of the Tribe from the 1960s and especially how it has, sometimes alone and always at the vanguard, taken the steps and fought the battles brilliantly in court and the halls of Congress to build on the opportunity that gaming offered to a desert tribe for economic development and the cultural betterment of its members.

A not insignificant part of the success of the Cabazon Tribe was due to the initiative, foresight and perseverance of John Philip Nichols and his family. Lane tells the story well. A long time ago in Albuquerque, New Mexico, I had the good fortune to strike an acquaintance that has lasted many years with John Philip Nichols and his late wife, Joann. To say that Nichols and his wife were activists is an understatement. To say they were a team would not be emphatic enough. They had dedicated their lives to betterment of the common man, those who too often are forgotten, and were at that time beginning their efforts with the Cabazon Tribe that has ultimately resulted in the Tribe becoming one of the most prosperous in the United States. With the guidance, advice, and service of the Nichols family, now including his able sons, the Tribe capitalized on the opportunity offered by gaming and built a team that has made the Tribe a leader in Indian gaming development in this country. As Lane points out, this successful effort has not been without heartaches both to the Tribe and the Nichols family. But as anyone knowing the mettle of John Philip Nichols would expect, all has ultimately resulted in good for the Tribe and for his family.

Any tribe or individual who has any interest in the development of Indian gaming or the economic development of Indian tribes should make this book a must reading. More tribes should record their history, not only in the past but also in these later years. Lane's book is a good one to emulate.

Terry L. Pechota

Preface

The American Indians' fight for the right to live their own way of life amid laws serving White European values has been waged from the beginning against the worst of human weaknesses: greed and self-serving misperception.

Indigenous to the land where oppressed Europeans sought to govern themselves according to man's "inalienable rights" to religious freedom, equality and the pursuit of happiness, Native Americans first welcomed the Europeans to their land. But the Indians soon found, as would other men of color later on, that they were not to be part of this new government. The inalienable rights so cherished by these Europeans would not be accorded the Indians in peaceful co-habitation, simply because to the Europeans, Indians could not be looked upon as men.

In the 18th century, certain influential European men of letters took it upon themselves to recount in vivid detail their incredible observations concerning the native people in "discovered America." In 1768 and 69 one such man, the Abbé Corneille de Pauw—an early favorite of none other than Frederick the Great—wrote two volumes titled *Philosophical Investigations of the Americans,* and a subsequent third volume in which he described his horror at the Pope's acceptance of the Indians as men. The Indians' "constitution is weak," he said. "Their stature is smaller than that of Europeans. At first they were taken not for men, but for orangutans, or big monkeys, that could be destroyed without remorse or reproach. Then, to add ridicule to calamity, a Pope issued a Papal Bull in which he declared that, as he wished to establish Bishoprics in the richest countries of America it pleased him and the Holy Spirit to recognize Americans as 'true men. . . .' Without this decision . . . the inhabitants of the New World would still today be, in the eyes of the faithful, a race of dubious animals."

In their book *Was America A Mistake?* historians Henry Steele Commager and Elmo Giordanetti cite these passages as well as others from European scholars during the same period, including the Abbé Guillaume Thomas François Raynal, whom they refer to as "one of the most prominent figures of his century." According to these historians, Raynal wrote "one of the great books of the age," *A Philosophical and Political History of the Settlements and Trade of Europeans in the Two Indies,* from which they cite these quotations:

The men [Native Americans] had less strength and less courage, no beard and no hair; they have less appearances of manhood, and are but little susceptible of the lively and powerful sentiment of love. . . . Men who have little more hair than eunuchs cannot abound in generating principles. The blood of these people is watery and cold. The males have sometimes milk in their breasts.

Regarding this latter phenomenon [men with milk in their breasts], fellow scholar de Pauw agreed and had the answer to this anomaly:

I am persuaded that humidity of temperament in the inhabitants of the New World caused this defect . . . [making men] more like women, more cowardly, more timid, and more afraid of the dark . . . [milk in their breasts] must be brought about by the humidity in which the embryo is enveloped in the uterus, which prevents the bile from turning sour and from extravasating enough to render the chyle sanguineous.

If some of the more "learned" and "scholarly" Europeans held such beliefs, can it be surprising that America, when first inhabited by Europeans, became a *Killing Field*? That the invading "discoverers" of America wreaked mass slaughter on the people they found here is no longer in question, only the extent of the near-complete genocide. And the slaughter was opposed by few of the European invaders who called themselves Christians and claimed a noble mission of Christianizing the Native American "heathens" and "savages."

In his book *Land Grab*, John Tipton Terrell describes how in the fall of 1874, less than 100 years after de Pauw and Raynal published their works, former Christian minister Colonel John M. Chivington led a large force of Colorado Volunteers in the slaughter of peaceful sleeping Cheyenne and Arapahos. Terrell reported that his soldiers:

1. Murdered at least two hundred men, women and children. The number may have been much greater, for reports were conflicting. Investigators sent to the scene expressed the opinion that as many as four hundred had been slain.
2. Raped wounded squaws before killing them, then amputated their fingers, arms and ears to obtain rings, necklaces and other souvenirs.
3. Knocked out the brains of little children.
4. Cut out the private parts of both men and women and took them to Denver to be exhibited to the public.
5. Under an order from Chivington, scalped nearly all victims.
6. The colonel boasted that no prisoners had been taken. He was fully aware of the

identity of the Indians, knew that they had signed a treaty of peace and that they had been promised protection by military authorities.

A leading Denver newspaper of the day toasted Chivington and his troopers as heroes, stating "Among the brilliant feats of arms in Indian warfare, the recent campaign of our Colorado Volunteers will stand in history with few rivals, and none to exceed it in final results. . . . All acquitted themselves well, and Colorado soldiers have again covered themselves with glory."

This book is about one tribe of Native Americans, the Cabazon Band of Mission Indians. They were a part of the larger Cahuilla Tribe in Southern California, who, although located within the mission area established by Spanish invaders in the 1770s, were always free. They were never among the de facto slaves forced to build the 21 Spanish missions the length of California, many of which are still standing.

The Cabazons are brothers, however, to those who during 65 years of Spanish rule endured the suffering and almost total destruction of their native way of life. Records show only 29,000 births to 62,000 deaths among the Cahuillas during those years. The conditions perpetrated upon the Mission Indians by their captors, as related in one report by the Bureau of Indian Affairs, were without redemption:

Disease ran rampant in the compounds. In their hopelessness and suffering, Indian mothers were known to have smothered their babies at birth rather than condemn them to live such an existence. More insidious was the mass psychological depression that overtook the Mission Indians. They lost, as a race, the will to survive.

With the decline of the native population and its effect upon the labor supply, the Missions became, economically, a liability and were considered to have failed. They were abandoned in 1834, and the survivors of many Mission bands [now dependent upon their captors] soon perished. Bereft by mission training of inherited skills, with few vestiges of their old social structure to sustain them, they were the victims of starvation, disease and the Anglo-American massacres which were soon to follow.

Records show that when the United States took over California in 1848, an estimated 110,000 Native Americans lived there. By the end of the century only an estimated 17,000 remained alive, and a report of the Commissioner of Indian Affairs showed only 15,283 by 1890.

The Cabazons, to whom this book is dedicated, were among the victims of these massacres. When the United States acquired California through the signing of the Treaty of Guadalupe Hidalgo with Mexico, it had agreed to preserve recognition of the rights of Native Americans to their inherited lands. But when California became a state, two years after the 1848 discovery of gold at Sutter's Mill, more than 200,000 fortune-seekers flooded the state. These newcomers and their elected officials opposed ownership or even possession by Indians of any of their inherited lands thought to have any mineral value. To try to bring peace, President

Millard Fillmore sent three commissioners to negotiate a "just and equitable settlement with the Indians of California." Within a year, the commissioners met with 402 Indian leaders and executed 18 treaties as well as one supplemental treaty, which together became known as the Barbour Treaties, named after Commissioner G. S. Barbour.

Wanting nothing more than to be left to their own way of life, the Indians settled for guaranteed rights of perpetual use and occupancy of reservations totaling 8,815,900 acres, in return for their relinquishment of all rights and title to California land they already occupied. In addition to acreage, the chiefs were promised other specified goods and supplies, tools, livestock, clothing, services and educational support, and were assured Washington would honor these treaties. So the Mission Indians left their homes and moved onto the reservations promised. But on July 8, 1852, the U.S. Senate refused to ratify the treaties, leaving the bands stuck on "strange" land now coveted by land-hungry Europeans.

With the California legislature pushing Congress to "remove the Indians" from all of California, and the Senate refusing ratification of the treaties, the message to the gold-seekers was clear. It became "open season" on killing Indians. In fact, when killing at random wasn't enough, there were those who actually organized "Indian hunts."

The treaties now forgotten, legislation was passed in 1853 granting preemption rights to lands, including Indian-occupied lands, to new European settlers. In an attempt to soften the blow, a law was passed almost 25 years later in 1875 allowing Indians to homestead public lands if, but only if, they gave up their native way of life, a condition that applied to no one else.

In the 1890s, a new commission named after Commissioner Albert K. Smiley surveyed Indian lands and conditions. As was done for tribes across the country, the Smiley Commission "set aside parcels of generally poor land for the remnant Indian bands" under the Mission Relief Act of 1891. In an attempt to document the current state of Indian affairs, the Indian Appropriation Act of 1905 authorized an investigation of Indian conditions, and C. E. Kelsey was made a special agent to conduct the investigation. He surveyed every Indian settlement between the Oregon line and Mexico, and reported that of a 17,800 population only 5,200 were living on reservations, the remainder being scattered; only 3,000 of the 11,800 non-reservation Indians owned any land, and 75 percent of that was worthless.

With much of their land unusable for agriculture the Mission Indians, including the Cabazons, had to scatter to survive. They faced many obstacles: to try to make it in a racist country, in a state that was especially harsh, cruel and inhuman to its Native American population, and (according to one native non-Indian resident of California's Riverside County where the Cabazon reservation is) in "one of the most racist counties in the United States—here where the history of no treaty with the Indian or Native American has been kept."

This is the Cabazons' story as they have lived it from the 1960s. It is a story of courage and tenacity and achievement in the face of frontal assaults and sabotage by several levels of government and yellow journalism. It is also the story of

Introduction

When it became apparent to the Nevada and New Jersey gaming interests that Indian gaming might continue to expand, billionaire Donald Trump immediately went public to demand the Congress do something to stop its growth. With an obvious eye for the well-turned phrase, the lawyer for the Connecticut Indian Tribe targeted by Trump's wrath instantly labeled the legislation the "Donald Trump Welfare Act." But the humor was short lived. It has now become apparent that the Trump assault on Indian tribes who have built up gaming on their reservations is just a beginning.

As of this writing, two Nevada Senators, Harry Reid and Richard H. Bryan, joined by New Jersey Congressman Robert Torricelli, the instant patriot, are pushing legislation that will fulfill Mr. Trump's wishes, at least as it concerns Indians.

Torricelli, the good Congressman who labors overtime for his masters in Atlantic City and elsewhere, has had the temerity to offer as his rationale for tightening the screws on Indian tribes his fear that organized crime might infiltrate Indian gaming. This is the same cry one hears from the Nevada gang.

I think it a fascinating commentary on America and American society that Mr. Trump, who has most likely never missed a meal in his life, is asking for government intervention to further impoverish Indian people, many of whom still have trouble securing a minimum of one meal a day—on good days.

Heaven knows that those of us out here in America may not be swayed by such sophistry, but one should not bet much of one's life's savings on whether or not this argument will convince members of Congress during the current legislative session.

Greater scams have been sold to the folks in Washington who, when they decide to vote against their own constituents' interests and in favor of the money men, are looking for a semi-plausible reason to offer when asked how they could possibly vote as they did.

The story of John Nichols and the Cabazon Tribe is, it seems, being told over and over again, as it has for the last several hundred years. The narrative started when White Europeans landed on the shores of America and decided this land was their land, and no one, especially the Indians who lived here, would stand in their way. If a deceptive treaty did not strip the Red Man of his land, then money and trickery of other sorts were tried. The final solution, when all else failed, was a technique still used today by macho occupants of the White House: send in the Army.

In current times, the military (Army, Navy, and Air Force) is a solution reserved strictly for misbehaving third-world villains, the likes of Col. Khaddafi and Saddam Hussein. As a television comic recently pointed out in a parody on President Bush talking to an unnamed questioner:

> "Noriega is a crook, a drug dealer and a thug."
> "How do you know?"
> "He used to work for me."

What our government reserves for the Indians today is a much subtler method of control (the Army is no longer needed, except perhaps at events like Wounded Knee): First, establish a condition of poverty unequaled in this country, then offer food, contingent of course on Indian submission to authority and proper Indian behavior. How wonderful it is for small, otherwise powerless bureaucrats to be able to exercise the power of a necessary commodity like money or food over someone who needs or wants it. How uplifting it must be when people who otherwise might never wish to speak to you come begging at your door. And how disappointing it must be when those miserable supplicants ultimately find a way to make a living on their own, no longer needing your money or help.

The industry of Indian gaming crept up on the White establishment so slowly and quietly that it went unnoticed until it had taken hold around the country. Never mind that it was a form of economic development the Indians only saw as a last resort, something to prevent starvation and degradation. Never mind that on several reservations, gaming began bringing in money needed for projects and jobs the government could not or would not provide. Never mind that the welfare rolls decreased after these people were offered the dignity of work for pay, and that alcoholism and divorce and suicide rates also dropped. These are things, when you're White and rich, as we presume Trump is, that have no meaning. What is important, if you're White and rich and in the gambling business, is that you chop off the hand of any competition wherever you can.

The yardstick by which the Congress should measure gambling legislation, but most likely won't, is the final destination of the money made by a gambling casino. The Indian tribes use it for jobs on the reservation, for alcoholic treatment centers for their tribal members, for other projects that benefit all tribal members. Let's see now. Where do the profits go that are made in Donald Trump's casinos?

their relationship with an avowed radical and revolutionary non-Indian named John Philip Nichols and his family—another tribe of sorts—and how a small desert town and tribes across the nation have been changed by their joint vision and brains, forever.

After the bankers are paid, whatever is left goes directly to Donald Trump's favorite charity: Donald Trump. Will this be taken into account by Congress? I, for one, will not hold my breath to see if such reason will ever be acknowledged by our elected officials.

The Cabazon Tribe was on the cutting edge of this whole business. The marriage of the Tribe with Dr. John Philip Nichols and his family was one of the great moments in history, not only for the Cabazons, but for Indian tribes around the United States. Desperate to find some kind of revenue way back when, the small band of Cabazons took a chance on their own idea and a development plan offered by Nichols. Slogging their way through court, through political thickets, the obstacles were enough to chill the ardor of most human beings. But the tenacity of the Tribe and the Nichols family finally saw success.

Nichols actually believed in the tenet of Indian self-determination, as expressed by the Indian Self-Determination Act passed in the 93rd Congress in 1975. It was a piece of legislation that has come to dominate activities by tribes around the country. In my own law practice, which is partly focused on Indian issues, I run across the Self-Determination Act in a great deal of my work. I remember a year after the law was signed I held hearings to see how it was working. The Bureau of Indian Affairs sent a middle-level bureaucrat to give testimony at the hearings of the Senate Select Committee on Indian Affairs, and after a few minutes of his testimony I understood why it was having difficulty. He was instructed, it soon became clear, not to answer my questions, and not to answer them in a way that I would not notice. I was persistent, however, so the upshot of a hearing that lasted several hours was that I learned the Bureau had actually hired additional people to administer a law designed to reduce the personnel in the Bureau. I suppose I was lucky to learn that much from him.

As a matter of public policy, I firmly believe that officially sanctioned gambling is not a good thing for society. That includes not only casinos in Las Vegas and Atlantic City, but also video lottery machines that are euphemisms for "slots" in any other setting. In South Dakota, the State itself, in its never-ending search for ways to pump money into its treasury, controls and shares in the profits of video lottery machines on virtually every street corner in the state. It is one thing to allow gambing in Deadwood and on Indian reservations where addicts are required to drive great distances to satisfy their urge, but it is another to seduce those of our citizens who live with visions of sugar plums and who will plunk their entire paycheck into a State-run slot machine, principally because in most cases the machines are conveniently situated in the same room where they buy their beer.

But if individuals such as Donald Trump and the variety of other private casino owners are to be allowed to pocket gambling money, then by God so should the Indian tribes if they choose to do so.

Here we are at the end of the 20th century, in a society so technologically advanced it's frightening, and we still haven't learned the lesson of our racist past. Is it possible that we haven't shed our desire to first gauge the color of someone's skin and, finding it not white enough, start tromping on them to take away whatever it is of theirs we want? I'm afraid, to answer my own question, that the answer is yes.

I've seen how remarkable the change is on the Cabazon Reservation, and I've seen the dramatic change on those reservations in South Dakota where the tribes have made money on gaming. It should make one's heart feel good to see people working at dignified jobs, to see them straighten their lives around, lives that were contorted by poverty. Why would anyone want to change that? One of the greater benefits of those tribes that are making money is the change in White attitudes toward them. I marvel at how, on the Yankton Reservation in South Dakota, the local business community and especially the bankers are considerably more respectful of the Tribe because of the millions of dollars the Tribe is bringing into the White community as a result of a well-run casino operation.

Whether they are White or Indian, every reservation needs someone as tenacious as were the Nichols family and the members of the Cabazon Tribe. The obstacles in the way of the advancement of the Indian people are greater than for anyone else, so tenacity is a prime commodity, an essential requirement. Reading this book is a lesson for all of us in the way in which people with good intentions and the required tenacity can actually make a difference. It has already made a great deal of difference, not just for the Cabazons, but for Indian people everywhere. What must be done now is to maintain, to persevere, to make certain that the small gains already made are not washed away by the hypocrisy of the barons of Atlantic City and Las Vegas.

Senator James Abourezk (D-SD)

RETURN
of the
BUFFALO

1

Prologue to Rebirth

In a speech on May 22, 1964, at the University of Michigan, President Lyndon B. Johnson challenged his listeners to "help build a society where the demands of morality and the needs of the spirit can be realized in the life of the nation." He called it the Great Society.

The Great Society, said the President, "is not a safe harbor, a resting place. . . . It is a challenge constantly renewed, beckoning us toward a destiny where the meaning of our lives matches the marvelous products of our labor. . . . It rests on abundance and liberty for all. It demands an end to poverty and racial injustice of which we are totally committed in our time." He urged the students and their parents and teachers to join his efforts to begin the creation of such a society, "to prove that our material progress is only the foundation on which we will build a richer life of mind and spirit."

Three months later, on August 20, 1964, the cornerstone of his plan was laid in the enactment of the Economic Opportunity Act—a movement that became popularly known as the War on Poverty. In the Findings and Declaration of Purpose section of that Act there appeared these words:

> It is, therefore, the policy of the United States to eliminate the paradox of poverty in the midst of plenty in this Nation *by opening to everyone the opportunity for education and training, the opportunity to work and the opportunity to live in decency and dignity.* (Emphasis added.)

That Act was the most unique law ever passed by a parliamentary body in any industrialized nation in the world, and among its claims to uniqueness were:

1. No other nation in the recorded history of humanity ever declared an

official government "policy" to eliminate poverty; it was a first.

2. It was not a "welfare" or "income transfer" program. Its clear intent was to open to every American—no matter what his class, race, religion or gender—opportunities that would enable "a permanent increase in the capacity of individuals, groups and communities to deal with their problems *without further assistance*." (Emphasis added.)
3. It required "maximum feasible participation of residents of the areas and members of the groups served," giving even the poorest American the right to exercise decision-making influence and power over the expenditure of federal dollars in local communities.
4. Finally, it created a new "federalism," initiating and expanding direct communications between the national level of government and local communities, often providing direct funding to existing or newly created nonprofit agencies and bypassing state and local elected officials and old-line, traditional agencies.

It was, however, just the cornerstone. What would follow can only be described accurately as a legislative "blizzard" of domestic programs designed to benefit *all* Americans and in particular the elderly, the poor, the young, the handicapped, and those most vulnerable to the worst practices of capitalism and industrialization. For a brief but shining moment the feeding of the "fat cats" was slowed, while Lyndon Johnson led those that President John F. Kennedy had earlier called "a new generation of Americans" in the Congress and federal bureaucracy in an outpouring of legislative "love" for the American people. It was a brilliant, if short-lived, performance producing more than 50 major pieces of social, domestic laws.

Among the laws passed were: Medicare and Medicaid, the Elementary and Secondary Education Act, Aid to Handicapped Children, the Teachers Corps, Water Pollution Control, Heart, Cancer and Stroke Program, School Breakfast Program, Rent Supplement, Community Health Services, Mental Health Facilities, Civil Rights Act of 1964, Voting Rights Act of 1965, Urban Mass Transit, Freedom of Information Act, Age Discrimination Act, Department of Housing and Urban Development, Department of Transportation, Food Stamp Act, Truth in Securities Act, Older Americans Act, Higher Education Act, Aid to Appalachia, *Indian Vocational Training*, Military Medicare, College Work Study, Guaranteed Student Loans, *Indian Bill of Rights*, Summer Youth Programs, Narcotics Rehabilitation, Clean Air Act and a multitude of environmental laws.

Johnson's call for a Great Society met with derision from his political enemies. His call for a domestic War on Poverty, while conducting an escalating real war in Vietnam, would prove politically suicidal. As the body bags from Vietnam multiplied, the support for a domestic "war" steadily deteriorated. While Congress and editorialists debated whether the nation could afford both guns and butter, young people facing military service escalated their protests, repeatedly shouting, "Hey! Hey! LBJ! How many kids have you killed today?"

It was, perhaps, both poignant and prophetic that the 1967 law amending the War on Poverty—the Economic Opportunity Act of 1967—was signed by President Johnson in December of that year in Cam Rahn Bay, Vietnam. For a brief period, Americans had been served by a Congress and a President that took time out from their slavish pandering to the nation's corporate elite long enough to serve the best interests of the "general welfare." And for that brief period, laws mandated that the "general welfare" included non-elite White Americans as well as African-Americans, Native Americans, Latino-Americans and Asian-Americans.

In 1979, several former members of that Great Society Congress looked back at what they had tried to do. The late Kentucky Congressman Carl Perkins, former chairman of the House Committee on Education and Labor, said he and his colleagues had had "a sense that we could solve all of our problems. Our national leadership—John F. Kennedy and Lyndon Johnson—contributed to a sense of confidence that government could solve problems and could be expected to serve the common good." The late Alabama Senator Lister Hill put it this way: "In the 1960s Congress was concerned about the welfare of the poor and the veterans. . . . We tried to do something for our fellow Americans, for our country." Former Senator Ralph Yarborough of Texas was most graphic in describing the Congress of his years as "the Congress of people like [the late Senator Wayne] Morse, [former Senator] Albert Gore of Tennessee, [the late Senator] Paul Douglas of Illinois, and [the late Senator Ernest] Gruening of Alaska. . . . The Congress then was more concerned with people."

"I make speeches around and I tell them clearly," said Yarborough: "The most expensive business of government is feeding the 'fat cats.' The main difference I see in the Congress of the '60s and that of the '70s is that the Congress of the '60s was more concerned about feeding the poor than they were about feeding the 'fat cats.'"

The word "rhetoric" fell into some disfavor in the two decades following the 1960s, especially when applied to the "general welfare" of Americans. Yet, in truth, rhetoric is vital to progress. No reform or revolutionary mass movement is possible without it. Rhetoric can inspire as well as depress, is important in forming and sustaining individual and group self-concepts, and helps define what is possible and what is not possible. Words alone are important and powerful in the human experience, and can create new worlds when combined with enhanced consciousness and purposeful action. The inherent creative power of words is augmented when delivered by an institution or a representative of perceived power, in both the deliverer and the receiver of those words.

By the end of the Kennedy-Johnson presidencies, America's legal caste system had been almost legally ended. Through rhetoric and action, governmental and private-sector institutions began a process of including Americans of non-European descent in jobs and other activities from which they had previously been excluded.

The "beginning" of the end of that legal caste system was the ruling by the

U.S. Supreme Court in its *Brown v. Board of Education* decision on May 17, 1954. The Court held "in the field of public education the doctrine of 'separate but equal' has no place. Separate educational facilities are inherently unequal. . . . The plaintiffs and others similarly situated . . . are, by reason of the segregation complained of, deprived of the equal protection of the laws guaranteed by the Fourteenth Amendment."

As the Kennedy-Johnson years came to a close, two laws were added, which for all intents and purposes almost ended America's caste system: the Civil Rights Act of 1964 and the Voting Rights Act of 1965. The final nail in America's Apartheid Coffin was driven in by the Voting Rights Act Amendments of 1970, which barred the use of literacy tests in all elections.

America had moved closer to becoming a democracy. The rhetoric had worked. In Appalachia and other rural hollows, in urban ghettoes and barrios, and on Indian reservations all across America, the rhetoric had been heard and believed. A new spirit blossomed. It was a spirit of hope and belief that a better life was possible, even for those previously left out of America's promise. And a new generation took advantage of every new opportunity or job that became available.

But to many Americans, the old way—America's caste system—was the American way, and many of their political, economic and religious leaders agreed, overtly or covertly. To these and other frightened or angry Americans, Richard M. Nixon applied the term "the silent majority" and rode their fear, racism and anger into the White House. To these Americans, the Civil Rights Movement and the Antiwar Movement threatened public order, and anarchy was just around the corner. They elected Nixon to fix things—to stop "crime in the streets," to end the Vietnam War, and to stop the flow of jobs, federal money and new opportunities to "minorities."

New York's current U.S. Senator Daniel Patrick Moynihan was one of Nixon's most prominent Cabinet-level advisors. A Harvard professor, Moynihan had served previous Democratic administrations and was considered by the press to be Nixon's "house liberal."

But in the five years before joining the Nixon administration, Moynihan had come to a philosophical "parting of the ways" with much of the leadership of the Civil Rights Movement. He had authored a paper that met with controversy among the leaders, titled "Employment, Income and the Ordeal of the Negro Family," published in the Fall 1965 issue of *Daedulus, the Journal of the American Academy of Arts and Sciences.* Its publication during the period of planning for President Johnson's 1966 White House Conference "To Fulfill These Rights" created a firestorm among Civil Rights activists and resulted in a rift that appeared irreparable for many years to come. The hostility was open and palpably intense.

In early 1968, Moynihan spoke at a Miami conference funded by the Ford Foundation's Ministers' Leadership Training Programs. Dr. Martin Luther King Jr., who supported much of the analysis in Moynihan's controversial paper, was also a conference speaker. In his book *Bearing the Cross*, David Garrow includes a description of how Moynihan's appearance was viewed and Moynihan's reaction:

> "Moynihan spoke in an atmosphere of total hostility," one Ford Foundation observer reported, and Moynihan later wrote to Ford President McGeorge Bundy to protest SCLC's [Southern Christian Leadership Conference] venture. Moynihan said the session was "the first time I have ever found myself in an atmosphere so suffused with near madness. . . . The leadership of the meeting was in the hands of near-demented Black militants who consistently stated one untruth after another (about me, about the United States, about the President, about history, etc., etc.) without a single voice being raised in objection. King, Abernathy and Young sat there throughout, utterly unwilling (at least with me present) to say a word in support of nonviolence, integration, or peaceableness." Ford's observer noted that it was an accomplishment that Moynihan "got out alive."

Almost two years later, Moynihan would pen another controversial paper, this time from the Nixon White House. It would become known as the "Benign Neglect Memo." Some have suggested it should have been titled "Moynihan's Revenge." It was, if Moynihan's words are to be believed, not a memo requested by Nixon but one volunteered by Moynihan. The memo's opening lines were:

> As the NEW YEAR begins, it occurs to me that you might find useful a general assessment of the position of Negroes at the end of the first year of your Administration, and of the decade in which their position has been the central domestic political issue.
>
> In quantitative terms, which are reliable, the American Negro is making extraordinary progress. In political terms, somewhat less reliable, this would also appear to be true. In each case, however, there would seem to be countercurrents that pose a serious threat to the welfare of the blacks and the stability of the society, white and black.

The bulk of the memo made an unscholarly effort (or a political one, some observers said) to support these opening statements, but then made an awful assertive leap, admittedly "with no real evidence," into the abyss of racial libel. He alleged that "Hatred—revenge—against whites is now an acceptable excuse for such things as crime, the fire-setting, the rampant school violence . . . among the black lower classes." He then added that this "alienation . . . is matched and probably enhanced, by a virulent form of anti-white feeling among portions of the large and prosperous black middle class. It would be difficult to overestimate the degree to which young, well-educated blacks detest white America."

Moynihan concludes by offering the President four suggestions, the first of which was to get some of his appointees together and talk about the subject.

> Second, the time may have come when the issue of race could benefit from a period of

"benign neglect." The subject has been too much talked about. The forum has been too much taken over to hysterics, paranoids and boodlers on all sides. We may need a period in which Negro progress continues and racial rhetoric fades. The Administration can help bring this about by paying close attention to such progress—as we are doing—while seeking to avoid situations in which extremists of either race are given opportunities for martyrdom, heroics, histrionics or whatever. Greater attention to *Indians, Mexican-Americans* and *Puerto Ricans* would be useful. A tendency to ignore provocations from groups such as the Black Panthers might also be useful. (Emphasis added.)

Moynihan's third suggestion could be interpreted as a plea for the President to use Moynihan's social-scientist colleagues to do "carefully done studies" and research on crime. Lawyers, he tells the lawyer president, are simply "not professionally well equipped" to manage or to do the research required. His last suggestion was directly related to suggestion two:

Fourth. There is a silent black majority as well as a white one. It is mostly working class, as against lower middle class. It is politically moderate (on issues other than racial equality) and shares most of the concerns of its white counterpart. This group has been generally ignored by the Government and the media. The more recognition we can give to it, the better off we shall all be. (I would take it, for example, that Ambassador [Jerome H.] Holland is a natural leader of this segment of the black community. There are others like him.)

Regardless of Moynihan's motivation or intentions, his memo was supportive of and consistent with the policy of the Administration he was then serving, but how consistent and supportive did not become clear to much of the American public until after Nixon's re-election in 1972.

The memo's usefulness to the Administration was demonstrated by the speed with which it was "leaked" to the press. The message to the press and to the American public—especially to the non-Black "silent majority"—was that a well-known liberal, trusted by and serving an avowed "conservative" president, was advising that president "enough already." Since in the words of the memo, "the American Negro is making extraordinary progress" and "young Negro families are achieving parity with young white families," it was now time to let "market forces" take over while attention was turned to "other minorities." Eventually other minorities would include Eastern European "ethnics." These other minorities don't show this "hatred—revenge—against whites," the memo implied and their "forum" had not "been too much taken over to hysterics, paranoids and boodlers on all sides," as Moynihan had described the African-American "forum." Taking this course "would be useful," he advised Nixon.

Of course, Moynihan was right; his suggested course was useful to Nixon. The President had inherited the Great Society Congress and a bureaucracy that had been energized by that Congress and two presidents to "do something" for the poor, the veterans, minorities, the non-"fat cats." And it would take Nixon some time to turn his inherited situation around.

Although he was possibly not totally aware, what Nixon also inherited were energized communities of poor Whites and those "Indians, Mexican-Americans and Puerto Ricans" to whom Moynihan unwittingly suggested giving "greater attention" as a way to diffuse racial tensions. The messages of hope and inspiration that were the hallmarks of the Kennedy-Johnson Administrations had touched the entire country, and previously left-out groups had benefited from the programs created to give substance to those messages, and were invigorated by them.

The brilliance of the Kennedy-Johnson Administrations was in their insight. They knew that beaten-down American groups had to be convincingly told and shown their government really meant its rhetoric. Among the programs resulting from this insight was VISTA (Volunteers in Service to America), which provided a government-supported vehicle for tens of thousands of students, some of the wealthy, lots of the middle class and elderly Americans to volunteer their know-how in hands-on service to the poor and disabled across our country. Another was the Neighborhood Youth Corps which engaged local governments and the private sector in providing partially subsidized jobs to poor in-school and out-of-school youths. Yet another short-lived program was Medicare Alert, which employed—in local communities—elderly Americans to go door-to-door to tell other seniors about Medicare, explaining that they no longer had to let illnesses go untreated because they could not afford a doctor or hospital care.

Acceptance of this new concern for the downtrodden came very slowly, however, for one long-suffering group. For Native Americans, forcefully isolated on often barren reservations, knowing of at least 400 treaties signed with the United States government that had been broken and dishonored, it had taken some special convincing to reassure them the government really meant to help this time. Nevertheless, the Kennedy-Johnson rhetoric and programs led many to regain hope, and by the time Nixon took office, positive things were happening with American Indians on and off reservations.

To implement the War on Poverty, the law had envisioned the creation of local nonprofit agencies known as Community Action Agencies (CAAs). When it came to power, the Nixon Administration found more than 60 CAAs in operation on reservations, with plans to channel more than $50 million annually of Office of Economic Opportunity (OEO) money through these Native American-controlled agencies. Those dollars would enable these agencies to get tens of millions more program dollars from other federal, state and local government agencies, as well as funds from private foundations. Some tribes, maximizing the self-determination language of the law, had already gained Native American control of programs previously administered paternalistically and often contemptuously by the Bureau of Indian Affairs. And, just as other Americans did, Native Americans benefited from programs offered by various federal agencies, even when their tribal organizations were not administering them. For this brief period, a door of opportunity opened and many American Indians stepped briskly through.

But for the masses of Native Americans, the cumulative years of oppression and isolation had taken a heavy toll. When Nixon took office, only 1.5 percent of programs operated by the Department of the Interior directly serving Native Americans were run by them. Only 2.4 percent of Indian Health programs, then operated by the Department of Health, Education and Welfare (HEW—the predecessor of today's Department of Health and Human Services—HHS), were run by the Indians themselves, which could be one of the reasons the Indians' expected life span at that time was so unbelievably low. The average age of death was 44, a third less than the national average. Infant mortality was 50 percent higher, the rate of tuberculosis was eight times higher, the suicide rate was double that of the general population and the scourge of alcoholism was plaguing Indians on and off reservations across the country.

In early 1970, the Bureau of Indian Affairs (BIA) was responsible for directly operating schools attended by 50,000 Native American children. However, through contractual arrangements by the BIA, only 750 of these children attended schools with Native American school boards. With such obvious governmental ignorance of the special needs of Indian children, is it any wonder the average educational level for American Indian children in 1970—for *all* Native American children under federal supervision (a total of 221,000)—was less than six school years? Equally appalling was the fact that their dropout rate was double the national average.

When Nixon took office there was also an abysmally high level of deprivation among the Indians. Unemployment ran as high as 80 percent on some reservations and, on an average, was 10 times higher than the national average. As a result, 80 percent of all Native Americans living on reservations had incomes well below the poverty line—with families living on average annual incomes of only $1,500.

Within about three months after receiving and "leaking" Moynihan's memo, Nixon delivered a message to Congress on July 8, 1970, concerning Indians. The term "self-determination" had been picked up by Nixon minority-group appointees from activists in and out of the Civil Rights Movement. They employed the term to distinguish their efforts to build on the positive gains made by minorities in the Johnson Administration, and it is in that light that Nixon's message to Congress should be read.

Nixon first put himself on record as an advocate of Indian self-determination, stating that federal policies pertaining to the Indian had "oscillated between two equally harsh and unacceptable extremes": those which threatened to terminate the Indian guarantee of special standing under the law, and those creating "excessive dependence on the Federal government." He cited the 1953 House Concurrent Resolution No. 108, wherein Congress declared "termination was the long-range goal of its Indian policies." His policy, Nixon asserted, would be self-determination without the threat of termination. Such a policy would mean, he declared, that "the historic relationship between the Federal government and the Indian communities cannot be abridged without the consent of the Indians."

It would also mean the rejection of our nation's "suffocating pattern of paternalism," he said. To address this problem, Nixon promised to propose "legislation which would empower a tribe or a group of tribes or any other Indian community to take over the control or operation of federally-funded and administered programs in the Department of the Interior and the Department of Health, Education and Welfare whenever the tribal council or comparable community governing group voted to do so." Under his promised legislation, Nixon said, "it would not be necessary for the Federal agency administering the program to approve the transfer of responsibility . . . [and] in those cases in which an impasse arises between the two parties, the final determination should rest with the Indian community." However, if the Indians wanted to hire "Federal employees who had formerly administered these projects, these employees would still enjoy the privileges of Federal employee benefit programs" under Nixon's promised legislation.

Nixon's message also promised to submit to Congress the Indian Financing Act of 1970 to stimulate economic development. More money was promised for Indian health programs as well as for other initiatives already undertaken in his administration. Nixon concluded his administration was "proposing to break sharply with past approaches to Indian problems" and "most importantly . . . we have turned from the question of *whether* the Federal government has a responsibility to Indians to the question of *how* that responsibility can best be fulfilled. We have concluded that the Indians will get better programs and that public moneys will be more effectively expended if the people who are most affected by these programs are responsible for operating them."

Nixon's speech contained great rhetoric, and that rhetoric would have a value. Unfortunately for Native Americans, inadequate and sometimes retrogressive action would follow. It was not a good combination.

According to former U.S. Senator James G. Abourezk (D-SD), the Nixon Administration was not alone in treating our nation's Native American population with either gross neglect or aggressive apathy. In his book *Advise and Dissent,* Abourezk described his initiation into the realities of this legislative issue:

> My entry into official Indian affairs coincided with the period of increasing Indian militancy. In January 1973, I had just been sworn in as a freshman Senator when I was appointed as chairman of the Indian Affairs Subcommittee of the Senate Interior Committee. "Scoop" Jackson, chairman of the Interior Committee, convinced me that he was doing me a favor by making the appointment. I strutted around for a while, boasting of the appointment to my friends and family, until I discovered that no one else wanted the job.

In evaluating action and inaction by several administrations he'd observed, Abourezk wrote:

> In addition to congressional apathy, I found very little sympathy for Indian concerns in successive administrations. For all his pretense as a liberal, Jimmy Carter did less for Ameri-

can Indians than Richard Nixon. Although Nixon did very little, he did sign an executive declaration that put him on record as favoring Indian self-determination.

However, during this period, the performance of the holdover Great Society Congress kept the greatest part of Great Society programs in place throughout most of Nixon's first term, even as Republican, "conservative" and other right-wing attacks on these programs escalated. By the end of the decade, these attacks, delivered in steady, emotion-charged propaganda packaging, would succeed in making the word "liberal" and the phrase "Great Society" near obscenities in the public's mind.

Throughout Nixon's July 1970 message to Congress, he spoke in strongly supportive terms about the new and sometimes bold programs put in place for Native Americans by the Office of Economic Opportunity (OEO) (the War on Poverty lead agency). For example, to "urban Indian centers" jointly set up by OEO and HEW to serve urban Indians, Nixon told Congress "these efforts represent an important beginning in recognizing and alleviating the severe problems faced by urban Indians," and he added, "to expand our efforts as rapidly as possible, I am directing the Office of Economic Opportunity to lead these efforts." To the politically uninitiated, these words and the following would seem to be his ringing endorsement and approval of OEO and its Indian programs:

> The Office of Economic Opportunity has been particularly active in the development of new and experimental efforts. OEO's Fiscal Year 1971 budget request for Indian-related activities is up 18 percent from 1969 spending. In the last year alone—to mention just two examples—OEO doubled its funds for Indian economic development and tripled its expenditures for alcoholism and recovery programs. In areas such as housing and home improvement, health care, emergency food, legal services and education, OEO programs have been significantly expanded. As I said in my recent speech on the economy, I hope that the Congress will support this valuable work *by appropriating the full amount requested for the Economic Opportunity Act.* (Emphasis added.)

But as all OEO-funded programs across the country, including Native American programs, would learn, Nixon's praise and promises were not worth very much. As soon as he was reelected in 1972, he showed the OEO and Native Americans his real face, his real agenda. He appointed Howard Philips director of OEO and gave him instructions to dismantle the entire agency and its programs.

To save the day, program operators across the country dug into their pockets and raised enough money to hire a lawyer to bring a lawsuit to stop the dismantling. The lawsuit was successful and Philips, who had never been confirmed by Congress, was removed from office.

By mid-1973, Nixon's energies focused on trying to save his presidency, and OEO and Native Americans faded from his vision. Therefore, the programs he tried to dismantle continued (with significantly reduced budget support) to serve the nation for several years to come.

Nevertheless, as right-wing propagandists began to dominate the nation's major media, doors of opportunity opened in that brief period of the Kennedy-Johnson presidencies began to close for all poor Americans, especially for those labeled "minority." Programs that were designed and operated in an unprecedented effort to eliminate poverty "by opening to everyone the opportunity *for education and training*, the opportunity *to work* and the opportunity *to live in decency and dignity*," became, in the mouths of Republicans, "conservatives," and other right-wing propagandists, a "throwing of dollars at problems," "a tax-and-spend liberal waste of taxpayers' money," or "a Marxist agenda." The Nixon presidency and the failed presidencies that would follow, through 1992, set the nation on a course of restricted opportunity for all Americans except the moneyed class.

After the Watergate scandal drove Nixon from power in 1974, Gerald Ford, born in 1913 (the same year as Nixon) succeeded to the presidency. Ford had become Vice President under Nixon after Spiro Agnew was forced to resign because of illegal activities during his prior governorship of Maryland. Ford's presidency became a two-year holding action as a result of his issuance of a pardon to Nixon. Most political observers agreed that the pardon effectively ended any real chance Ford may have had to win a term of office in his own right.

During the last years of Nixon's presidency and Ford's short stint, some Native Americans began to take actions that would be called militant in defense of their rights. In 1973 the American Indian Movement (AIM), led by Dennis Banks and Russell Means, took over the Sioux Reservation at Wounded Knee. Native Americans later occupied Alcatraz Island for 19 months. However, many Native Americans remained on the sidelines, resignedly expecting their newly given opportunities to vaporize into thin air as had so many solemn treaties with the government from the past.

Between these two factions of militancy and conservatism was another group that decided to test out these newly granted opportunities, even while distrusting the Feds. Many of this middle group were either urban Native Americans who had grown up away from the reservation, or those who had served in the armed forces and had seen life in other parts of America or in other countries. Although their initial steps were tentative, and accompanied by a "don't rock the boat" philosophy, they did take them. And, as each step proved fruitful, more and more were taken and confidence grew.

It was a great beginning for many, but in some ways it was an arrested beginning. Minorities and poor people, generally, awaited the end of the short Ford presidency as Ford actively tried to cut most federal programs serving the poor. And, even though Ford had come from the Congress and was a prominent member of the Republican minority in the House of Representatives, his relationship with Congress was much more confrontational than Nixon's had been. Thus, the end of his term was hoped for by many, poor and nonpoor alike.

Those who had lived through the Johnson years looked forward to another period of Democratic control of both the White House and Congress when Jimmy Carter took office in 1976. However, his would prove to be just the opposite of the Johnson years. Carter would not be a Lyndon Johnson nor a John Kennedy, nor was he cut from the same cloth as Democratic presidents since Franklin D. Roosevelt. To many, his was a Republican presidency in Democratic disguise. As for Native Americans, many others would agree with Senator Abourezk's blunt assessments that Carter, who "hardly knew Indians existed . . . did less for American Indians than Richard Nixon."

When Carter took office in early 1977, the country was trying to recover from the 1974–75 recession that had especially aggravated joblessness among minorities and women. Less than a month after Carter's inaugural, the U.S. Commission on Civil Rights issued a report on "The State of Civil Rights: 1976," and among its findings was that the traditional two-to-one ratio of minority to White unemployment rates persisted and the earnings gap between males and females had widened. Most significantly, the report confirmed a 10.7 percent increase in Americans living in poverty, the largest since 1959 when poverty-rate data first became routinely available.

While governor of Georgia, Carter had been an active supporter of full employment and a member of the non-profit Full Employment Action Council. The Council had revived the interest in full employment as a national policy first set into law as the Employment Act of 1946, sponsored by the late Congressman Wright Patman of Texas. However, due to big-business opposition the policy was never implemented.

The Full Employment Action Council, co-chaired by a Labor representative and Coretta Scott King, widow of Dr. Martin Luther King, Jr., was formed to put teeth into that 1946 statement of federal policy. But before the end of his first year in office, Carter would effectively undermine the Council's legislation. (The legislation enunciated in the Humphrey-Hawkins bill was named in honor of the ailing Senator Hubert H. Humphrey, who would soon die of cancer, and Congressman Augustus F. Hawkins of California.) As a result, Full Employment remains to this day a policy never implemented by our government.

For Native Americans, 1977 proved not to be the best of political years all around. On January 24, Senator Abourezk held a press conference to announce he would not run for re-election in 1978. Stating, "I've never believed that I am indispensable," Abourezk attributed his decision to a desire to spend more time with his family. He had been one of South Dakota's most popular vote-getters in a quarter of a century.

Abourezk had been a strong liberal voice in both the House and the Senate. In all his years of elective office, the liberal Americans for Democratic Action (ADA) rated him 90 percent or more every year but one. His had often been the strongest voice championing Native American rights. He had led the negotiating team that went to Wounded Knee and met with AIM in 1973. His Senate committee was principally responsible for passage of the Indian Freedom of Religion Act, a Congressional Resolution, and the Indian Child Welfare Act. Regarding the latter, Abourezk called it "perhaps the most far-reaching bill that we passed. . . . [It] required that tribal court must decide where a child belonged, taking the decision out of the hands of the white welfare agencies and white courts." His leaving the Senate would leave a void in that body, but would ultimately free him to provide valuable services to Native American tribes in other ways.

By the end of April 1977, it was clear that the great expectations many groups held for the Carter Administration had been dashed. In an April 1977 article chronicling these disappointments, the *Congressional Quarterly* magazine pinpointed the reason for the Indians' pessimism with the administration under the subheading "Indians: No Participation." The article quoted Ernest L. Stevens, director of the Joint Congressional American Indian Policy Review Commission and staff director of the new Senate Select Committee on Indian Affairs, who said "the hallmark of the Carter administration has been no participation by Indians. They haven't named one key person in Indian Affairs since they came in. . . . How do they come up with an Indian program without having somebody up front? This administration is relying on career bureaucrats, not Indians." According to Stevens, Carter and Interior Secretary Cecil D. Andrus were expected to "do some things in that awful bureau over there," referring to the BIA. Almost tongue-in-cheek he gave them the credit due, however, likening the improvements made in the BIA under their direction to its time under Nixon's leadership, saying "not having moved in 100 years, they moved a couple of inches."

In the *Congressional Quarterly* article, Abourezk was a bit more optimistic, but in hindsight there could have been a little political satire beneath his statement: "I'd say from my limited experience that they're doing all right. I don't see where they've turned any Indians down." In his book, written after leaving the Senate, Abourezk described trying to get the Carter Administration to appoint a full-blooded Indian to "become Assistant Secretary for Indian Affairs." But, he said, "Interior Secretary Cecil Andrus instead appointed Forest Gerard, Washington Senator Henry "Scoop" Jackson's former staff member, who was the perfect part-Indian bureaucrat to appoint if you wanted nothing to happen in Indian Affairs. Nothing happened, despite Gerard's protestations during the Indian Committee's confirmation hearings that he would implement recommendations made by the American Indian Policy Review Commission." (Perhaps the Carter people chose to reward the Senator [Jackson] who would still be around, rather than the Senator [Abourezk] who would be leaving.)

The 95th Congress, elected in 1976, brought 67 new members to the House and 18 to the Senate. It was the youngest House since World War II and the average age of senators dropped from 55.5 to 54.6 years of age. (The election of California's 70-year-old S. I. Hayakawa over 43-year-old incumbent John V. Tunney kept the average age of the Senate from dropping more precipitously.) And yet, as corporate political action committee (PAC) money became more influential, Congress moved inexorably away from a people-program agenda.

Yet in 1977 it was that same Congress that restored most of the proposed cuts in Indian programs recommended by the Carter Administration. On June 9, 1977, the House passed an appropriations bill for the Interior Department that contained significant increases over the Administration's budget request for Indian programs. It added more than $110 million to support Indian "progress toward self-determination," and supported programs such as the self-help Indian Action Teams, reforestation and irrigation efforts, and Indian Health Services, including $20 million to reduce an "unconscionable" backlog of 23,000 cases of noncritical delayed surgeries. At about the same time, the BIA came in for almost scathing comments by the House Appropriations Committee, who in its Committee report said the BIA was "more concerned about covering up its inadequacies" than in giving Indians effective services.

Early in his term of office, President Carter began to deal with the longstanding problem of land claims by Native Americans. Specifically, he appointed retired Georgia Supreme Court Judge William B. Gunter to devise a legislative solution to the massive claims by two Maine tribes, the Passamaquoddy and the Penobscot. The federal government had been prodded to act on behalf of the tribes by a 1972 lawsuit filed in Maine over a 1794 treaty and several other earlier treaties involving the two tribes and the states of Maine and Massachusetts. By mid-July, Judge Gunter made his recommendations: the tribes were to be given 100,000 acres of land outright and the right to buy another 400,000 acres.

The Indian Claims Commission had been set up in 1946 to hear and resolve such claims. Originally given a 10-year life, the agency's life had been repeatedly extended; a Colorado-based group, the Native American Rights Fund (NARF), had become a spearhead for legal efforts to recover tribal lands. Gunter's report was important because it was initially seen as a possible precedent for settlement of about 18 other claims by tribes up and down the Eastern Seaboard. The initial response of some authorities, however, was not encouraging. Maine's Governor James B. Longley found it "very difficult to rationalize the settling of a human or equal-rights issue outside of a court of law." And he posed the question: "Why should a present generation of Americans be forced to pay for alleged wrongs which might or might not have occurred even before their grandparents were born?" It was to be a question repeatedly used by right-wing Americans from then on about claims of other American minority groups, but the answer repeatedly arrived at by most courts is simply and fortunately: because it is right and just.

The year 1977 would prove to be an extremely difficult one for the Carter Administration and the country as well. Theodore C. Sorensen, Carter's original nominee to head the Central Intelligence Agency (CIA), and one of the bright stars of the Kennedy White House, was forced to withdraw his name from nomination. Sorensen's chance to head the CIA had been killed because he had insisted the nation would not be hurt by publication of the Pentagon Papers and might be more damaged by concealing them.

Later, another close aide to President Carter, Office of Management and Budget (OMB) Director Bert Lance, would be forced to resign over allegations involving illegalities and irregularities during his presidency of the Calhoun (Georgia) First National Bank. He would later be acquitted of all charges, but the allegations and his forced resignation cast another cloud over the Carter term.

And big-business flexed its legislative muscle during the year. It was to be the first thrust in an open frontal assault against organized labor. Formally organized in 1974, the Big Business Roundtable brought together the chief executive officers of 180 of America's major corporations, including IBM, AT&T, General Electric, General Motors, du Pont and others among the top 500 firms.

Labor leaders correctly saw the Roundtable as a direct threat to working people. Robert Georgine, then president of the AFL-CIO Building and Construction Trades Department, was quoted as saying: "It is apparent that the real purpose of the Roundtable is to destroy local unions and take away the gains they have made through the collective bargaining process." In fact, one of Labor's major legislative goals for the year, the common-site picketing bill, went down to defeat because of the effective lobbying of the Roundtable. Jack Curran, then legislative director of the Laborers' International Union, said they "hurt us badly" in the common-site battle defeat.

The first Carter year was a year of ferment. It soon became clear that, to make matters worse, the most undisciplined form of capitalism was soon to be foisted on the nation as the nation's moneyed interests prepared and organized for plunder of the nation's treasury.

For Native Americans, the year ended with an Emergency Legislative Meeting in Phoenix, Arizona sponsored by the National Congress of American Indians. The meeting was called, with almost 200 tribal representatives in attendance, to plan strategy to stop what was becoming "Indian Backlash" legislative momentum. Led by Washington State Congressman Lloyd Meeks, who had been a member of the American Indian Policy Review Commission, five congressmen had submitted nine bills correctly characterized as anti-Indian; 13 other congressmen had joined them as cosponsors of Meeks' bill and/or that of his Washington State Republican colleague Jack Cunningham; and lobbying for the Congressmen and Senators was the Interstate Congress for Equal Rights and Responsibilities (ICERR). The ICERR had targeted a number of Senators to pressure to introduce the Meeks bill in the Senate in 1978, especially Senators from Washington, Montana, South Dakota and Nebraska.

A statement prepared for that year-end Emergency Legislative Meeting, attended by Second Vice-Chairman of the Cabazon Band of Mission Indians "Art" Welmas, asserted:

> The backlash bills are a direct response to pressure from non-Indian groups who make no secret of their objective: to do away with our treaty rights, our reservations and our tribal governments. Many of these groups are, in fact, racist, though they would deny this. All of

them would repudiate our legal rights and powers. They would have this country turn its back on solemn promises made to the Indian nation. Their slogan is equal rights. What they mean is destruction of Indian rights.

This anti-Indian movement is motivated by intolerance and greed. The decisions of the courts of this land affirming and reaffirming our rights are unwelcome messages to them. They are unwilling to abide by the rule of law which holds that we have a right to govern our reservations so they may be preserved as a homeland for our people; that we are entitled to the return of lands or fair compensation where these lands were unlawfully taken from us; that we have a right to use the water essential to the survival of our reservation land base and that we have a right to the share of the fish guaranteed us by treaties.

We hear these anti-Indian spokesmen proclaiming that they are seeking to uphold the principle of equality and of representational government. But, in fact, we know what they want is to continue to control and exploit land, water, fish and the game unhindered by Indian rights, in the future as in the past.

Despite the politicians nipping at their heels, December 1977 was both an end and a beginning for the Cabazons. On December 10, just four days after the "backlash" meeting, the official tribal meeting minutes record for the first time, in a most offhand way, a connection with the man who would eventually pave the way for the Tribe to realize such a visionary financial future that it would one day make headline news alongside business mogul Donald Trump. The minutes state: "Motion [was] made by Art Welmas to hire Dr. [John Philip] Nichols if we get TA [Technical Assistance] money. Seconded by Gene Welmas. Motion carried."

Things would never be the same again.

2

They Met in the Desert

Joseph Benitez, a Chemehuevi tribal member born on February 2, 1935, was brought by his family while still an infant to live on the Cabazon Reservation near Indio, California. In a February 10, 1963, election, he became Spokesman for the Cabazons, succeeding Remeijo Callaway. In an unidentified newspaper clipping kept in Cabazon files, Benitez described growing up on the reservation:

> Life was pretty primitive in those days. There wasn't much on the reservation except sagebrush and rabbits. We didn't even have electricity until the 1950s. Housing was limited to makeshift quarters. . . . There was no running water. Just sagebrush and rabbits. . . . We walked two miles to school every day, even in the summer heat, and thought nothing about it. . . . A highlight of our lives was the monthly trip to [the nearby] Torres-Martinez Reservation where the Indian Agency handed out rations for our food allotment. We always could count on a good meal after that.

Like Native Americans all across America, Benitez benefited from the opportunities produced by Johnson's Great Society. Using his training (he earned his associates degree in business administration and later completed a Dale Carnegie course) and his position as Tribal Chairman, he became Project Director of Riverside-San Bernardino County Indian Health Inc. The organization operated a medical and dental clinic serving Indians in San Bernardino and Riverside Counties. He was, among other activities, a member of the Health Care for California Indians Panel of the California State Health Department, Chairman of California Rural Indian Health Board Inc., and a member and Secretary-Treasurer of the National Indian Health Board.

According to a report sent to the Bureau of Indian Affairs, the 42-year-old Benitez was re-elected Chairman of the Cabazons on May 14, 1977, along with four other officers: William R. Callaway, also 42, First Vice-Chairman; Art Welmas, 48, Second Vice-Chairman; and John A. James, 46, Secretary-Treasurer, a post he would hold for 24 years before later being elevated to Tribal Chairman.

Receiving unanimous confirmation that day in May 1977, each received a total of eight votes, representing 72 percent of the Tribe's eligible voters and putting America's election turnouts to shame. Only 11 tribal members were 21 years of age or older and eligible to vote of a total tribal membership of 28, and on the Election Certification form sent to the BIA the addresses listed indicated that only two of the four officers lived in close proximity to the reservation.

Benitez was 20 years old when Martin Luther King, Jr. burst into the nation's consciousness as leader of the Montgomery, Alabama, bus boycott. One year earlier, a unanimous Supreme Court ruled that segregated schools were unequal per se. For all minorities, including Native Americans, what came to be called the Civil Rights Movement pricked the moral conscience of the nation and stirred the juices of hope and possibility in all oppressed people. Benitez and others reaching adulthood in those precious few days of a kind of universal altruism in our nation's history were fortunate, indeed. And they were especially fortunate if they were prepared by education and/or leadership skills to take advantage of the new opportunities now made available to them. Benitez was one of those fortunate few, and in later years would appropriately credit the Civil Rights Movement in a newspaper interview, saying: "They made it work for all of us."

In 1976, Benitez attended a training course in accountability in Sacramento, California. Conducting that training was Dr. John P. Nichols, president of the training group Pro Plan International Ltd. Inc. Impressed with Nichols's training and broad experience in management, Benitez entered into discussions that would lead to a 1977 contract for Nichols's services with Riverside-San Bernardino County Indian Health Inc. (RSBCIHI). Prior to finalizing negotiations for the RSBCIHI contract, Benitez and Art Welmas would both attend another of Nichols's training sessions—a five-day course in resource development—and both would agree Nichols could also be valuable in providing badly needed resource development services to the Cabazons.

Born on December 10, 1929, Arthur James Welmas was six years older than Benitez and was his half brother through their mother. He too benefited from programs made possible through the social activism taking place in the country. Welmas had attended St. Johns Mission in Arizona for the first eight years of his education, with the final four of his 12 years spent at California Indian Union High School. He would later attend barber school as well as Manpower C.E.T.A. Training School. Welmas served in the United States Marine Corps, entering in 1947. He left the Marines in 1951 as a Corporal in the Infantry and enlisted in the Air Force. While in the Air Force he received top secret clearance, worked on nuclear projects, fought in the Korean Conflict, and returned to civilian life in 1955 as an Airman Second Class.

During the years following his discharge, Welmas became actively involved in tribal affairs and travelled to meetings near the reservation in Indio from his home area of Escondido, just north of San Diego, California. By the '70s, he was very active in Indian affairs generally, and especially with the American Indians for Future and Tradition, an organization in the San Diego area. He also became employed as a job developer in an Indian Center in San Diego as well as Public Meeting Coordinator, Revenue Sharing, for the City of San Diego, the latter of which required him to coordinate and disseminate public information to Indian groups.

Both Welmas and Benitez, along with fellow tribal officers and members, had envisioned the real possibilities the new federal and state programs offered for themselves, other tribal members and the Tribe itself as an entity by 1977. Because of the new ferment in the country, the BIA was forced to back away from what had been an oppressive paternalism. Most Native Americans, including active Cabazon members, now saw the possibility of regaining tribal independence and control over their affairs from demeaning, racist bureaucrats who arrogantly viewed them as less than European Americans.

Funds to which tribal members were entitled by law had often been doled out by BIA personnel as if the tribal members were children. In one letter dated June 8, 1966, so clearly demonstrating the absurdity of this relationship, then Tribal Chairman Benitez—who had learned how not to rock the boat—wrote a Mr. Haggerty of the BIA Riverside Area Field Office, saying:

> It might come as a shock to you, but we can't afford to pick up the telephone and make long-distance calls whenever we feel like it. I already have over $50 in phone bills for this year. That is one reason we feel it is necessary to establish a tribal budget. *We are trying to take our place as responsible adults and citizens, and it takes money to run a tribe.* We find it necessary and expensive just to keep in touch with the Bureau, and in the years past a lot of mistakes were made just because the older people didn't know they could call or write your office, and have you people help them. This is one of our *failures* we are trying to overcome. (Emphasis added.)

The tribal budget Benitez was referring to was adopted by the Tribe in January 1966, and came to a request for only $350, allocated as $200 for committee expenses, $100 for telephone calls and $50 for miscellaneous.

On May 6, 1967, one year later, the Cabazons approved a resolution that canceled that $350 proposed budget, which had still not been confirmed by the BIA, and adopted a new one for $1,500 in conjunction with BIA designation Riv-67-34. A second resolution, apart from a few minor spelling errors, clearly states the objectives of the Tribe, yet the BIA treats the document as so nebulous and technically incorrect it could not be acted upon until a later date. The tribal resolution read, in part:

> (WHEREAS), On this date it was requested that the telephone bills be combined and forward[ed] to the office [meaning BIA] to be re-embersed [sp] for the calls that have been

made in the interest of the tribe.

(WHEREAS), These bills were charged to the Chairman, Joseph R. Benetez [sp] it is to mandate to him the amount of ($36.66) for compensation. The toll recepts [sp] are also forward[ed] for proposed record value.

(THEREFORE BE IT RESOLVED) That after presentation and vote of (9) for and (0) against, this resolution was adopted for the payment of the telephone bills that have occurred over a time of several months.

Both resolutions were signed and certified by the Tribe's officers, Chairman Benitez, Vice-Chairman Callaway and Secretary-Treasurer James.

A full *18 months* after the $350 budget was adopted by the Tribe, the first of the typical BIA responses came in a memorandum from the Sacramento Area Office to the Riverside Area Field Office, dated July 3, 1967. That response was as follows:

Following are comments on the subject documents, which we did not have the time to review when you were in the office last week:

Cabazon resolution (Riv-67-34) on cancellation of budget. The original was received with your transmittal dated 6/14/67. As we interpret it, the F.Y. [Fiscal Year] 1968 tribal budget of $350, which was adopted 1/26/66, has been cancelled. It so happened that we did not act on any F.Y. 1968 tribal budgets until recently. In the meantime, a Cabazon budget of $1,500 was adopted, and we have the resolution and will act on it. Photocopy returned herewith.

Cabazon resolution (Riv-67-36) authorizing a $1,500 budget. We are retaining the original resolution and Budget Schedule D, which was attached to it. We will prepare Schedules A and B, obtain approval of the budget, and request an allotment of Cabazon funds under the Annual Authorization, as was recommended in Schedule D.

Cabazon resolution (Riv-67-37) authorizing payment of telephone bills. The resolution is not in good form, because the Resolved clause does not state who is to be paid. However, if you have telephone bills which are marked Paid, and if you can determine that the bills were paid by Mr. Joseph Benitez, Chairman, you could accept the resolution as authority to reimburse the Chairman. If you did not obligate F.Y. 1967 tribal funds by submitting an MOR document to OS in Albuquerque, it appears that you will have to delay payment until the F.Y. 1968 budget has been approved, and until funds have been allotted. The original of the resolution is returned herewith.

On September 21, 1967, obviously still awaiting transmittal of the approved budget funds, the Tribe approved another resolution. Barely concealing its frustration and anger at being treated like unworthy wards by a bureaucracy reflecting either incompetence or contemptuous arrogance or both, the Tribe passed Resolution Riv-67-63. The resolution asserted that it would serve the Tribe's "best interest" for these hopefully soon-to-be-received funds to be "placed in a local bank" and that the "General Council feels it wastes time waiting for approval of resolutions for payment of minor expenses." Since the BIA, in approving the budget, "recommended that a limitation be placed on travel expenditures," the Tribe's resolution provided "travel authorization be limited to $1,000," an obvious message since the entire budget was only $1,500.

This exchange between the Tribe and the BIA was classic. It was the universal oppressor-oppressed group relationship, blind and stupid arrogance meeting suppressed fury. But 1967 was not 1977, and a lot happened in those intervening years, the most important being that Native Americans began to stand tall, making it more difficult for would-be oppressors to ride their backs.

One such person was a 44-year-old Minnesota Chippewa named Russell Bryan. Bryan purchased a trailer and had it shipped to family tribal land in Squaw Lake Village on the Leech Lake Reservation in Minnesota. The county in which the reservation was located imposed a county personal property tax of $147.95 on the trailer. When contacted by Bryan's wife Helen, the Leech Lake Reservation Legal Services agency initiated legal action in 1972, fought their case up to the U.S. Supreme Court on the all-important issue of tribal sovereignty, and won.

The Court unanimously held that Public Law 280, which in 1953 gave some states, including California, the criminal and civil jurisdiction over reservations, did not weaken Indian reservation sovereignty by giving those states power to impose taxes. Writing for the Court, Justice William J. Brennan, Jr. stated that Congress did not intend that the law "should result in the undermining or destruction of such tribal governments as did exist," thereby converting them "into little more than 'private, voluntary organizations'—a possible result if tribal governments and reservation Indians were subordinated to the full panoply of civil regulatory powers, including taxation, of state and local governments."

It was a significant victory. A modern, unanimous Court had upheld sovereignty 23 years after Public Law 280 was passed, keeping that law properly limited in its scope. The victory for the Bryans was a victory for all Native Americans.

The concept of sovereignty was and is of great importance. When invading Europeans, hungry for ownership of land they couldn't get in their native Europe, made their genocidal sweep across what was to them newly "discovered" territory, they drove Native Americans from what they saw as the best and richest portions onto reservations. But over that land the invaders viewed as the least valuable, Native Americans were granted limited sovereignty. The Supreme Court wrote in the 1832 case of *Worcester v. Georgia*:

> The Indian nations have always been considered as distinct independent political communities, retaining their original national rights as the undisputed possessors of the soil, from time immemorial, with the single exception of that imposed by irresistible power, which excluded them from intercourse with any other European potentate than the first discoverer of the coast of the particular region claimed; and this was a restriction which those European potentates imposed on themselves as well as on the Indians. The very term nation, so generally applied to them, means "a people distinct from others." The Constitution, by declaring treaties already made, to be the supreme law of the land, has adopted and sanctioned the previous treaties with the Indian nations, and consequently admits their rank

among those powers who are capable of making treaties. The words "treaty" and "nation" are words of our own language, selected in our diplomatic and legislative proceedings by ourselves, having each a definite and well-understood meaning. We have applied them to the Indians as we have applied them to other nations of the earth. They are applied to all in the same sense.

Sovereignty would, by definition, eliminate the justification for supervision propounded by the Bureau of Indian Affairs since its inception. The BIA's struggle with the War Department for power over Native Americans had started in 1849, when the BIA had been transferred out of the War Department to the Department of the Interior. The BIA saw its mission as civilizing and Christianizing heathens. Such long-held views die hard, and in *Land Grab*, John Upton Terrell tells of a conversation he had that reflects how long such negative views toward Indians survived in institutions and succeeding generations of the employees of these institutions:

Only a short time before I wrote these words a white official of the Bureau of Indian Affairs stationed on the Apache Reservation at San Carlos, Arizona, said to me, "Hellfire, when we conquered the West, the Indians didn't even have the wheel. Archaeologists and ethnologists and all the other nutty scientists who study and write about Indians make me sick. Why should we bother our heads about such ignorant, low-type people? Why should we spend millions trying to educate them when they got nothing between their ears but bone? The whole country would have been better off if they had been wiped off the earth."

It was varying degrees of this kind of institutional and individual contempt, hostility and arrogant stupidity that emerging Native American leadership had to confront. And, like African- and Latino- and Asian-Americans, Native Americans began to say "enough is enough!"

Like other tribes, the Cabazons quickly learned the new—for all American poor people—languages of bureaucracy, in all sectors: federal, state, local and private. Benitez and Welmas, both staff members in bureaucratic agencies, were deeply involved in volunteer organizations and other groups as well. John James, while employed by the telephone company for more than a quarter century, served as a board member of an Indian health agency and was a Communication Workers of America (CWA) union shop steward as well. As a result of these three men's involvement with the Cabazons, new knowledge and new opportunities brought new hope and old dreams alive once more.

The minutes of Tribal meetings during these years reflect an increasingly sophisticated approach to their concern for preservation of their land, protection of their rights on the land and a determination to keep the minimum blood quantum qualification percent for Cabazon membership at one-quarter Indian. A review of the official records, beginning in 1963, also reflects a strong interest in ways to create businesses on the reservation, businesses that would provide jobs and wealth for the Tribe and its members.

As the 1970s advanced, this latter concern and accompanying activity increased, perhaps also related to the fact that "self-determination" was the popular phrase being coined by government and private philanthropic agencies and foundations of the time. During this period Congress also passed, and the White House approved, Public Law 93-262, the Indian Financing Act of 1974. This law authorized the appropriation of an amount "not to exceed the sum of $10,000,000 for each of the fiscal years 1975, '76 and '77" for the purposes of Indian Land Grants; and "not to exceed $20,000,000" for an Indian Loan Guaranty and Insurance Fund as well as Interest Subsidies and Administrative Expenses; and another "$50,000,000 exclusive of prior authorizations and appropriations" for an Indian Revolving Loan Fund.

The Cabazon minutes show the Tribe's Business Committee, which met regularly and took care of its business between meetings of the full Tribe, discussed on March 25, 1973, the establishing of a store on tribal land to earn income. At the September 6, 1975, meeting, discussions were held about Indian World, a profit-making business, and the possibilities of working out an agreement between the Cabazons and two other tribes—Torres-Martinez and 29 Palms—to push joint projects.

A year later, on September 25, 1976, the Tribe's Business Committee discussed formally setting up an office in Indio. The Committee also gave approval to "hire Charles Riggs as director and Amelia Callaway Giff as secretary . . . with pay." A month later their regular meeting was held "in the new Band office in the Johnson Building, Indio."

For the next year, the Tribe tried to get a Jojoba Project off and running on tribal land in cooperation with the University of California at Riverside, and attempted to get funding from different sources for various other projects such as planning, water restoration, block grants, 701 housing, revenue-sharing and an Overall Economic Development Project (OEDP). More than $300,000 was sought in a June 1977 application to the Economic Development Administration (EDA) of the U.S. Department of Commerce for "construction of a building to house tribal government offices, tribal business offices, education rooms, museum and social and cultural activities." It was agreed the preliminary architectural work for this project would be done by a firm at no cost, contingent on securing funding for the rest of the project. A $1,000 grant was received through BIA in June 1977 to hire youths to work on tribal farm projects, including both jojoba and sesame crops. During the tribal meeting of September 10, 1977, discussion was held regarding possible amendments to the Articles of Association with the BIA. One suggestion was that it might be of value to write to other tribes about changes they could have made in their Articles. Then someone not identified in the minutes, although today believed to have been John James, suggested the Tribe "also ask about gambling on the reservation." Already the potential benefits of Indian sovereignty were beginning to occur to tribal leaders.

The other major proposal in the final draft stage at this time was an enumeration of the goals of their submission to OEDP. The goals set forth were as follows:

1. Develop the reservation's agricultural resources to the fullest extent possible, consistent with Cahuilla respect for the land.
2. Develop commercial enterprises on the reservation without exploiting the Cahuilla's cultural heritage.
3. Obtain adequate housing for every member of the Band, especially those who wish to reside on the reservation.
4. Provide a job for every Band member who desires one.
5. Improve community services for all Band members.

Among the specific projects listed as having "the highest probability of fulfilling the Band's goals" were: agricultural development, with varied crops; the utilization of "206 acres of tribal land . . . on Interstate Highway 10" for such commercial ventures as "light manufacturing, a motel-and-restaurant complex, a recreational vehicle park, a mobile home park, and a trading post with native arts and crafts"; housing, employment expansion; and other community services, including the construction of a community center.

The year 1977 was one of positive ferment for the Cabazons. Not only were things beginning to look up, but the Cabazons were beginning to confidently and aggressively look up and out. They knew they needed more than a Mr. Riggs to help them achieve their goals; they needed someone who could take them to another level. As 1977 ended, Riggs resigned and negotiations were under way with Dr. John Philip Nichols.

Who was Nichols and why were the Cabazon leaders so impressed with him? Nichols was and is a self-described radical, born December 15, 1924, in Racine, Wisconsin. In his own words, a radical is "a person who doesn't have a false God. A true radical," he said, "is a Brother, and he is not going to hurt another Brother, and he will die for his Brother. He might not even know the man, but a Brother will die for what is right and that's the essence of radicalism. So, I have always been a radical. He does not do things to be liked. He does things that are right for the working class."

Nichols was an only child, the only child of "radical parents," who were open and activist socialists, he said. From about the time he was 8 years old, he remembers his mother asking him daily, "What have you done for the union today?" And later she added the strong, positive assertion that "any person who is worth his salt goes to prison for the union and for his beliefs."

He learned early never to automatically trust or believe in authority figures. His parents taught him to first find out what their intentions are. Do they intend to use their power for love or hate, to build or destroy? Using the Bible as a teaching tool, Nichols's parents—and especially his mother—taught that Jesus was a revolutionary whom the politically powerful destroyed, turning one of his followers into a snitch or fink. In his parents' lexicon, a snitch or fink—an informant—was the lowest form of human life, whether in Ireland working for the British or in the American workplace working for the bosses and undermining his peers or the union. Nichols also learned that anyone who acted without prejudice, who helped the poor, the disenfranchised or people of color, quickly became an enemy of the ruling class.

Nichols's mother was a member of the International Workers of the World (IWW). She had grown up in a logging camp and had earned a master's degree in teaching. A believer in the one-great-union concept, she helped organize railway clerks in Montana in the years 1913–16. From 1933 to 1936, during the Great Depression, she helped form and organize industrial trade unions. She was a close associate of Emma Goldman and John Reed.

Between the ages of 8 and 14, Nichols worked in the clay pits and coal mines during summer months. He was what the older miners called "an engineer." His job was to go into sections of the mine on skids, in places too small for adults, where the coal veins were only two-and-a-half to three-feet high. Armed with a pick, he would loosen the coal and separate the larger from the smaller pieces. By 10 years of age he had learned to use dynamite. He recalls now how for many years his skin seemed always to be the color of coal dust.

Nichols also vividly remembers meeting the great John L. Lewis, president of the United Mine Workers Union, and Alan Heywood, along with Philip Murray of the Steelworkers. He credits Lewis with teaching him three important lessons: one, he (Nichols) needed to have an operation to have his eyelids removed so that as a union leader his eyes would be open 24 hours a day to protect the workers from the bosses who were always trying to break the union; two, he must learn never to show his emotions, no matter how much pressure or stress he was under; and three, he must always be true to his family, the movement, the local union, then God and maybe country—in that order.

Nichols describes his father as a taskmaster who passionately believed in the work ethic and taught him the value of earning a living by the sweat of one's brow. He believed and taught Nichols that a person must always be loyal to his fellow workers, never lying to them, and if a worker got sick it was a person's responsibility to carry his fellow worker on his back until he got well. Nichols's father believed that only through unions could workers achieve strength. He realized the owners and bosses were not the only real enemies of workers, however. Included as enemies were the lackeys of bosses, the police, the press, the muckraking reporters, banks, utility companies and rent collectors. His bible was James Warbasse's book *Consumers Cooperative Societies* (published in 1922).

Nichols's paternal grandfather was an early homeopathic physician who at one time taught pharmacology at the University of Wisconsin. During World War I, he had become close to members of the Sioux Indian Nation when he served as chief medical officer for their reservations in North and South Dakota. After the war, he remained with the Sioux for another year and after returning to Wisconsin, he had many Sioux visitors and operated a free clinic for other tribal Indians living in Northern Wisconsin. These patients and visitors made a strong impression on young Nichols.

Growing up during the Depression, Nichols never enjoyed what is today thought to be a "normal" childhood. He would later say, "I never had a childhood. I never played games. Life was a serious business." To support his family during the Depression, Nichols's father—with Nichols as his work partner when possible—worked as a farmer, in a steel mill, a brewery, raised pigs (5,000) and rabbits (30,000), and was also at one time a sausage maker. His mother worked as a teacher whenever her radical background was not held against her. As Nichols would later describe her situation: "My mother taught school as a substitute teacher . . . but the problem was, if you're a radical there's not a lot of jobs, and you'd be the last substitute called after everybody in town was sick and nobody else was left around." One year, however, she taught school the whole year: she was his fifth-grade teacher in a one-room school.

When attending a 1937 union-organizing picnic, Nichols learned about the violence a "radical" movement can attract. "My dad came. There were people down there and they were doing this sort of experimental thing running their own shop, and that's when the police came and fired on us. People got killed and wounded. . . . If I didn't know who to hate before I sure knew who to hate after that. . . . Everybody wants to be loved. Turn the other cheek? Sometimes it doesn't work that way. I saw that later in life while working with Mennonites in Paraguay.

"Paraguayan soldiers came in and raped the Mennonites' wives and the Mennonites would say, 'Do you want her again?' I would see the Mennonites get hit and they would turn their cheeks. It didn't work that way because it didn't change the soldiers. It just degraded the family. There comes a point that you have to stand up for what you believe and that was something I learned early."

During the Spanish Civil War, Nichols's father went to Spain ("at great personal sacrifice to our family," said Nichols) after joining the famous Abraham Lincoln Brigade to fight in that war. "My father became a friend of George Orwell (author of the book *1984*) in that period," Nichols said. "Orwell had gone to Spain [to fight] . . . against fascism and he started to see that . . . communism was as big a danger. It was all . . . totalitarianism. The communists were willing to shoot the [Spanish] Republican Party leaders because they were more concerned about their [communist] control, and they weren't really concerned about the survival of Spain. So, my father came back a radical still, but a much wiser radical."

Another lesson to have great import in Nichols's life came through his "Uncle Jake—Jacob Anderson," he said, who taught him, "You always wrote a person, any person you met, a card. . . . I was a little kid then. . . . Uncle Jake said you write everyone, so I wrote all my relatives every year, and with what little allowance, whether it was 10 cents a week or eventually a quarter—whatever it was—I bought postage stamps."

When Nichols was 8, he took part in his first presidential election, sending 250 postcards out for Roosevelt. And on one occasion he recalled, "My father took me to Mexico to meet Trotsky (Leon Trotsky, the Russian revolutionary). . . . I wrote to Trotsky—every place I met anybody from the time I was a kid . . . I wrote everybody I met. . . . I started writing Bishop Cox of the Methodist Church, one of the great men on the social gospel. . . . The reason I wrote all the letters . . . was for knowledge." And when Nichols was a child and a teenager he "always asked these people if they had any books they were through with that they thought might be worthwhile. I'd be willing to pay for them, but I would like to buy them as cheaply as I could. I mean, I didn't ask them to send them for nothing . . ."

"What correspondence taught me was that there were a lot of people a lot smarter than I was . . . but the other thing that I learned from an early age on was I was being investigated by my mailing list. . . . By the time I was 12 years old, the FBI had come to my house."

Nichols's writing habit would continue throughout his life. As his international contacts grew, so did his mailings. He also kept a list of important dates in the lives of many persons with whom he corresponded, such as birthdays and anniversaries. The telephone became increasingly important as an adjunct to his writing over the years, as his heavier schedule and diminished energy made contact by telephone more convenient.

Nichols, a professional social worker with an earned doctorate in religious education, became a labor union member and shop steward at 16 years of age while working at the Stokley Brothers Canning Company in Plymouth, Wisconsin. At 18 years of age, he again became a union shop steward with the International Union of Brewery, Soft Drinks, Grain, Distillery, Water Workers of America.

In 1953, at age 29, Nichols worked jointly with the National Community Services Committee of the CIO (Congress of Industrial Organizations) and the International Union of Brewery, Soft Drinks, Grain, Distillery, Water Workers of America. The International split, with half of the membership becoming members of the Teamsters Union. Nichols went with the Teamsters, joining the staff of Ray Schoessling, who was then head of the Chicago Joint Conference of Teamsters Union Local 25 and Brewery Workers Local 133. He later became Secretary-Treasurer of the International. Nichols also worked on the staff of Harold Gibbons, who became Executive Vice President of the Teamsters, and Nichols got to know Jimmy Hoffa, its President, personally.

During the investigation of Jimmy Hoffa by the U.S. Senate Select Committee on Racketeering, Nichols temporarily moved to Washington, D.C., at the request of Gibbons to assist in solving some of the problems created by the investigation. After a short stint in the nation's capital, Nichols "decided to make a change" in his "vocational activities and travel abroad," which he said, "was a heartfelt desire of my wife and older children. . . . After stopping in Recife, Cuba, Rio de Janeiro and Santos, Brazil, we decided we would make our living in San Paulo, Brazil." Within two months, Nichols had become sales and advertising manager of Refrescos Do Brasil (Coca Cola) and subsequently became its manager. When he left Coca Cola, he worked for another major corporation, Anderson Clayton, as an idea man in their marketing department.

Nichols then returned to the United States for a short period. While waiting to return to Latin America, he took a temporary assignment as Executive Director of the Lower Eastside Neighborhood Association in New York City. Securing a position with Church World Service as staff representative, Nichols was assigned to Ayuda Christiana Evangélica (ACE) and the Concilio Evangélica de Chile. He would be based in Santiago and would be supervised by Obispo Enrigue Chavez.

For more than four years, Nichols worked with health and social-welfare treatment facilities and on economic-development projects of Chile's almost 900 local committees, covering a 2,300-mile area serving 2,000,000 Chilean Evangelicals. Among these projects were setting up and working small mines for precious stones such as lapis lazuli and various kinds of metals, deep-sea diving, the collection of abalone, the cultivation and gathering of seaweed for the Far East market, sawmills, millwork factories and native crafts work centers.

From that operations base, Nichols did consultation work for evangelical groups in Peru, Brazil, Guatemala, El Salvador and Bolivia, and similar economic-development work with COMBASE, a group representing Protestant, Evangelical, Mennonite and Pentecostal churches in Bolivia.

In 1967, 10 years before contracting with the Cabazons in California, Nichols was a consultant to the Chilean Council of Churches delegation to the World Congress of Pentecostalism in Rio de Janeiro. He was also a delegate from Chile to the World Congress of Evangelicals held in Berlin, West Germany, in 1966. Assisted by his wife Joann, he was ACE's official coordinator for disaster relief within Chile and throughout Latin America. While serving in that position in 1965, 80 percent of the country was declared a disaster because of the devastation from nationwide earthquakes and tidal waves produced by another mammoth earthquake. During this time, he and Joann coordinated the feeding of 3,000,000 people, the rebuilding of thousands of houses, the distribution of planeloads of clothing and blankets and the establishment of post-disaster cooperative economic-development enterprises.

Before returning to the United States, Nichols made several trips to countries in Africa as an economic-development consultant after the Declaration of Rancaqua was drafted. The Declaration was a faith statement for Evangelicals and Pentecostals. Nichols, Obispo Chavez (Pentecostal Church of Chile), the Reverendo Coelho Ferraz (Presbyterian Church of Brazil), and Reverendo Geraldo Valdevia were among the drafters of the Declaration. To raise money for Evangelical economic- and social-health-development projects, Bishop Chavez, Nichols and other staff made multiple trips to the Orient and throughout Europe.

In late 1967, Nichols sought and was granted a five-year leave of absence by the board of ACE so he could return to the United States for his children's education. The leave was twice extended so that he could represent ACE with resource-development activities in the United States and Europe.

Upon his return to America, Nichols, Joann, and Dr. William Willner formed Pro Plan International Ltd. Inc. in Tallahassee, Florida. Willner was a lawyer, the retired Director of Grants and Contract Management of the National Aeronautics and Space Administration, and a professor of public administration. Together, Nichols and Willner wrote and published two major training books: *Revenue Shar-*

ing in 1973, and *Handbook of Grants and Contracts for Nonprofit Organizations* in 1976. Included in the latter book were the Federal Register regulations, published November 4, 1975, governing the Indian Self-Determination and Education Assistance Act, Public Law 93-638. The year it was published, Joe Benitez and Nichols met for the first time, and one year later Benitez, Welmas, Nichols and the Cabazon Band's Business Committee had reached a meeting of the minds. Given Nichols's broad-reaching experience, all that needed to be done was to formalize an agreement on paper and secure the money to pay for his services.

It was this meeting of the minds, between the courageous, rotund, radical visionary known as John Philip Nichols and the small Tribe of poor-but-awakened and equally courageous Cabazon Indians and their families, that would revive and change an obscure, economically dying, racist Southern California desert town named Indio into a city of hope.

The Wildcat and the Coyote had been wed, as Cahuilla custom recommends.

3

The Early Successes and Struggles

As in a marriage, when two groups enter into a contract each brings to that relationship a history, and much of the history of each is unknown to the other, no matter how extensive the résumés or initial discussions. Each must get to know and learn how to be comfortable with the other in order for the developing relationship to enable both groups to function at an optimal level.

The process is more difficult when past similar relationships and contacts between seemingly similar groups had proven exploitative to one of the parties. This had been the case throughout the history of all Native American relationships with European Americans from the beginning, especially over money. So accepted was this exploitation at one time, as later press response would prove, the only question—usually asked with a wink between fellow European Americans—seemed to be, "How much are you beating the Indians out of?"

Therefore when John James, then Tribal Secretary-Treasurer and later Chairman, was asked his initial reaction to Nichols and his family he didn't hesitate to respond: "I thought they were hustlers, that they had a get-rich-quick scheme [for themselves] and they'd be gone. . . . Then I talked with some people and they let me know that Doc [Nichols] was serious. . . . I thought to myself, well, let's give him a try and just see what he's going to do. I found out he really knows all those people [he claimed to know], people [even] I never heard about, [and] he got them all lined up [to help us]. . . . The next thing you knew, you got six offers [of help], whereas we couldn't get one offer. So, that impressed me."

James, who is close to Nichols in age, is known for his bluntness. In relating his memory of an early conversation he had with Nichols, he said, I talked to him straight out. I said,

"If you are hustling, if you're just doing this to get rich quick and haul out of here, it ain't gonna work because we're here permanent; we're not moving." And Nichols said, "Pro Plan, which is my family, just wants your backing. Once we get things rolling, if things aren't running the way you want them to run, you're welcome to fire us. You're just hiring us is all you're doing." I said, "Well, let's put it this way, you gotta be in for the long haul." And he said, "Well, I'm talking about a 10-year plan, beginning with steps—a one-year plan and a five-year plan, then a 10-year plan—with a tentative additional 10 years on top of that." I said, "God knows where we're gonna be in 20 years. That's a long time." He said, "You'd be surprised. It goes real quick . . . especially if you're successful. One trick is to bypass the BIA and go directly to Washington." And that's what we did.

James said Nichols also warned tribal members they could expect and should be prepared for negative governmental and private-sector reaction to their success. James recalled that Nichols said, "You know they're going to be on us. They're not only going to be tapping your phone. They're going to be following you around. You go somewhere and you've got credit cards, they're going to be checking your credit. They're going to be down at your bank. They're going to be over there where you got your car. They're going to be talking to your neighbors. You're going to have everybody from the locals all the way up to the FBI and they're going to treat you like Fidel Castro's brother."

James was also suspicious of the motives and intentions of Glenn Feldman who soon became the attorney of the Cabazons. James said his initial reaction to Feldman was negative since "we didn't know this guy. . . . He'd worked with the federal government and that smelled. We had to ask ourselves if the government had sent a spy down to cut our throats. We found out it was the other way around. He didn't like the way the U.S. government was treating the Indians and the sneaky things they were doing to us and that's why he took us on. In other words, it was a labor of love as far as he was concerned. He loves to hang them, the very guys he used to work with, because he realized what they are and what they've been doing."

James was not alone in his initial reaction to Nichols. John Welmas, son of Art Welmas, and later to become a member of the Tribe's leadership, also related his early reactions to suggestions that Nichols was taking advantage of the Tribe and taking its money. He said,

I thought that way too, and I'll be the first one to say this because I didn't really know (if you don't know you're going to assume what you want to assume), and at first you think, "He's got everything." When we started out nobody really had anything (you know, I didn't even own a car . . . I didn't have a place to stay) and when you see somebody who has a home and a car, I don't want to seem to be stereotyping, but when the Indians are coming back here to the reservation and they don't have zero, and you see this guy working for the Indians and he has a house and what have you? Well, you say, "Why can't I have that? He's probably stealing money." But then you get to know everybody and you find out it's not like that at all. Basically, everybody does that; if they don't know the facts they assume something negative is happening, just like the press has done over the years. They don't know and won't believe that we Indians have made all the decisions all along, and that if anybody was taking anything we'd be the first to know. But the press just likes to assume the worst about us, since I guess it sells papers.

On January 6, 1978, Nichols as President of Pro Plan International Ltd. Inc. submitted a letter proposal to develop the Ten-Year Master Plan for the Cabazon Band of Mission Indians. The cost, payable in three installments, was $10,000.

The proposal was approved in February and the agreement was signed on March 1, 1978. Under the terms of the agreement, Pro Plan contracted to:

A. Devise a TEN YEAR MASTER PLAN to:
  1) Analyze existing tribal council procedures.
  2) Analyze existing tribal council and its committee structure and strengthen the effectiveness of said structure.
  3) Evaluate new economic development structure.
  4) Include recommendations and cash forecast over a 10-year span.
  5) Evaluate and project developing social needs.

B. Develop a Procedural Manual to include:
  1) Reporting systems.
  2) Accounting regulations.
  3) Board policy.
  4) Analysis of facilities.
  5) Relationship of tribal institutions to government.

C. Review the following systems:
  1) Procurement.
  2) Equipment and supply management.
  3) Compensation.
  4) Facilities management.
  5) Planning and budgeting.

On March 15, 1978, the two parties signed another agreement that stated:

1. Pro Plan International Ltd. will provide secretarial, bookkeeping and administrative services to the Cabazon Indian Tribe and Nation.
2. Pro Plan International Ltd. will provide an office for the Cabazon Indian Tribe and Nation in the Pro Plan office complex at 82-640 Miles Avenue, Indio, CA 92201.
3. Utilities charged to the office complex will be split between the two parties.
4. Each party will be responsible for his own telephone costs.
5. The Cabazon Indian Tribe and Nation agrees to pay to Pro Plan International Ltd. the sum of $2,000.00 on the fifteenth day of every month for the above listed services.
6. Travel costs for Pro Plan International will be charged to the Cabazon Tribe and Nation when incurred on their behalf and authorized by the Cabazon Tribe and Nation.

Upon execution of the contracts, Nichols employed a Study Team to develop the Ten-Year Master Plan; included on the team were Joann Nichols, William McGrath, Faith Reardon, Terry Hughes, Frank Greenberg and Dr. William Willner. Although initially the Plan was to be submitted by the end of September 1978, the Accountability and Procedures Manual was submitted in August, and the Ten-Year Master Tribal Reorganization Plan was submitted on November 15, 1978.

A 260-page document, the Plan covered every aspect of tribal life and government, establishing the basis for a government equivalent to a "nation" within a nation. It provided for an executive, legislative and judicial separation of powers and functions. It established an orderly system of committees, and, very important, provided that working members of the Tribal Council would be salaried rather than per diem, although per diem would be paid non-working members.

In the Tribal Council meeting of April 29, 1978, new OEDP priorities were presented and approved, with William Lunsford given authorization to submit them in June to the U.S. Department of Commerce. Mr. Lunsford was from the Southern Reservation Planning Organization, a group that was assisting tribes in developing their OEDP proposals for funding. The four new priorities were: (1) agricultural development of guayule, a small shrub grown for the rubber attained from it, because according to Nichols, $60 million of federal funds were projected to be appropriated for guayule, (2) jojoba expansion, (3) shrimp agriculture, and (4) a smoke shop. An application was also approved for a Community Development Block Grant from The Department of Housing and Urban Development (HUD) to build a community hall, a two-lane access road and an agricultural feasibility study.

Although their feet were now firmly planted in a new economic direction, their ideas flowing freely and plans turning into reality, the Council soon discovered tribal outsiders were not the only potential source of detriment to their goals. The minutes began to record a series of battles the Council had to fight within its own ranks, the first with Alfred "Fred" Alvarez, a contributing but renegade member of the Tribe who "commented on the economic potential in growing marijuana for medicinal purposes and the feasibility of applying for money for such a project." Mr. Benitez, who was chairing the meeting, "responded that he did not feel there is a place in the Cabazon Plan for this at present."

Although Alvarez's suggestion would appear innocuous and even altruistic to persons who did not know him, since marijuana growth and use can be officially supported for treatment of specific health conditions, the tribal members did know him. They took into account that he was a self-proclaimed illegal drug user, dealer and a member of the Hell's Angels motorcycle gang. The push to grow marijuana was to be a constant and persistent effort by Alvarez until his eventual assassination, by parties unknown. An effort would later be made by tribal dissidents, including Alvarez's father and sister, government officials and the press, to try to implicate tribal members and associates in his death in order to cripple the progress of the Tribe.

Throughout 1978, Pro Plan, through Nichols and Joann (who was manager of the tribal office and took Tribal Business Committee and Council minutes) presented partial drafts of what became the Ten-Year Plan final document. In its June Council meeting, drafts of a tribal resolution regarding business regulation of sales of tobacco products, a tribal business permit and business agreement were presented and approved.

Before Nichols began with the Tribe, the Cabazons had been involved in developing a jojoba plantation on tribal lands. At one time discussions were held regarding the eventual planting of as much as 120 acres in jojoba, a major economic-development project that gained interest after a 1977 National Academy of Science report concluded that great economic benefits would flow from jojoba growth and marketing in the nation's Southwest. Because of the worldwide depletion of sperm whales, a substitute for its valuable oil had been sought and apparently found in the oil of jojoba beans. Declared the National Academy: "Jojoba oil resembles sperm whale oil in chemical composition and physical behavior. If a sufficient supply of jojoba oil were available at a competitive price, it would be used as a substitute for sperm oil."

The February 1979 issue of *New Directions*, the official publication of the Santa Barbara, California, Chamber of Commerce, added fuel to the excitement when it featured a cover photograph of green jojoba and a cover story titled "Jojoba: Its Future is Limitless." In the article, *Business Week* magazine is cited as publishing about how under a "$70,000 state research grant, plant scientist Dr. Demetrious M. Yermanos would plant up to 200 acres of reservation land in Southern California. And the Bureau of Indian Affairs has drawn up a five-year plan calling for 10,000 acres of jojoba to be planted on various Southwestern Indian reservations." Although the Cabazons were not mentioned in the article, their reservation was instrumental in getting Yermanos his grant, a grant pushed by then Governor Jerry Brown.

The U.S. Department of the Interior (DOI) even got in on the act. In a September 11, 1978, letter from Dr. Gordon Law (Assistant and Science Advisor to the DOI Secretary) to Dr. Randolph T. Blackwell, Director of the U.S. Department of Commerce's Office of Minority Business Enterprise (OMBE), $100,000 was sought to set up a Center for New Crop Agriculture and Appropriate Technology (CATE). Law's letter said OMBE's decision "to assist" in setting up CATE was welcomed "because the four tribes (San Carlos Apache, Arizona; Cabazon, Morongo and Pauma, California) participating in this interagency project . . . are urgently in need of the kind of assistance this center would provide." As Joe Benitez would write in an October 1978 memo to the Tribal Council, criticizing Nichols for not submitting a jojoba proposal to the BIA, "there has been three years of development of 120 acres and technical assistance by the University of California/Riverside." For two years or so it was full-court press before the bottom dropped out of the seemingly unlimited market. Just as with other BIA initiatives, Indian adrenaline had been pumped up without a payoff.

By September 1978, the Cabazons would be awarded a Community Development Block Grant to construct a community building. Construction was scheduled to begin in November.

In the September 16, 1978, meeting, the first step was taken by the Tribe to apply but limit their own tax on businesses on reservation land. Art Welmas made a motion, seconded by William Callaway and approved unanimously, "that no industry be assessed a tax above two percent." It was a first, but giant, step in becoming a revived nation.

In that September Council meeting, Nichols reported that three attorneys were "checking into the legality of selling tobacco products" at a prospective Cabazon Smoke Shop. He told the Council "the opinions of the attorneys vary, but they all agree the State of California will take the Band to court." Since Pro Plan had advanced money to pay attorney's fees, he said, "Pro Plan would want to recover its legal costs."

Financial projections on the Smoke Shop were distributed to the Council. Nichols told tribal members that "direct mail of cigarettes is much more profitable and that Mr. [Al] Pearlman has offered the front-end moneys for advertising in national publications for direct mail." The now-deceased Pearlman, then owner of Washington Wholesale Drug Exchange, a pharmaceutical manufacturing and distributing company in Washington, D.C., would prove a valuable asset to the Tribe in these early efforts.

Discussions had previously been held regarding a Smoke Shop joint venture between the Cabazons and Little Beaver Enterprises of the Yakima Tribe. It was becoming increasingly apparent that Chairman Benitez was leaning toward this venture and "recommended," according to the minutes, "waiting to make any decisions until a meeting" could be held "on the 30th of September at which Little Beaver Enterprises would be represented."

At the September 30 meeting, Robert Ramsey and Charlie Pims of the Yakima Nation attended representing Little Beaver. After full discussion, a motion was made by Art Welmas, seconded by John James and approved unanimously, "to negotiate with Little Beaver on the Smoke Shop." Shortly thereafter—following approval of a motion requested by Benitez for a 60-day extension request to the BIA of the Ten-Year plan—Benitez "requested that Pro Plan International leave the meeting." This was a recorded first.

One month later, on October 28, 1978, the first item on the Council's agenda was the Smoke Shop and Little Beaver Enterprises. Art Welmas had obviously undertaken to personally review the facts surrounding this prospective business. He reported that "he had spoken with Rudy Saluskin (of the Yakima Nation) and that there appeared to be a lack of clarity between Ramsey and Saluskin and that at present the Smoke Shop is legally risky. He stated he would like a letter to the Tribe from Little Beaver showing interest." Then the minutes state "Mr. Welmas requested that all negotiations with Little Beaver be put in writing." Since Benitez had been the prime negotiator between Little Beaver and the Tribe, his reports to the Tribe were now in question.

After Benitez reported on his contacts with a Jim Fletcher who, according to Benitez, was "continuing to work on the housing program with the Farmers Home Loan Administration," Art Welmas asserted he "wished to be invited to all meetings with Jim Fletcher on housing and building. He suggested that all information on building be left in the office for tribal use." A little later Eugene Welmas made the motion, it was seconded by William Callaway and passed unanimously, that "Art Welmas be included on the signature cards of the Community Development Block Grant bank account." Then Art Welmas moved "that any voucher for over $150 must be approved by the Tribal Council. This was seconded by Eugene Welmas and passed unanimously."

The tension in the meeting and the actions taken to limit the power and freedom of the Chairman to act alone had been prompted by the previous executive session in which Benitez had asked for Pro Plan to be excused, and by a letter dated October 15 that Benitez had sent to Council members openly attacking Pro Plan and Art Welmas, whom Benitez painted as a Pro Plan defender. According to the letter, Pro Plan was not performing sufficiently to justify its $2,000 monthly contract fee, and Dr. Nichols specifically "does not spend that much time in the office to develop different resources," he said. Attached to the letter was an unexpected bill totaling $1,036.75 for Benitez's own consultant services, which he claimed he rendered to the Tribe during August and September. And, adding to this sudden and apparently angry move, when Art Welmas expressed the opinion in defense of Pro Plan that "the basis of all present tribal problems is money and a lack of communication between the Tribal Chairman and the managerial service," asking Benitez "if he would work with the Pro Plan managerial service," Benitez replied that he would not. Welmas then asked for the resignation of Benitez and stated this was "to be put on the agenda at the next meeting." Everything was now out in the open—it was either Pro Plan or Benitez.

Minutes from the subsequent October 28 meeting highlight two other significant actions that were approved. Although the Tribe owed Pro Plan money for its services through November 15, 1978, Nichols asked for approval to work "on a credit basis until the Tribe is in a better financial situation." A motion to this effect was made by Art Welmas and seconded by William Callaway and the motion passed unanimously, showing solid support for Pro Plan. Then "Art Welmas made a motion that a Certified Public Accountant be brought in to do an audit covering the past 12 years [while Benitez was the chairman]. The motion was seconded by Fred Alvarez. Pro Plan said it would donate the CPA services of John Goff of Moonie & Associates and that he will be available the first week in December 1978. The motion passed unanimously."

The next meeting of the Tribe was held November 4, 1978. After approval of the minutes, an executive session was called and all non-tribal members left the meeting. Reconvening an hour and a half later, the Chairman introduced and welcomed Beverley Jean Welmas as a new member of the Tribal Council. Most of the remainder of the meeting, attended by Al Pearlman, was devoted to discussions about Pearlman's potential involvement with two possible tribal business enterprises.

Pearlman was pleasantly blunt about why a wealthy and successful business like Washington Wholesale Drug Exchange would be interested in joint venturing with a small Indian tribe. According to the minutes of that meeting, Pearlman said "a minority small business has two special benefits: (1) many government agencies are encouraged to buy 15 percent of their goods from a minority company; and (2) in some instances a minority company is allowed to bid 5 percent above the person making the lowest bid and still receive the business." This "edge" was especially attractive to someone in Pearlman's business, due to the large sales made by pharmaceutical companies to government agencies and to agencies receiving government funding, including private and government-run hospitals, community health facilities, clinics, and drug rehab centers in every state in the nation.

(In years to come the press would question why a large security firm like Wackenhut, in seeking U.S. Defense Department contracts, would also want to form a joint venture with the Cabazons—"such a small Indian tribe." Well, in addition to the "edge" Pearlman outlined, Wackenhut had the additional incentive that Congress had passed a law mandating 5 percent of all defense-procurement dollars be spent with minority firms.)

Actually, according to the minutes, Pearlman had two main business interests in the Tribe. A tribal corporation, Shaman, had been formed to "purchase pharmaceuticals in bulk, package them following FDA guidelines, and . . . sell to state, county and city governments." He described in detail the kind of building and training required and brought a contract for the Tribe to consider. His second business interest was mail-order sales of cigarettes. Pearlman assured the Tribe that the "building, road and what else is needed would be put up front by" him, and he would be "reimbursed out of profits." He stated he would want "an exclusive contract" to get started, and the Tribe and he would also need a reservation post office, a warehouse and truck.

Twenty-one days later, the Council met again, and after preliminary approval of the previous minutes and amended Articles of Association, the members got down to the major business they obviously came to perform: the changing of the guard. It had been clear for at least some two months that a new Chairman would soon be needed to replace Benitez. It was only a question of when, and members had come to this meeting to say the time was now. The minutes record the action this way:

> Linda Streeter asked if new elections should be held. Mr. Benitez indicated that amended Articles (of Association) did not replace the old Articles. He asked for the opinion of [Dr.] John Nichols and John Nichols replied it would be a question the Board itself would have to decide. Art Welmas indicated that he felt that if the Area Director had approved the new Articles, an election should be held. Linda Streeter made a motion to elect new officers and Art Welmas seconded the motion. . . . The motion carried. Mr. Benitez then asked how the Council proposed to hold its new election. Art Welmas stated he thought the election should be held immediately and then business could continue. . . . Mr. Benitez opened the nominations for Tribal Chairman. According to the Articles, the incumbent is automatically put on the ballot. Fred Alvarez nominated Art Welmas and Leroy Alvarez seconded the nomination. Mr. Benitez asked John and Joann Nichols to count the ballots. The vote was 6 votes

for Art Welmas and 1 vote for Joe Benitez. Mr. Benitez turned the chair over to Art Welmas. Nominations were opened for 1st Vice-President. Leroy Alvarez nominated Fred Alvarez and Linda Streeter seconded the nomination. Nominations were closed. The vote was 5 votes for Fred Alvarez and 1 unreadable.

Nominations for 2nd Vice-President were opened. Art Welmas nominated Sam Welmas and the nominations were closed. He was automatically elected since the only other incumbent nominee had previously been elected Tribal Chairman. Nominations were opened for Secretary-Treasurer. The incumbent, John James, was nominated. Nominations were closed and he was automatically elected. Linda Streeter then moved to cast a unanimous ballot for Sam Welmas as 2nd Vice-Chairman and John James as Secretary-Treasurer. Fred Alvarez seconded the motion and the vote was unanimous.

Benitez was out. Although he would remain in the meeting and participate, he was not happy, and eventually sought unsuccessfully to fight the election through the BIA. To make the bitter pill even more difficult to swallow, it was announced before the meeting ended that "John Goff, CPA with Moonie & Associates, would arrive the first week of December, 1978, to do an audit of the Cabazon books [compiled during Benitez's chairmanship] and to look at the Accountability and Procedures Manual." This work would be the beginning of the end of Benitez's participation in all tribal matters.

On January 6, 1979, by Resolution No. 18-79, approved by the Tribal Council, a committee was appointed "to prepare a bill of particulars against Joseph R. Benitez" on charges of "failure to carry out his Chairmanship responsibilities, with gross neglect of duty, and misconduct reflecting on the dignity and integrity of the Band." The process would be a long one, resulting in Benitez being found guilty on five charges and sentenced by the Cabazon Tribal Court.

The complaint filed before the Tribal Court listed these five causes for action:

FIRST CAUSE OF ACTION

Article 8(A) of the Articles of Association of the Cabazon Band of Mission Indians authorizes the Chairman of the Cabazon Band "to execute on behalf of the Band all contracts, leases or documents which have been approved by the General Council."

In early 1978 while he was Cabazon Tribal Chairman, the defendant did enter into negotiations with the Naegele Outdoor Advertising Company Inc. (Naegele). Such negotiations concluded in March 1978 whereupon the defendant executed an agreement with Naegele on behalf of the Cabazon Band of Mission Indians.

This agreement was extremely disadvantageous to the Cabazon Band, in that it purportedly authorized Naegele to erect outdoor advertising structures on the Cabazon and Twenty-Nine Palms Reservations under terms which did not adequately compensate the Cabazon Band.

Such agreement was never authorized or approved by the Cabazon General Council.

Said agreement has been determined by this Court in a separate proceeding to be invalid.

In acting as he did, the defendant has violated the Articles of Association of the Cabazon

Band as well as Cabazon tribal law and custom.

SECOND CAUSE OF ACTION

In connection with and in consideration of defendant's execution of the agreement referred to in paragraph 6 above, defendant and Naegele did enter into a second agreement in early March 1978 for which defendant personally received the sum of approximately $6,304 from Naegele.

In so acting, defendant engaged in a conflict of interest inconsistent with his duties and responsibilities as Tribal Chairman, in violation of the Articles of Association of the Cabazon Band, as well as Cabazon tribal law and customs.

THIRD CAUSE OF ACTION

Article 8(D) of the Articles of Association of the Cabazon Band requires that the Secretary-Treasurer shall certify the enactment of all ordinances and resolutions and further requires that he co-sign tribal checks.

During his chairmanship of the Cabazon Band, the Defendant caused checks, contracts and resolutions to be signed and enacted without the signature of the Secretary-Treasurer.

In so acting, the defendant has violated the Articles of Association of the Cabazon Band, as well as Cabazon tribal law and custom.

FOURTH CAUSE OF ACTION

During his Chairmanship of the Cabazon Band of Mission Indians, the defendant received travel advances from the Band which were never reimbursed.

The defendant's actions were in violation of Cabazon law and custom.

FIFTH CAUSE OF ACTION

The defendant has signed and caused to be filed with the United States District Court, Central District of California, one or more declarations which contain material which is false, defamatory and which reflects negatively on the integrity of the plaintiff and its business enterprises.

In so acting, the defendant has violated the Articles of Association of the Cabazon Band, as well as Cabazon tribal law and customs.

Before this action against Benitez was brought before the Tribal Court, it had been heard and acted on by the Tribal Council. A Special Committee to Investigate Charges Against Joseph R. Benitez was established by the Tribe and, after extensive consideration of the audit by David L. Moonie & Co., CPA, it met on May 23, 1980, and unanimously authorized the presentation of the charges to the General Council for action. The next day the Cabazon General Council acted and forwarded to Benitez the following itemized charges:

Pursuant to the authority of Section 6A3 of the Articles of Association of the Cabazon Band of Mission Indians and pursuant to the principal [sp] that an Indian Tribe shall have authority over all matters relating to its members, the following grounds for disenrollment of Joseph R. Benitez from the Cabazon Band of Mission Indians are stated:

Section 1.2 (c)

The member has used his position as an officer of the Band for unauthorized personal gain to the detriment of the Band.

Charges

1. Housing Improvement Program: Excessive disbursement of Housing Improvement Funds for personal use (1973-1978) as shown by David L. Moonie & Co., Certified Public Accountants.

Total H.I.P. Income: $18,536.81

Received by:

Joseph Benitez	$6,045.94
Marc Benitez	$1,500.94
Wm. Callaway	$2,307.39
John James	$ 68.00
Amelia Giff	$ 500.00
Arthur Welmas	$ 156.09
Recipient Uncertain (21 Purchases)	$5,956.74

2. Naegele Outdoor Advertising Sign Co.: Entered into personal contract with Naegele Outdoor Advertising Co. in the amount of $6,304.00 on March 6, 1978, prior to signing a contract between the Band and Naegele on March 21, 1978. Neither contract negotiated with Naegele was ever approved by the General Council. The contract between the Band and Naegele is considered detrimental to the Band, because over the life of the contract, the Band will receive $92,000 and Naegele will make a profit of many millions, an unconscionable return on the investment. By this contract, signs were allowed to be erected on Twenty-nine Palms Reservation causing possible legal problems and financial claims on the Band.

3. Received travel advances from the tribe which were not reimbursed.

Section 1.2 (d): The member has knowingly violated the terms, conditions or obligations of the Articles of Association, to the detriment of the Band.

Charges

1. Business was conducted and contracts, resolutions and checks authorized without the signature of the Secretary-Treasurer as required by the Articles of Association. Tribal records attest to this.

Section 1.2 (f): The member has knowingly engaged in such other misconduct or gross neglect of duty as to seriously reflect on the dignity and integrity of the Band.

Charges

1. Refused to follow dictates of General Council—e.g. return of Master Charge and purchase of a tractor.

2. Certified resolutions without knowledge of elected Business Committee.

3. Refused to cooperate with contracted administrative service, thereby jeopardizing the proper conduct of tribal business.

4. Changed tribal name on letterhead to Chemehuevi-Cahuilla without General Council discussion or approval, seriously jeopardizing the tribe on legal documents.

5. Lack of responsibility to tribal members regarding 148 docket funds.

6. Generally impeded tribal advancement re Indian self-determination by looking for personal remuneration rather than tribal, in position as tribal chairman.

7. Falsely stating to the Business Committee and the General Council that he has not received remuneration from tribally related activities during July, August and September of 1978.

8. Enrollment of non-Indian on tribal roll.

9. Claimed Shaman International Health Systems Inc. as former employer in order to obtain unemployment compensation, misconduct reflecting on the dignity and integrity of the Band in violation of state and federal law.

In a June 1, 1980, letter to the Tribe, Benitez requested a postponement of the Tribal Council's originally scheduled hearing, which was granted. A September 23, 1980, letter to Benitez rescheduled the hearing on October 11, 1980. Finally, after more maneuvers by Benitez and his attorney, the hearing was held on November 15, 1980. Made available to Benitez and the Tribe for that hearing was an updated review of financial records by George M. Johnson, CPA.

On the first charge regarding disbursements of Housing Improvement Program funds, the Council found Benitez guilty by a vote of 7 for, 6 against, with one abstention. On the charge involving contracts with Naegele Outdoor Advertising Company, there was extensive discussion. According to the Tribe's official minutes:

A preliminary statement was made by Steve Rios (Benitez's attorney) whereby Joseph Benitez would plead guilty only to conflict of interest regarding his personal contract with the Naegele Company. Arguments for the defense on the Tribal contract included the following:

A) The Cabazon Band historically did all negotiating for the 29 Palms Band;

B) The Cabazon Band knew that $42,000 was set aside for 29 Palms;

C) Other Council members were present during some of the negotiations;

D) Joseph Benitez did not have proper advice;

E) Joseph Benitez informed Naegele at a later date that some signs were not on Cabazon land.

For the prosecution, George Johnson, CPA, read his audit report regarding the Naegele contract.

The minutes of the Cabazon General Council in casting judgment read: "Fred Alvarez moved and Leroy Alvarez seconded to accept a finding of guilty on the full charge against Joseph Benitez, such finding to include guilt on conflict of interest, on bad judgment, on nondisclosure of tribal contract negotiations to the General Council, on jeopardizing tribal relations with 29 Palms Reservation, and to condemning that type of behavior. . . . Joseph Benitez was found guilty by a vote of 14 for, 0 against, 0 abstentions."

On the unreimbursed-travel-advance charge, "Motion was made by Fred Alvarez and seconded by Leroy Alvarez to accept a guilty plea to non-reimbursement to the Tribe of $524.52 as presently shown by the audit and to instruct Steve Rios, counsel for the accused, to prepare a letter under [over] the signature of Joseph Benitez, to be sent to the agencies previously contacted by the Tribe, requesting that they release to the Tribe a listing of all expense moneys (travel, per diem, etc.) which have been paid to Joseph Benitez from 1968 through 1978, for which restitution will be made to the Tribe after further auditing. The vote was 12 for, 0 against, 2 abstentions."

On the charge regarding the conduct of business and the authorization of resolutions and checks without the signature of the Tribal Secretary-Treasurer, Attorney Rios initially told the Council that Benitez "was pleading not guilty and that there was no evidence to support the charge." After reviewing the audit report, which showed that 554 checks totaling $185,757.56 were not signed by the Secretary-Treasurer, but by Benitez alone or by Benitez and William Callaway, Rios said, "Benitez would plead guilty to technical violation of signing of checks and no contest on signing contracts and resolutions." One point made by the CPA was that he "found several voided checks in the file which were signed by William Callaway only. In my opinion, this would indicate that Mr. Callaway was pre-signing checks, thereby giving Mr. Benitez sole control over the disbursements of funds."

Action by the Tribe on this charge was taken, according to Tribal Council minutes, after "Fred Alvarez stated that Manuel Medina (who operated a tractor on the Tribe's jojoba acreage) had told him he had given money to Joseph Benitez and indicated a guilty plea on the charge from Joseph Benitez should be offered. Motion to accept a guilty plea on the complete charge was made by Sam Welmas and seconded by Floyd Welmas. Joseph Benitez was found guilty by a vote of 12 for, 0 against, 0 abstentions."

Following this vote, Chairman Welmas, in response to the request of Attorney Rios for "more time to research evidence," asked for a continuance of the hearing to accommodate Rios and to allow the General Council more time before "voting on the rest of the charges and on sanction." By unanimous vote, the Tribe continued the hearing to a later date. However, the matter was eventually transferred to Tribal Court for further action.

The later final judgment of the Tribal Court was "Joseph Benitez, Defendant, cannot vote in Tribal functions or meetings, official or not, cannot hold any positions for or with the Tribe and cannot participate in any Tribal affairs for a period of not less than twenty-five years, five years for each cause of action." The initial judgment was rendered on March 7, 1985, with final judgment being made on Benitez's appeal in a written opinion signed by Judge Brenda Montez on November 14, 1985.

The Benitez case was handled by the Tribe in a manner highly protective of his civil rights. It was also handled in a manner that was in his best interests as well as in the best interests of the Tribe. If the Tribe had chosen to do so, several matters could have been handed over to outside authorities for criminal prosecution. But to do so would have violated their fierce determination to keep federal officials out of their affairs as much as possible.

Even though they would find out Benitez had agreed to allow both the cities of Indio and Coachella [adjacent to Indio] to annex part of Tribal lands, the Council did not take vindictive action against him; they went to court and got the "annexation" nullified. Proof of Benitez's perfidy regarding Indio's attempted annexation was provided in the Findings of Fact and Conclusions of Law, signed on May 18, 1981, by United States District Judge Laughlin E. Waters. With the cooperation of Benitez, the City of Indio had argued to the judge that it had legally annexed part of the reservation. That part came under the jurisdiction of all city criminal ordinances prohibiting gambling, and the Cabazon cardroom was located on the part they thought legally annexed.

Judge Waters held under part 5):

In 1970, at the request of certain landowners, defendant City of Indio began to process Annexation No. 23. This Annexation included said privately owned land and a portion of the Cabazon Indian Reservation was processed pursuant to the Annexation of Uninhabited Territory Act of 1939. In furtherance of such annexation proceeding, the City adopted Resolution 2234 of the City Council of the City of Indio and City of Indio Ordinance No. 563.

6) Representatives of plaintiff [the Cabazons] were given opportunity to protest the proposed annexation at a hearing held on April 15, 1970.

7) The [then] President of the Cabazon Band of Mission Indians, Joseph Benitez, attended the protest hearing held on April 15, 1970. Neither Mr. Benitez nor any other representative of plaintiff protested the proposed annexation at that hearing.

The proof was conclusive. Benitez not only did not try to protect the Tribe's land from being annexed in 1970, he joined with the City of Indio in 1981, in their lawsuit with the Tribe, to help the City of Indio keep what it tried to take 11 years earlier. He filed a sworn affidavit supporting the City in opposition to the Tribe and to gaming activities.

At the first meeting in 1979, on January 6, the Tribe passed resolutions removing members Benitez and Callaway as signatories from all bank accounts; removing members Benitez, Callaway and James from specific accounts and replacing them with Art Welmas, Fred Alvarez, James and Sam Welmas on new signature cards; and asking for return of the Tribe's MasterCard by Benitez. Resolutions were also approved providing for the establishment of a postal sub-station on reservation land; approval of an ordinance establishing the Cabazon Housing Authority; and approval of a Citizens Participation Certificate for pre-application for their Community Development Block grant application. Art Welmas, James and Fred Alvarez were approved as the initial Board members of the Housing authority, with Eugene Welmas to serve as alternate.

The contract between the Tribe and Pearlman's corporation, P.N. (Pearlman-Nichols) Associates, was approved as well as a resolution authorizing the exchange of land with a James O'Brien for the purpose of providing access to the site on which the Tribe's community building was to be built.

Other significant resolutions included the endorsement of member Sam Welmas as a candidate for the Laymen's Institute of the World Council of Churches in Switzerland. The drafting of a resolution to lower the voting age to 18 for tribal members was approved and a "motion was made by Linda Streeter and seconded by Leroy Alvarez that P.N. Associates be asked to build a multi-sales center using the building plans as presented by Fred Alvarez and that the Community Building be constructed according to the plans presented by the building designer John Farmer, with $300 to be allocated to C.V. Steel Co. to work more on Fred's plan."

Fred Alvarez again pushed for marijuana cultivation, this time in a motion that combined "Indian traditional plants such as jimson weed, peyote and marijuana." His motion was amended by a member to read that "a resolution to this effect would be sent to an attorney for the correct wording." It was apparently the Tribe's way of telling Fred "no" and "yes" at the same time, since he was making positive contributions to the meetings in other areas. Before the end of the meeting he would ask that "the Band reaffirm its confidence in Pro Plan and support Pro Plan in its attempts to assist the Band to get going again."

Before the end of the month, on January 18, Fred Alvarez would have received signed resignations from Benitez and William Callaway as well as the Tribe's MasterCard that had been in Benitez's possession, even though both were still protesting the November election that ousted them from office. At the next Council meeting on January 27, these resignations were approved and those elected in November were appointed to fill their unexpired terms, bringing their actions in accord with the Tribe's Articles of Association.

Two matters were discussed at the end of the January meeting that would prove important for the future of the Tribe. A motion was made to contact former U.S. Senator James G. Abourezk to help expedite the Tribe's application for a postal sub-station on the reservation, and to "hire him if he donates his services." Within two months Abourezk's law firm would become the Tribe's legal representative under retainer. Motion was also approved to "establish a tribal law enforcement agency." It would be the beginning of what would eventually become a full-blown Tribal Department of Public Safety. Finally, the Tribe voted to pay a continuing education stipend for the daughter of Gene Welmas who "might be interested in transferring from Inter Mountain to Sherman School," a reaffirmation of a Cabazon legacy that strongly and generously supports education for its members.

Before this meeting, Art Welmas and Nichols had flown to Florida and Washington on a business trip. Welmas reported to the Tribe regarding a number of meetings: with cigarette buyers, with Assistant to the Secretary of Interior Gordon Law, with Bill Miller of BIA, the National Center for Community Action, visiting the Smoke Shop of the Seminole Tribe, speaking with the leaders of the Miccosukee Tribe and on observing the operation of the pharmaceutical warehouse of the Washington Wholesale Drug Exchange firm.

After Welmas's return from this East Coast trip, and three days before the next Council meeting, the January 3, 1979, edition of the Indio *Daily News* and the January 4 edition of Riverside, California's *The Press Enterprise* ran stories on baseball legend Leo Durocher. What the Tribe and Nichols read would be good news and bad news for their fortunes for many years to come. Under the headline "Casino Permit Winners to Hedge Bets" *The Press Enterprise* reported:

> The successful applicant for Coachella's first casino gambling permit said yesterday the proposed cardroom will not open until after the March 6 election that will decide the fate of the city's three-month-old gambling ordinance.
>
> Linda Desser said yesterday that the opening of the proposed Desert Sands Casino will not take place immediately because of the large investment needed to remodel the structure to meet the minimum size required by the gambling ordinance.
>
> Desser and (partner Dudley) Gray's rival for the license was a partnership consisting

of Leo Durocher, the former major league baseball player and manager who now lives in Palm Springs; Rocco Zangari of Palm Springs; and Dr. Henry Baron, a Sharon, PA resident who also owns a home in the resort city.

The *Daily News* reported under headlines reading "Strikeout for Lippy Durocher—Casino Okay Given to Desser":

Leo "The Lip" Durocher struck out last night, when he and his partners Dr. Henry Baron and Rocco Zangari failed in their attempt to obtain Coachella's sole casino permit.

Councilmen voted 3–0 on a motion by Lester "Batch" Cox Jr. to issue the permit to Linda Desser and her attorney partner Dudley Gray, who are now expected to launch a massive campaign to uphold the September 19 ordinance which legalized poker, pan and lo-ball in the city.

The press would later imply the Tribe knew or should have known of Zangari's alleged criminal background, but if either newspaper knew of any reason Durocher or Zangari should not have gotten the nod, not one word was printed. If either paper knew of any ties these men had with the criminal world or the Mafia, not one word was printed. These two articles, dog-eared copies of which are still contained in warehoused files of the Tribe, would have a profound impact on the future and fortunes of the Cabazons within less than a year and a half.

During the March 10, 1979, Council meeting, the Tribe unanimously approved retaining the law firm of now former U.S. Senator James Abourezk as the Tribe's legal representative for a retainer of $3,000. Four days later a letter and check were sent to Abourezk retaining him with the understanding the Tribe was "to be billed at a rate of $200 per hour when your [Abourezk's] services are involved, and at a rate of $75 per hour when Mr. [Glenn] Feldman . . . is involved, as per your discussion with John Nichols." As history would unfold, the coming together of the Cabazons, Abourezk and Feldman would prove a great moment for Native Americans throughout the United States. This team—a small, gutsy tribe, a selfless, savvy political leader, and a brilliant, meticulous liberal attorney—would spearhead legal battles causing reverberations throughout the judicial system.

In the March 10, 1979, Tribal Council meeting, a Gambling Ordinance for the reservation was adopted as was a Liquor Ordinance, each with a unanimous vote. Also approved unanimously was another motion "to adopt tax rules on cigarettes at 1/2 cent Cabazon use tax and 1/2 cent Cabazon sales tax per package for domestic sales and the same for direct mail." Finally, it was unanimously approved "to take 1 (one) cent a card from each Bingo game and donate it to designated religious groups."

By the end of March, many elements were in place for the Tribe's economic-development thrust. A HUD grant to construct a community facility had been approved. A joint-venture contract with Al Pearlman's firm had been executed. Ordinances had been approved for tribal sales of cigarettes, liquor and gambling by tribal resolutions. A Washington-based law firm had been retained. An initial tax structure for use and sales had been given approval. Efforts were under way to identify and purchase a trailer. What was now needed was a businessman with the energy, smarts and guts to make this iffy startup work.

During the visit of Nichols and Welmas to Florida and Washington, D.C., Nichols introduced Welmas to Nichols's son, John Paul, who was the Greater-Miami-Area manager with the Howard Johnson's chain of hotels and restaurants. (Upon leaving the Cabazons 10 years later, John Paul returned to the hotel industry and is currently employed in hotel management.) Nichols also brought John Paul and Pearlman together.

In an interview at tribal headquarters in Indio, John Paul remembered events in those early days, and his arrival in April 1979. He came here originally, he said, "to run a specific venture":

My dad had been trying to get me to work for him for many years and I had always resisted. While my dad was a very good idea man, I didn't think he was a very good businessman. More importantly, I wanted to develop my own wings. He brought a couple of investors, specifically Al Pearlman and Bill Blank, to Florida, and they essentially wanted to convince me to come out here [to Indio]. I had seen what the Seminoles had been doing with cigarettes in North Florida. That really allowed me to visualize the potential impact. I came out here [to Indio] to take a look in February 1979. It was beautiful. The Date Festival was on, there were snowcapped mountains, and the weather was great. I made a mistake in coming back out in late April when it was 110 degrees and the weather had changed, but at that point in time my position was a contractual relationship with the Tribe, where I was one of the principals of P.N. Associates, which was effectively a joint venture created by Al Pearlman and the Nichols family.

It was my job to run the cigarette enterprises and related businesses that it might develop. I was an employee/principal of that organization which had a contractual relationship with the Cabazons to manage those businesses. We came out with, I think it was $50,000, $60,000, if I remember right, of Al Pearlman's money. We started in a 24-by-60-foot rented trailer with a diesel generator—there was no development out here. The only person that had any development on the reservation was the past Tribal Chairman and past Vice-Chairman for many years. They were the only ones living on the reservation. That was it. That's how it developed originally and obviously transitioned many, many times from that original 1979 concept—which was to be a White contract business, if you will, on an Indian reservation—into something that became far more complex 10 years later.

John Paul explained that among other ways, they kicked off the mail-order part of the new business with an article in the *National Enquirer*:

John Paul: The article in the *National Enquirer* didn't start with the first day. It was really six months into the operation before that happened. The difference between what we were doing and what I guess most of the tribes were doing was: one, we were really trying to take an isolated area (keep in mind 12 years ago this little piece of reservation was not anywhere near Indio—they put the Happy Wanderer [RV park] there [now adjoining the Casino] so they could be the most isolated RV park in the desert). We had to figure out a way of attracting people out here, so we marketed intensely—for a small community—which was unusual. In fact, that brought some awareness, because most people in the valley here didn't know there was an Indian tribe in Indio. We also had a certain twist to the business as we were the only tribe in the country that developed a mail-order business for cigarettes; that's where the national notoriety came because we were different. We would ship to North Carolina, New York, Montana or Florida—the home of the N*ational Enquirer*—and that caused some attention. [And] it was our need to advertise in some national publications, including the *National Enquirer*.

We contacted the editorial board of *National Enquirer* and said, "Hey, we have a story for you." The fact that we were advertising with them I realize isn't supposed to make a difference, but it does. We got their attention and we did have a cover article. The story line was "Indians make $10,000 a day." The problem was that in a funny sense, that story caused us more problems than help because the perception was that we were making $10,000 of profit a day, which we would have loved to have made, but in fact it was $10,000 in sales.

Author: What was and is the advertising approach by the Cabazons' businesses to the surrounding areas?

John Paul: Socially responsive advertising is the best way I can put it. One way was we were beating the tax man, and everybody likes that; I don't care who you are. To put it in perspective, our best customers were the local police. They loved it; they thought the idea was great. They'd come by in squad cars and buy cigarettes left and right. And any time you can legally or fairly beat the tax man, or the little guy can do that, I think that's a good sell. I think people want to contribute to that. The other way we did it really, and this is both on a national basis and locally, was what I call locally conscious advertising, which is sort of a help-raise-a-poor-reservation-up theme . . . American [Indian] rights, etc., and I think that, on a national scope, was a more effective way of advertising. Basically, if you are going to purchase from us, even though it's a great price reduction for you, it's still in the long run helping an Indian tribe raise up by their bootstraps. Was this unreal? No. I think it was real, and most socially responsive advertising is. We could have marketed it differently, but that appeared to work.

Author: How long did it take to really develop these businesses?

John Paul: The local cigarette business took off instantly. When I say instantly, 40 days later we were selling $100,000 worth of cigarettes a week out of a 24-by-60 trailer; it was just amazing! The mail-order business had a much tougher road. The reason for that was the legality of that business was much more questionable. I mean we think we were right, but the laws involved were far more complex. There was a lot of federal legislation that questioned our ability to do that. The problem we had there was this: with major mail-order advertising, a quarter-page ad may cost you $20,000. In the *National Enquirer* I think our minimum ad was $3,000. These are very small ads, just blurbs. The *New York Post*, a major newspaper, cost us $3,000 or $4,000 an ad. Repetition is the name of the game. You just can't put an ad in a national publication from an obscure Indian tribe in Southern California and expect people to send you money the first time, so you have to build goodwill, if you will, build comfort on their part, and it takes a while and many thousands of dollars to develop a pattern of order.

When you do, you hope it is long lasting, but the attorneys general of the states we were involved in were contesting our right to do that. They said, "hey, we are going to tax you; we are going to find out who you are; we are going to go to court; we are going to get lists of these people; and we are going to bill you." They would literally take out ads next to ours and put that there. So here's the problem: We were spending up to $20,000 on an ad. They would have an ad right next to ours put out by the state or a disclaimer by the publication because they were under pressure from the state. You know, if I'm a consumer and I'm reading this obscure little ad from some Indian tribe in Southern California and I'm reading the state attorney general's position right next to it, I'm not going to buy from that Indian tribe. So the mail-order business never developed the volume it warranted, in my mind, nor did it return the cost. The cigarette side of it was astronomically profitable, and in fact it was such a simple business. We sold other stuff too though—jewelry, peanuts, nuts and liquor are a whole different issue that we got into.

We looked at what other products we could offer that had a significant state tax that we could pass on partially to the consumer, pass on partially to the Tribe (not all of it was passed back to the consumer) that fit the product line we were selling. Can't sell cigarettes and toys; doesn't make sense. Essentially, we were selling adult products, hopefully, in the sense that we were catering to people who were responsible for their own behavior towards their bodies, etc.

We had secured a federal liquor license [because although] we had the ability [financially] to purchase liquor, there was still an antiquated law on the books that required Indian tribes to get a federal liquor license. It was a law passed in 1953 to protect poor Indians who get drunk on the corner; it's sort of a father image they [the government] still have that's really an anachronism—but nonetheless you need to have it [the license] to be able to [sell liquor on the reservation]. So we secured the Tribe's approval and we looked around and found out how we could do this.

The Tribe was seeking to buy in bond liquor where no prior use tax had been added in order to take advantage of the Indians' sovereign status to pass this savings on to consumers. But as a business, John Paul said:

It was a far more difficult proposition than cigarettes because there was only one outfit in the country, in Oklahoma City of all places, that could sell us in-bond liquor [without a prior use tax imposed by the state]. We could never get anybody in California to sell to us [directly] except some wineries, when in fact there was no [use] tax on the wineries. They were like any other retailer, so there was no tax advantage.

But, Oklahoma City or the Central Liquor Company there, had its own in-bond warehouse. You could literally transship from the warehouse directly, with just the federal bond stamp, to the reservation without any state seal ever being necessary. And, their specific state law allowed them to sell anywhere in the country, which is very unusual because the liquor industry typically prevents that from happening.

[However], the cigarettes were always the big draw. . . . Cigarettes had to sell the liquor because there weren't enough savings [on liquor]. Let me put it this way, the tax savings that we could pass on were offset by the volume savings that the big boys like the Liquor Barn, Fedmart—big chains which were selling in those days—could offer. Now the advantage was significantly different in that there was, for instance, $2 on a carton of cigarettes that had a [retail] price of $7, whereas it was $2 on a gallon of liquor that had a [retail] price of more than $15. So the relative percentage of savings for the consumer [on alcohol] was less.

Even though we could save the [use] tax, when we bought one semi-trailer load, they [the big chains] bought 20 semis; therefore their overall cost structure was low so there really wasn't that big of an advantage. Yes, we could beat supermarkets, and we could beat local retailers, but we couldn't beat big discount houses price wise; we were even-Steven.

So, it really became a marketing and promotion thing. We'd advertise locally the same specials you'd see advertised anywhere else—"buy a case, get a discount"—and it did become very successful. We were going through a semi-load of liquor out of this building [the current tribal office] a week. It was just amazing! We would sell 1,000 cases of Popov Vodka! The consumers were typically from Rancho Mirage, Palm Springs, what I would call the upper class, affluent consumers who wouldn't come out necessarily to buy cigarettes, but certainly would come to buy discount liquor.

This building [Cabazon tribal headquarters] was built to accommodate the cigarette business. Obviously, we eventually transferred here from the 24-by-60 trailer to make a much larger cigarette store. This building then had a wall right down the middle, and [one] side of it was a warehouse. We had pallets and pallets, three levels high of one thing only, cigarettes, and we had an assembly line. We could pull 800-number orders. We had a bank of telephones and actually had another 800 number in Georgia.

When we got into liquor we obviously ran into some space problems—the space requirement for storing 1,000 cases of liquor was far more substantial. We then got another 48-by-60-foot trailer and located it in the parking lot, ran some electric lines over there, moved the mail-order business over there and used all of this back warehouse for liquor and cigarettes: a retail store. We then started carrying extensive Indian jewelry. I'd say for a while there we literally had the best Indian jewelry collection anywhere in this area of the country, other than Arizona, certainly in Southern California.

A lot of people started coming [to shop] independently. We started carrying health-food products, really trying to become a second Hadley's, if you will. It was a different gimmick in that they sell everything health food; we would sell liquor and health food. It was kind of a dichotomy of some sort.

Towards the end, I think we were doing several hundred thousand dollars a week in rough sales. [But] it's a very low margin business. You had to sell lots of stuff to make some money. There wasn't a major profit here. The whole thing was based on volume sales. If the volume was off we were dead. The name of the game was selling lots.

The Smoke Shop opened in May 1979. Treasure Welmas and Mark Nichols [Dr. Nichols's youngest son] were its first clerks. Among its other early employees was Brenda James Soulliere, then a senior in high school. Children of John James, Brenda and her brother Bruce grew up in Banning, California, 30 to 45 minutes west of Indio.

Brenda had a long love affair with horses during her pre-teen and teenage years and became an accomplished horseperson, eventually representing the Tribe in the Rose Bowl Parade. She and a small group of friends formed a horse-lovers circle when they were from 8 to 13 years old, and as she described it:

We were riding the local parades as a group. We organized bake sales to raise money to pay for our costumes and we collected cans and turned those in to raise money. Then we got material, and most of us sewed, so we made our saddle blankets and our satin shirts and bought the matching blue boots and matching hats. It was a lot of fun. You know, one time we had like 12 riders.

Brenda kept up her interest in riding, and in 1982 won the High Point Championship. That was one year after she became a member of the Tribe's Business Committee. But in the early days of 1979 she began by working in the Smoke Shop:

I was going to high school and working a part-time job up in Banning and a full-time job here in Indio. . . . I would get up around 6:00 or 6:30 in the morning; get dressed for school and ready to eat; put on my jeans and stuff; and go down and shovel out my horse corrals. Doing it every day there wasn't a whole lot to shovel, so, I'd get done there and go to school. . . . I had a class from 8:00 to 9:00 a.m. . . . My senior year, I could have graduated in half a year. If I really pushed I could have been a three-year graduate. But I didn't. I wanted to stay with the rest of my class.

So, anyway, I only had to take one class and that was just to stay in school until I graduated with the rest of my class. So, I would be in class from 8 to 9, then I would jump in my car and go down to Indio and work a 10 to 6 p.m. shift in the Smoke Shop. I'd get off at 6:00 and I would drive back to Banning, go home and put on my McDonald's uniform and I would go to work at McDonald's from 7:30 to 12:30 [a.m.].

I did everything there [at the Smoke Shop], it seemed like. I started off being a cashier, then learned how to stock the cigarettes. When there was a small trailer we had storage in the back, so whenever we needed them we'd just bring them out front. We had to keep track of inventory . . . to greet customers. We learned how to take credit cards. . . . One of the things I always remember about working in the Smoke Shop is that all through high school I never, ever learned to figure percentages, but when they decided to do 10 percent, 15 percent off cigarettes at the Smoke Shop I learned them. Otherwise the customer would have to tell us, and how do you know they're going to be right?

At the first Council meeting after the Smoke Shop opened, John Paul made his first report, indicating 124 brands were being carried and $100,000 insurance coverage on inventory was in force. He also briefly discussed plans for saturation advertising.

Gambling was also discussed and, after a full reading of the Gambling Ordinance by Dr. Nichols, the ordinance was passed with 2 abstentions. According to the minutes, Nichols "indicated that Attorney Feldman suggests starting out with pan and lo-ball poker and bingo, and that slot machines may come a year later. John James suggested a limo service between the airport and the casino and between hotels and the casino."

What is remarkable about this meeting may be the power of positive thinking exhibited by the members of the Council. Here they were, in June 1979, only one month into the operation of a Smoke Shop out of a trailer, and already they had envisioned a casino on land that had no improvements except a trailer, not even an access road or a parking lot. As John Paul was to say, it was "all dirt. We had no money. Every dime we had went into growing the business, and the perception was—right or wrong—a parking lot doesn't make money. I think we did the right thing. We could have spent a lot of money on a parking lot and today the Tribe would probably have a nice empty parking lot and no business. We had to put cash where it would generate cash."

But most important is the fact that the ideas for *most* of the businesses of the Tribe came from the tribal members themselves. The idea of gambling or, as John James calls it, "gaming," came from James. And it was James who pushed it. The role of the Nichols family and those they brought in to assist the Tribe was to make the Tribe's ideas happen, to find the money, the investors, the technical help—whatever was needed to turn visions and ideas into reality. And, if special care or treatment was needed to help a member get over a rough passage in his or her life, to find that special care or treatment. A major resource for treatment of alcohol abuse developed by Nichols was the Des Moines, Iowa, Methodist Medical Center, subsequently used by both tribal members and Nichols's children.

By the end of June, according to the Tribal Council minutes, John Paul reported "liquor would be sold in two to three weeks with the OK of Attorney Feldman, and mail-order sales of cigarettes should begin in one to two weeks if the boxes arrive as ordered. John Paul Nichols projected the enterprises should show clear profit after four months. A check for [tribal] taxes collected in the first month of operation in the amount of $833.16 was submitted to the Business Committee."

By mid-July 1979, a 95-percent increase in business was reported by John Paul. Advertising "for direct mail of cigarettes" was scheduled to begin in July "in Massachusetts and Texas and in August in Washington State." It was also announced that a loan "to finance the permanent all-steel-frame building" which was to hold "retail sales, warehousing, etc." was signed by Chairman Welmas.

At its September Business Committee meeting, a resolution was adopted providing for "monthly allotments of money to tribal officers." This was the first implementation of the John Philip Nichols-introduced concept of paying tribal leaders for managing the business affairs of the Tribe, similar to paying corporate management. This first implementation was, indeed, a modest beginning. The resolution read "in the months of October, November, December of 1979 and January of 1980, the Tribal Chairman will be allotted $250 monthly, 1st-Vice-Chairman $160 monthly, 2nd Vice-Chairman $80 monthly, Secretary-Treasurer $80 monthly, and that the funds are to come from the Discretionary Account."

In August, the sealed bid submitted for construction of the proposed community building was rejected as too high. The bidder was notified that he could resubmit when the bid was re-advertised, and in early September, sealed bids were opened in response to the re-advertisement. The two bids received were tabled, pending discussion with the HUD representative.

Although it was reported that their community building had been included in the Indian Health Service's (IHS) FY '79 Budget, the tribal members were firmly not interested in receiving any IHS funds. That position reflected the general disdain in which the IHS was held by the Cabazons and many other tribes. Art Welmas's view regarding health care for the Tribe mirrored the thinking of its leadership. The minutes state: "Art Welmas indicated that a health plan for the entire Band is essential and should be implemented as soon as funds are available from the sales project," a reference to the developing Smoke Shop. He emphasized this urgency in the September 8, 1979, meeting, citing the health plan as "the priority need" of the Tribe. (Health—a private insurance plan providing maximum, quality coverage for all tribal members—was and remains a top priority for the Tribe. As of this writing, every member of the Tribe enjoys the benefits of such a plan. The priority need of 1979 has been fully realized.)

The Smoke Shop sales were in high gear during the fall of 1979. Al Pearlman told the September meeting of the General Council he "felt the investment of his money had been well worthwhile," indicating, according to the minutes, "that the retail shop sales are excellent and mail-order sales are slower than expected, due to a problem of advertising." John Paul made the financial report of the business, structured as Cabazon Indian Reservation Sales (CIRS), showing "projected sales are to go to $4,000 a day in the next few weeks and could go as high as $12,000 a day during the tourist season."

The exploration of gambling as a tribal business was also going forward. Dr. Nichols briefly reported to the General Council on a meeting held with Morris Shenker, then chairman of the board of the Dunes Casino in Las Vegas. Nichols reported that "Shenker showed great interest and is to put the Band in touch with his attorney to continue negotiations." At the last meeting of the Tribe's Business Committee in September 1979, the minutes reflect that Dr. Nichols reported further on meetings with the Dunes, stating they were "very interested in putting in a turn-key operation, providing the casino, personnel, training, restaurant, etc., but $6,000,000 investment funds must first be found." Dr. Nichols continued by reporting on meeting with a representative of the Mormon Church in Salt Lake City, and of their interest in Indians and their economic development.

During the Business Committee meeting of September 21, 1979, another step was taken in implementing the concept of paying tribal management. One-third of the projected $8,000 monthly export income was determined to be disbursed as follows:

Tribal Chairman	$1,000 per month
1st Vice-Chairman	$820 per month
2nd Vice-Chairman	$420 per month
Secretary-Treasurer	$420 per month

And "Dr. Nichols indicated he felt pay to tribal officers will increase as they put in more time."

In the same meeting, Fred Alvarez once again pushed his pet marijuana project. The minutes state he "asked permission of the tribe to grow 50 marijuana plants on land where the graveyard is, and name each plant after a state. Sammy Welmas replied that a burial ground should be left alone. John James indicated that each tribal member would need to be consulted. Dr. John Nichols suggested that Fred "put his plants in Mexico on the land of the Yaqui and name each plant after Indian leaders." Once again the tribal members rejected Fred's suggestions. But Fred had another pet project, the development of a motorcycle racing track, and once again the Tribe put him off, with Dr. Nichols suggesting "the separation of 29 Palms and Cabazon land. After the legal questions regarding a bicycle race track are answered, an ordinance is to be drafted concerning the use of Fred's property for motorbike use." No action of any kind was taken by the Tribe.

At the November 1, 1979, meeting of the Business Committee, Fred Alvarez requested and received approval to invite biker friends to occasionally ride around his property. According to the minutes, "he gave full assurance it would not be a commercial enterprise." Fred also expressed an interest in and requested approval to put "a trailer park on his family's 120 acres" of land. Approval was granted and Dr. Nichols offered to work with him on this project.

In this meeting John Paul told the Tribe "alcohol will be sold within three weeks if it receives final approval. He said P.N. Associates has agreed to advance $25,000 to buy the liquor and currently Oklahoma has the best prices. Discussion was held on selling closed bottles from the retail center and by open bar from the casino." He also reported "immediate response to the *Enquirer* article has been very good"; there had been a "40 percent increase in revenue in October over September"; and inventory on hand was valued at $100,000.

It was also reported that arrangements were being made to enroll members in a Blue Cross plan to insure "an association and a business together for $40 per month, per person, $100 deductible per year." Members were informed that when the special form was made available each interested person would have to fill it out to be included.

When Durocher's group lost in its bid to operate the sole cardroom projected to open in the city of Coachella, the Tribe—through Dr. Nichols—contacted him through his former baseball team to suggest "a better way." Durocher, a longtime St. Louis Cardinals baseball player and L.A. Dodgers coach, had long been admired by both Charles Welmas and Dr. Nichols. At the November 1 meeting, Nichols told the Tribe "he had spoken with Leo Durocher and his representative concerning a casino and that more meetings are scheduled for next week. Indian gambling games are to be researched." Thus began a beneficial but stormy relationship: in addition to Durocher came one of his partners, an experienced casino operator named Rocco Zangari, whose alleged past would later be used by the press and others against the Tribe.

By the end of 1979, those opposed to Cabazon mail-order sales were beginning to have an impact. As John Paul said in his interview, the attorneys general of several states had become aggressive in their insistence that their states' taxes on cigarettes must be paid. Their insistence prompted publications, including the *National Enquirer,* to raise questions with the Tribe. Attorney Feldman asked and got a response from the U.S. Department of Justice concerning the Jenkins Act, questioning: "Does the Jenkins Act . . . apply to a federally recognized Indian tribe which is engaged in the interstate sales of cigarettes?"

Until the receipt of the U.S. Department of Justice response, which was received in early November, Feldman's stock answer was mailed in response to questions from states or businesses such as the *Enquirer:*

The Cabazon Band of Mission Indians is a Federally recognized Indian Tribe with a governing body, the Cabazon General Council, which is recognized by the Secretary of the Interior. The Band occupies the Cabazon Indian Reservation, near Indio, California, established by Executive Order in 1876.

In an effort to foster tribal self-determination and to improve the economic well-being of the Band and its members, the Cabazons are implementing an ambitious ten-year development program on their reservation. Their retail cigarette sales, being conducted under the name Cabazon Indian Reservation Sales, is an important first step in that effort.

Like other Indian tribes, the Cabazons are regarded as "domestic dependent nations" within the United States, and may exercise their "inherent rights of sovereignty" so far as consistent with federal law.

Pursuant to these sovereign powers, the Cabazon Nation has enacted a comprehensive ordinance providing for the taxation of cigarettes and other tobacco products sold on their reservation. The Cabazons have also established, and are operating as a tribal enterprise, a retail Smoke Shop on the reservation. The Smoke Shop sells to the general public, both Indian and non-Indian. All federal and tribal taxes have been paid on the cigarettes sold at the Cabazon Smoke Shop.

Tribal tax revenues and a portion of the net profits from the cigarette sales are being used for a variety of self-help projects on the Cabazon Reservation, such as funding a comprehensive health-insurance program for all members of the Band. . . . There is no federal law which prohibits mail-order sales, or the print advertising of cigarettes for sale by mail order. In fact, a number of specialty cigarette manufacturers have been advertising and selling their cigarettes through the mail for years.

The only federal statute that in any way regulates mail-order cigarette sales is the "Jenkins Act, 18 U.S.C. 375-378." This statute provides that any "person" who sells cigarettes in interstate commerce must register with the tax administrator of the state into which cigarettes are to be shipped and must file monthly reports with the tax administrator giving the name and address of each person within that state to whom cigarettes have been shipped.

No federal court has ever ruled on the question of whether the Jenkins Act applies to a sovereign Indian tribe. It is the position of the Cabazons that it does not.

The Jenkins Act, by its own terms, applies only to any "person" who sells cigarettes in interstate commerce. The term "person" is defined in the Act as an individual or any of a number of ordinary forms of business association. In fact, the definition of "person" in the Jenkins Act is precisely the same definition of the word which applies generally throughout the United States Code (see U.S.C.1). Neither definition mentions an Indian tribe.

The question then becomes whether Congress, by its definition of "person" in the statute, intended that word to include an Indian tribe.

Indian tribes, like the government of the United States, are regarded as sovereign entities. Thus, the term "person" can be construed to encompass an Indian tribe only if the language of the statute can be found to be a waiver of sovereign immunity.

There are numerous United States Supreme Court decisions, dating from 1840 to the present, which have held that the term "person" in a statute, without more, does not include a sovereign entity. The Court has repeatedly held that if Congress intended to include a sovereign, it would have done so expressly.

Finally, however, it should be noted that if a federal court should ultimately determine that the Jenkins Act does apply to an Indian Nation, the Cabazon Band of Mission Indians will comply with that ruling.

The Justice Department response to Feldman stated it was "presently unable to agree with your conclusion that the Jenkins Act does not apply to Indian tribes":

To begin with, the definition of "person" in 16 U.S.C. 375 (1) is not limited, as your letter appears to suggest, to the entities listed therein. That statute says only that the term "person" includes those entities. The courts have often pointed out that "includes" is a verb of enlargement and not a verb of limitation of enumeration.

Next, to describe Indian tribes as "sovereign entities" and "immune from suit" does not settle the question of the Tribe's liability under a Federal criminal statute because, as you well know, Indian tribes are not "possessed of the full attributes of sovereignty." The attribute of sovereignty most often in issue is that of self-government, that is, whether the particular state or Federal statute in question interferes with the right of a tribe to govern itself. Federal criminal laws of general applicability extend to conduct by Indians on reservations. . . . Exceptions to this general rule are essentially limited to intra-Indian offenses, where the sovereign power of tribes to punish their own members has been left undisturbed by Congress. Clearly, a violation of the reporting requirements of 15 U.S.C. 376 is not an intra-Indian offense.

The purpose of the Jenkins Act is to assist the states in collecting cigarette taxes due on cigarettes sold through the mails from other states. The Act is also aimed at eliminating an unfair competitive advantage of mail-order cigarette dealers over local dealers in the taxing state. Your suggestion that the Act does not apply to your client tribe's mail-order business would create the precise situation the Act is aimed at preventing.

We fail to see any way in which the Jenkins Act infringes on tribal "sovereignty." That an Indian proprietor can be required to collect and enforce state cigarette taxes on cigarettes sold on tribally owned reservation land to non-Indians was decided in Moe v. Salish & Kootenai Tribes, 425 US 463 (1976). The Jenkins Act requires only the filing of the tribe's name, trade name (as operator of the "smoke shop"), address and copies of invoices with tobacco-tax administrators of states to which cigarettes are shipped. To the degree this is a "burden" it is no greater than that imposed on other mail-order cigarette businesses, and it is certainly a lesser burden than sanctioned in Moe, supra. There is no apparent interference with tribal self-government that would be caused by such compliance.

We are aware, of course, of the district court's decision in Confederated tribes of Colville v. State of Washington, 446 F. Supp. 1339 (E.D. Wash. 1978) in which certiorari was granted and which was argued before the Supreme Court on October 10, 1979. Should the decision in Colville alter Moe in a way relevant to the applicability of the Jenkins Act, we would reconsider our position.

As the following letter, dated November 19, 1979, seems to make clear, the Justice Department and the various officials of the states were singing out of the same hymnbook. The letter, from the Chief Enforcement Agent of Connecticut's Department of Revenue Services, was in response to an earlier letter sent over the signature of Art Welmas. Welmas's letter asked for an explanation of how the Jenkins Act related to any liability the Tribe could possibly have to that state. The state responded:

First, the definitions as stated in the Act do apply to the Cabazon Band of Mission Indians and are covered under the definitions of: persons, corporations, companies, associations, firms, partnerships, societies and joint stock companies, as well as individuals.

Secondly, the State of Connecticut has the clear and legal right to demand taxes at the rate of $.21 per package or $2.10 per carton as outlined in Connecticut General Statutes, Chapter 214 (copy enclosed for your reading).

Thirdly, and as a point of information, no recognition or permission to sell cigarettes to Connecticut residents without collection of taxes exists in this State, to Indian tribes, federally recognized or not.

Federal rights granted to Indians concerning property, care and assistance are governed by individual treaties granted by the Government of the United States to that particular tribe. Keep in mind that these treaties in most cases pertain to a particular piece of land clearly designated as a federal reservation.

In essence those residents entitled to reside on that federal property and their dependents, because of their inherent rights, are entitled to certain privileges and assistance as set forth in federal law.

There is no Federal Indian Reservation in Connecticut. All land presently used by Indian tribes is done so in agreement with the State of Connecticut, and for the most part is used for historical purposes. There is, however, residential use afforded certain Indians having one-eighth (1/8) Indian blood of that particular property.

My inquiries reveal there are no BIA- or IHS-sponsored programs extending into Connecticut. The BIA and IHS limit their services to Indian people from specific tribes, the so-called federally recognized tribes; none of these federally recognized tribes are located in New England. Inquiries also show that Indians in general, residing in Connecticut, [p]resume no specific services beyond the amenities available to citizens at large.

In summation, our findings are that you are required to comply with the Jenkins Act and must, forthwith, provide this office with a complete list of names, addresses and number of Connecticut citizens who have purchased cigarettes from your organization.

Failure to comply with this Act within the specified time will be deemed a violation of the Act and prosecutorial efforts will be sought by this Department.

The bottom line was clear. The future of the cigarette venture, especially mail-order sales, awaited the decision of the Supreme Court in the Colville case. That was the situation as 1980 began. In the Tribe's first meeting of the new year,

John Paul reported that advertising would begin in the *National Enquirer* "in a few weeks, at a biweekly cost of around $3,000." But he also reported that although gross sales showed a total of $416,298 between September 29 and November 24, there were expenditures of $419,407.

In the two January meetings of the Business Committee, Mark Nichols would be given tribal approval to research the Tribe's history as a sovereign people. As Historic Preservation Coordinator, he became the person who interacted with government agencies. A motion was also adopted to claim the Mecca Hills as the historical land of the Tribe; this project would be of continuing interest and effort by the Tribe and Mark.

On February 9, 1980, the Tribe's new community building was formally dedicated after the meeting of the General Council. It was a Love-in meeting, with both Al Pearlman and the certified public accountant, George Johnson, highly commendatory regarding the progress of the Smoke Shop. Each was lavish in his praise, Johnson calling the progress a "miracle" and Pearlman calling it "a fantastic job," the "best retail operation he had seen in 40 years."

Among the guests at the meeting, as they were listed in the minutes, were possible investors such as Norman Lewis and Dr. Schrausser of CellLife; Jack Hindle, Carol Stephenson and Tim Birch of Mer-Lion Shipping and Trading Co.; Edna MacDonald, Director of Special Projects, Washoe Tribe; Hershel Webb and Anthony Shelde of the Pima Nation; Bob Marin of P.N. Associates; as well as former U.S. Senator James Abourezk and Glenn Feldman, the Cabazons' attorneys; Jim Fletcher; and Carlos Mendoza of HUD.

In a significant action during this meeting, a Bingo ordinance was adopted after a report by Feldman, who reported "he and Art Welmas had met with the District Attorney in Riverside regarding gambling." Said the minutes, "Mr. Feldman indicated there is ample legal basis for having Bingo but that negotiations with county authorities is important." Unfortunately, as events would unfold, neither county, city nor state authorities would see the Tribe's many offers to negotiate on various issues as important. The Tribe would be treated as an enemy.

Chief Hervasio Cabezon, circa 1890. From the collection of the Smithsonian Institution, Washington, D.C.

Gene Welmas, Chairman, Tribal Agricultural Resources Committee. Drawing by Heidi Zinn, photograph by Jesse Alvarez.

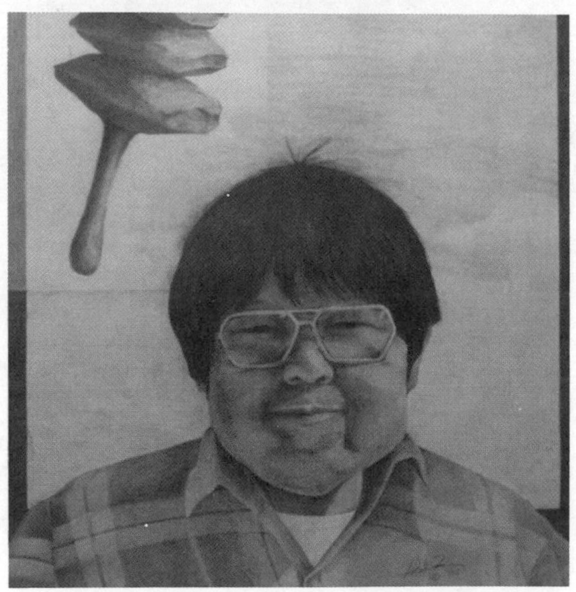

Sam Welmas, Tribal First Vice Chairman. Drawing by Heidi Zinn, photograph by Jesse Alvarez.

Cahuilla Bird Singers, 1979.

Cahuilla Bird Singers, 1979.

Cahuilla Bird Singers, 1979.

Back row- Virginia Welmas-Nichols, Gene Welmas, Floyd Welmas, John James, Treasure Welmas, Fred Alvarez. Seated- Art Welmas, Fernando Hernandez, Linda Ducas, Leroy Alvarez.

Beverly Roosevelt, Tom Laughlin, Virginia Welmas-Nichols. Photograph by Jesse Alvarez.

Cabazon Indian Smoke Shop, 1979.

Gene Welmas.

Desert Oasis Casino, 1986.

Tribal members donate their time and food to a local charity at Thanksgiving, 1993.

Joann Nichols, Sam Welmas,
Dr. Nichols.

Fred Alvarez.

Tribal Security Officers Charles Welmas,
Gavino Pluma, Floyd Waters, 1984.

First Tribal Bingo Hall in California, 1983.

The U.S. Supreme Court Cabazon Decision celebration dinner, 1987.

Ralph Fellows, Art Welmas, Dr. Nichols.

L to R- John Paul Nichols, Cameron Mitchell, Robert Loggia, Dr. Nichols, Robert Nichols. Photograph by Jesse Alvarez.

Leroy Alvarez, Ambrose I. Lane, Sr. Photograph by Jesse Alvarez.

Charles Welmas holds an urn during
a tribal reinterment ceremony, 1992.
Photograph by Taylor Sherrill.

Joann and Dr. Nichols, 1982. Photograph by Taylor Sherrill.

Charles Welmas, Elisa Welmas, Virginia Welmas-Nichols, Tamara Montoya, John Welmas. Seated- John James, 1993. Photograph by Taylor Sherrill.

John James, 1980. Photograph by Taylor Sherrill.

Brenda Soulliere, Fiesta Bowl, 1982. Photograph by Taylor Sherrill.

Indian leaders circa 1890. Front row- Cap. Habiel, Cap. Will Pablo, Chief Hervasio Cabezon, Cap. Manuel, Cap. Jose Maria. Back row- Cap. Ramon, Cap. Jim, Cap. Lastro. From the collection of the Smithsonian Institution, Washington, D.C.

Mark Nichols and Dr. Nichols, 1993. Photograph by Ward P. Riggins III.

Cabazon Band of Mission Indians General Council, 1994. Photograph by Nancy Duteau.

4

The Pain and Joys of Growth

CASINO

The 1980s would be filled with the roller-coaster emotions of exhilaration and depression, of victory and tragedy.

By June 1980, the Supreme Court had ruled that tribes must collect state cigarette taxes when cigarettes are sold to non-tribal members. At the Tribe's July meeting, John Paul Nichols reported "The State Equalization Board has adopted the position that retail sales of cigarettes are to be phased out. . . . Existing funds are to be carefully budgeted for conversion of the building to a card room." Later in the meeting, a review of the report for the quarter ending June 30th showed "an influx of $60,000 was necessary for the renovation of the building that would be converted to a card room." Art Welmas recommended that all officers go on "half payment of their fees" to help alleviate the pending financial crunch.

By September 1980, planning for the card room, now consistently referred to in the minutes as the casino, had moved into high gear. John Paul and his mother Joann (who managed the Tribal office), met with officials from local and state government to inform them of their plans to open a casino. According to the September 11, 1980, minutes of the Tribe's Business Committee, the meeting had been "called by the Indio Chief of Police concerning the planned card room on the reservation," so those in attendance were "representatives of state and county law enforcement." During the meeting, "State and county said they would support any business which is within the law." But "the City of Indio stated it was not favorable and would try to enforce city laws if possible."

Nevertheless, after hearing John Paul's report the Business Committee continued its planning, convinced of the legality and moral rightness of its position. It set in place its own tax structure, authorized the temporary use of its community building by the Smoke Shop for retail sales, accepted the filing of an application to open a casino, approved the waiver of payment of the tribal application fee, and accepted the presentation of the permit to run the casino as well as the license to be issued. The projected opening was set for October 15, with plans to operate 24 hours daily.

During this meeting, Dr. Nichols made two significant reports, the first of which described recent trips he had taken to Taiwan, Korea, and Japan and of his "meeting with coal and lumber purchasers" in those countries. His trips there were financed by Wallace Shipping Chartering Limited, a company trying to market coal to those and other countries, and it was paying a monthly fee to use Dr. Nichols as a consultant. These fees were being used by Nichols and the Tribe to meet office expenses and stay alive as an economic development entity.

Nichols's second report, according to the minutes, "discussed the advantages of forming an Indian security company and becoming eligible to apply for contracts with minority preference. He indicated that Wackenhut Inc. and Intersect Inc. were both well-known security firms which have been interested in working with an Indian firm." After his presentation "Fred Alvarez moved to draft a resolution calling for the formation of Cabazon Security Company. The motion was seconded by John James and passed" unanimously.

These reports were significant for three reasons: they support the fact that (1) Dr. Nichols's most important role with the Tribe was not as manager, but as a resource developer, with his wife Joann as manager until her death; (2) the interests of both the Cabazons and companies like Wackenhut were financial; and (3) Dr. Nichols directed funds he earned as a consultant to tribal use instead of personal enrichment. (Today, as a result, he lives in retirement in very modest circumstances.)

Just as Al Pearlman had been looking for a business "edge" in his initial interest in a joint venture with the Cabazons in a wholesale prescription drug facility, so were firms like Wackenhut and Intersect. In 1980, spending for defense exploded in America and competition for those dollars became ferocious. To any business, a 5 percent "edge" in bids of millions of dollars is a much-sought-after advantage.

As planned, the casino opened on October 15th. Three days later, as promised, the City of Indio Police Department closed it down in a highly publicized raid. The legal war had begun that would lead to the U.S. Supreme Court almost seven years later. In a recent interview, John Paul recalled the events that led both sides to that day and what followed:

We started talking about doing it in August, and it really was a very innocent process. We thought Bingo was too risqué; that's why we didn't get into Bingo. I mean, hell, that's my view. We picked something we thought we could win with in California. That's how the mind set was.

About the time we were closing the cigarette business, a newspaper story came out in the *Daily News*. It said Leo Durocher and a guy named Rocco were trying to get a license in the City of Coachella for a California-style cardroom. And, in fact, City Council had passed

an ordinance saying that they could legalize a cardroom. But the City fathers, the conservatives, forced a referendum, went directly to a vote, and the cardroom lost. . . . I believe it lost because somebody who had a cardroom down at Salton Sea fought it tooth and nail and funded the opposition.

Out of the original article, my dad and I and Art Welmas were sitting around one day and said, "If they [the Indio City Council] can do it [vote to allow a cardroom] why can't we?" It wasn't exactly a rocket scientist's idea. We had the newspaper and the whole intent was to replicate what they were doing. Out of that, Dad or Art wrote a letter to the L.A. Dodgers—we didn't even know where Leo Durocher lived—and we got a phone call a few days later and Leo said, "I want to bring this guy Rocco down. Let's get together." That's how the whole thing started. It's as simple as that. Once we had the initial discussion, we said, "Hey, we can do this!" and that was essentially where it went.

Leo was our initial contact. None of us had any experience in the poker-cardroom-casino business. In fact, my brother Phil was the only one who played a little poker in college, but we had no knowledge of the industry whatsoever. We thought Leo Durocher, a huge baseball name, a legend, Hall of Famer, would be a great host. And we thought Rocco, if he's associated with Leo Durocher, was okay. It was a very innocent approach. So it was part of a package deal. Leo said, "I'll be the host. If you want to use my name I want to get paid 'x.'" Rocco was given a deal: I think we paid him a salary of $40,000 plus 10 percent of net profit, if there was net. What did we know? It sounded like—hell, we weren't making any profit then. His job was to run the gaming side only. The construction and all that we did ourselves with the funds we had from the cigarette business.

Once we started talking about a building, we were contacted by the local police chief, Sam Cross, and he said you can't do what you are doing. We said, well, we think we can. We'd like to meet and explain to you why. He said no; it's illegal; we'll shut you down. We said, it's really different. So, we had a meeting and my mother and I went.

The police became aware of the plans for the Cabazon card room, surmised John Paul, through contractors:

We were building. We were putting a casino in. It was a California cardroom, just like 50 or hundreds of others in California. We were hiring employees, ads in the paper, just all that stuff. This is now September of 1980. The cigarette business was closed about a month now. We were transitioning.

We go over and meet at the City of Indio police station with Sam Cross, County Sheriff, County Council, City Manager, etc. So Mom and I are sitting and talking to them. We're telling them why we think we have these rights. We have an attorney with us. We figure this is a slam dunk; these guys aren't going to fight us anymore. We were getting nowhere.

We asked Sam Cross, why can't we have a civil disagreement—why can't we just walk into court and say we have a difference and do this without having to play cops and robbers? Why can't we settle our differences in a civil manner? I remember him saying, "The blue army never tells the red army." Why we were the red army, I don't know. And he said that like "This is a game. I'm the blue army; I got all the uniforms; and we will squash you."

In fact, we had a test game. Five of us would sit around and play . . . on tables [in the card room]. Police would come in, see us playing and leave. They would literally walk in.

We wanted to get busted, but we didn't want to jeopardize any customers. The whole idea was to get into court. We needed an action.

To make a long story short, I think it was October, some day in October—Saturday night—103, 104 people came to the cardroom. It was the third or fourth night open and that's when they came in; I think there might have been 35 cops altogether. There were a lot of cops. It was way overdone with riot helmets—gear, visors—coming in every nook and cranny. I think some of them might have been hiding in the bathroom and changed clothes. . . . They seized the tables, arrested a few people; everybody was cited. They really hadn't figured out what they were going to do [ahead of time]. I don't think they realized how many people were there and they said they couldn't arrest all of them, so "we have to cite some of these people. . . ." They were City of Indio [cops] but I'm sure they had support from the county. A few people had some warrants for traffic tickets. One guy was arrested and that was the guy who was on the famous picture on the front of the paper. . . . He was just a young kid who said, "I'm not going anywhere." 'Cause he had handcuffs on, made it look as if everything happened that way. Another girl was photographed being held in a stranglehold.

They took all the chips, tables. Why they took those tables is beyond me. And that was it. The war started. Obviously we closed that night, secured everything. We immediately, the next day—actually I don't know if it was the next day or not, but no longer than a couple of days later—we went to Federal Court with an emergency Temporary Restraining Order (TRO) request. Obviously we were not granted it. They scheduled a hearing a few days afterwards—I think it was two or three days afterwards—and we went to Judge Laughlin Waters for the TRO and were granted, in fact got, the Temporary Restraining Order and an order to give us back all the tables and chairs.

The next famous newspaper picture is that they are giving us back all this stuff—of course, we all made some mistakes that we shouldn't have made. And then we proceeded to operate for many years under the protection of the Temporary Restraining Orders, preliminary and permanent injunctions. The one exception to that—I have to get the court cases straight here—was Laughlin Waters. In fact, four or five months later he ruled against us. He said the City of Indio is right and you are wrong.

He had given us a preliminary, so we went for the permanent injunction, and he said I rule against you. We were dumbfounded. We had no money; we were dead broke. We had $5,000 in the cage. . . . The way I look at it in retrospect is we were all taking gambling lessons, learning the business; very expensive process, but you learn very quickly. So we said it can't hurt to ask for a stay of the injunction pending appeal on the fat chance that—I think it was one in 1,000—that Laughlin Waters would give us a stay pending appeal out of the clear blue sky. So we were closed for a few days after the [denial of a] permanent injunction. If he had not given us a stay pending an appeal, that would have been it. Nobody had any money. We couldn't keep fighting. . . . No funds to survive. We all would have gone somewhere else for jobs. We had to live, both tribal members and non-tribal members. But Laughlin did grant the injunction pending the appeal 10 days to the day later, and that was it. From that point on, we won every court case.

In a related interview, tribal attorney Glenn Feldman remembered the legal chronology this way:

Author: I have the minutes of November 12, where John Paul announced that the casino was going to reopen because of the Temporary Restraining Order.

Glenn: No, your terminology is a little off, that's all. We went in within two or three days after October 18 and asked for a Temporary Restraining Order, which is the quickest type of relief you can get from a judge, and he denied it. The next step in the process is to ask for a Preliminary Injunction, and that's what he granted us on November 10, and under the terms of the Preliminary Injunction the casino reopened; the cardroom reopened; and it remained open under the injunction until May 19, 1981, when he ruled against us on the merits of the cases and said that the Preliminary Injunction is hereby dissolved.

Now what happened after that, as I recall, is we then immediately filed with Judge Waters a motion for a Stay Pending Appeal, which is sort of a bizarre legal device where you say, judge, even though you just ruled against us and said we are not entitled to have this casino open, we want you to give us a ruling which allows it to remain open while that decision is appealed. It is very unusual and very rarely granted, but he did grant it.

Author: He granted it?

Glenn: He did grant that so that he allowed the casino to remain open while the cases went up on appeal to the Ninth Circuit.

Author: Okay, then that makes sense. Then there was the hearing on October 5, 1981, where the City of Indio filed papers asking for a lifting of that injunction. . . . And you won that case?

Glenn: Yes.

Author: And in winning you had to submit an audit to the court?

Glenn: What happened I think is that the City got Linda Streeter [-Dukic] and Joe Benitez and a few others to file affidavits saying this is a crooked operation; we are not getting any money (same things that they have been saying for the last 15 years); we don't need it; it's a Nichols family rip-off; they are taking all our money. And the City used those affidavits to come back to the judge and said, look your Honor, you need to reconsider. This is not a good thing, it's a bad thing, and the Tribe is getting ripped off; here are tribal members who are willing to say that. We submitted a variety of affidavits from, I'm sure, Art Welmas and John James, all the existing tribal leaders at that point, to refute that and yes, my recollection is that the judge did not agree to it. But he [the judge] said, I want to find out more about what is going on: I want an audit, I want financial reports, I want to see this stuff. So my recollection is we did an audit; we got all kinds of information and submitted it to them. Then the City came back and said, no, this is no good; it's all hocus pocus. The end result is the judge basically said, well I'm satisfied; we are going to leave this injunction in place while the Ninth Circuit considers the appeal.

Author: Then what happened? Follow the case.

Glenn: Then, sometime in 1982, the Ninth Circuit issued its decision and reversed Judge Waters on the annexation issue. It held that the annexation of tribal land by the City of Indio was void from the very beginning. There was no time limit as to how long we could challenge that and the court held that, as a result, the City of Indio's ordinance against cardrooms could not be valid in this case because the land was not within the city of Indio.

And they said because we reached that decision, we don't need to deal with these other Indian law issues about sovereignty and preemption and that sort of stuff that

Judge Waters had ruled against us on. They said we simply don't need to address those at all because we ruled that the land is not within the City of Indio and the City's ordinance can't be applicable. And that came down, it seems it was in the Fall of 1982; I don't have dates in front of me. And then within days, the County came in and raided and shut the place down, arguing, well, if it isn't in the City of Indio, it is certainly within the county of Riverside, and we've got the same anti-poker ordinance. Therefore, we are going to shut this rogue operation down.

Author: Follow that action.

Glenn: The County came in, shut them down; I mean the same thing. There was a raid. People got cited. They shut the whole operation down. We then, within two or three days, went back in before Judge Waters and that time he did give us a Temporary Restraining Order—because between the time of the original suit and the time we went back in to see him, the Ninth Circuit had decided the Barona case which held that tribes did have the right to operate gaming facilities on the reservations without state interference. And so based on the *Barona* Decision, which I think had just come down a month or two before, he said, while I ruled against you the last time, I see that the Ninth Circuit has now upheld your position and therefore I will give you the Temporary Restraining Order and allow you to reopen. And that Temporary Restraining Order remained in place. It then became a Preliminary Injunction, and that remained in place while we litigated the case against the County and the State, which we won then before Judge Waters.

Author: When did the State come in? You are finished with the City, now you have the County.

Glenn: Yes, we sued the County, because the County was the one who came in and shut the place down. The original suit was *Cabazon Band of Mission Indians v. County of Riverside*. At some point in the district court case, the State came in and intervened in the case. In an amicus brief you are just an outsider saying, "we've got an opinion; here's what we think." By intervening, they actually became a party in the case and at some point in that case, they came in, intervened on behalf of the County, and from that point on actually ran the case. It then became the State and AG's [attorney general's] office handling the case, and the County counsel basically backed out and became a second-team player. Judge Waters eventually granted our motion for Summary Judgment, meaning we won the case before him. He ruled in our favor based on the *Barona* Decision, and the decision went up to the Ninth Circuit. The Ninth Circuit upheld Judge Waters's decision and ruled in our favor.

I think the Ninth Circuit decision came down in early '86 because the State then filed their Notice of Appeal to the Supreme Court, and I learned that while I was traveling from Washington to Phoenix. I was on the road in Amarillo, Texas, when I got the phone call that the Supreme Court had agreed to hear the case. That would have been early June of 1986. We filed our briefs during the summer and fall of '86, the case was argued to the court in December, and the decision came down in February of '87; we remained open that entire period.

As I recall, the only time that the operations were closed was for that period from about October 18 until November 10, right at the very beginning, and then for two or three days after the County came in and shut them down before we could get the TRO.

What Feldman did not say was that when the case reached the Supreme Court

the State of California was no longer alone in its appeal. It was joined by 28 other states and appellants.

Tribal officer Brenda James Soulliere and Mark Nichols, who would later become the Tribe's Chief Executive Officer (CEO), also remembered the psychic trauma of the raids. They were barely out of their teens when these events happened. For Brenda the raid took place the first month of her tenure on the Business Committee. She remembers it this way:

I can remember a lot about that. I was in the cage. I was just getting ready to leave, and the other girl was coming on. All of a sudden, somebody shouted, and all of these green jackets came in, and I started to walk out. She [the girl in the cage] started freaking out, "What's going on? Don't leave!" I thought, "I'm going to go out there and see what's going on." I couldn't leave her freaked out trying to hand out money to everybody. So, I stayed there, and then they were banging on the door to open the cage, and I didn't know whether I should or not. Finally, I opened the door. They came in and . . . oh, they went through my purse. They said, "Oh, we're just looking for a bazooka," and they went ahead and went through my purse. I didn't like that idea. They confiscated the money and the chips and, I believe, I had to sign something of what they were taking. I remember there was one of our customers; her name was Roth I believe. She was a survivor of Auschwitz, I believe it was, because she had the numbers tattooed on her wrist or hand or something. She thought it was happening all over again. She was yelling. She was an older lady.

They took our picture. We didn't really know what was going on. It's just that there were sheriffs everywhere taking all of our things. So, we just had to wait and let it go by, and we told everybody, basically, we'd have to call them when we reopened. That's pretty close to a week.

We had to get an injunction to open back up. They arrested Philip [Nichols]. I guess he had an old warrant or something. They took him out in handcuffs. That was kind of scary. I was only 21 myself. You know, I had no idea what I did, or what we did as a group. So, we just . . . we came to work, I guess, in a trance, but we sat around a lot, and I think we all came in about every day and sat and talked about what we were going to do and how we were going to do it. Little by little, things started coming back. We were able to kind of rebuild ourselves.

They took everything that wasn't nailed down. I think I was there when they started bringing everything back. So we just kind of went on. We did the best we could, put everything back together and went on about our way. That's when the lawsuit started. We said, "You know, we're not going to sit back and take this." That's when all the legal battles really started.

CEO Mark Nichols remembers it this way:

I was here for both raids. As I recall the first raid . . . as a matter of fact, Dr. Allan Hulsizer was working with us during that time. I was working on that book project with him on Cahuilla living. This wasn't a business venture. This [the whole tribal business metamorphosis] was really kind of a grassroots revolution is the way I would more properly or aptly describe it, and he wanted very much to be part of it.

He was definitely part of the old school. He had been working with the BIA and it was just really an incredible experience to think in terms of Indians and being private entrepreneurs in their own government. You could see that even for a man that was 80 some years old, he was lighting up.

We had set it up, too, because when we first started, we tried to find out whether the City of Indio was going to, in fact, take a position on this thing. The earlier decision that had been made was to go into the cardroom business because we were concerned that if we went into a Bingo business we would wind up getting into some sort of litigation, which we didn't want to deal with. We had seen what had happened in Florida, and we decided we would take the safe route; we'd go after a cardroom. After all, they are all over California; who could argue with local option?

We actually had very good relationships with newspaper reporters. We had one, her name was Rita Lewis, who had done a lot of work with us on the Smoke Shop so we asked her to come out and do some coverage for us. We set up a couple of poker games, had the newspapers come out and snap pictures. I remember the front page of the *Daily News*, and it had this 85-year-old Dr. Hulsizer peering over a pan-poker hand, and it says "Tribes Test Legal Challenge" or something. That was the gist of it. We didn't have anybody [police] come out, although we were all sitting around waiting for them to come. . . . We sent them letters; we told them; we said if there is a problem with this, let us know. And they wouldn't. They said they didn't think it was legal, but they wouldn't tell us. So we set up some of these games.

I think we had been open a good three weeks or so before the raid came, and . . . it was such an exciting thing. We were all out here every night watching it. Seeing we had a lot of low-end games, it really became quite a community sensation at the time.

I was back in the restaurant sitting with my dad and a Mormon bishop; I think we had another minister there . . . a couple of other folks. John Paul was busy running around working. When the raid came down we were all basically in the facility. When they threw off all their flack jackets and turned and walked around, they said, "Police!" It was amazing. They had completely infiltrated the crowd. We were just oblivious. I guess they could have been gangsters to rob us; we wouldn't have seen them either. But we were just having a good old time in the corner of the building—we were sitting around a table there. . . . The place was packed. We had 100-plus people in the facility.

All of a sudden some people [police] walked in the front door, people walked in the side doors, and the back door on the side which was closest; and in walked a helmeted policeman and somebody behind him. There were at least two behind each door. Then somebody who had been out in the middle of the floor put up his hands and they announced, "This is the Indio Police Department," or whatever; "This is a police raid and everyone in here is under arrest for gambling!"

At that point there must have been six or seven additional people that had been in the crowd that pulled off their jackets and turned them inside out and they were all wearing jackets that said "Police." So there were probably, I'd say there were probably 21 officers or so that were in the building like that. In addition to that, I understand there were police cars parked and a series of other detectives.

We had customers that were basically going into a panic and a lot of concern. We had a very respectable crowd in here—Jewish pan ladies and all kinds of folks that the last thing they wanted to do was be part of a raid.

The press were here at the time because the next day on the cover of the *Daily News* was a picture of a policeman in a riot helmet with a young girl in a choke hold with a baton, slightly off the ground kicking. Here's a perfectly nice person that you've known all this time, and all of a sudden she was down being choked and dragged out the front door. So they were there to snap that picture. It was on the front page of the *Daily News*. It said "102 Arrested in Gambling Raid" or something like that. I remember the 102; that was sort of like the header in the paper.

The County of Riverside [raid] is a little less clear for me frankly. In fact, I think what I did is, maybe I came out once I heard about the raid. I was here when they were taking all the tables out and so forth and running off with all the stuff. (Unlike my father, I don't have a perfectly photographic memory.)

They were wearing green jackets with yellow letters that said "Sheriff," whereas the Indio Police had the dark blue jackets with yellow letters that said "Police." But yes, I was here, but I think I came out once it had happened. I don't recall the actual announcement on the floor.

While the war between the Tribe and local/state authorities raged over gambling, another struggle for survival was being waged daily. How could the combined offices be kept open? How were staff and Business Committee to be paid? Where was the money going to come from to pay for health insurance?

The answer was clear: Dr. Nichols had to raise the necessary funds. This meant continuing his consulting efforts and using these personal funds to meet expenses. It also meant using a "scatter gun" approach to resource development, trying whatever made sense and hoping something worked.

THE WACKENHUT CONNECTION

In September 1980, a new tribal corporation, Cabazon Security Corporation Inc., was formed. Its purposes were, according to its Articles of Incorporation, to "foster tribal self-sufficiency and self-determination" and to "improve the economic base of the Cabazon Indian Reservation through the development of a profit making enterprise, specializing in safeguarding and protection." It was to be the beginning of a three-and-a-half-year relationship between the Cabazons and a subsidiary of one of the nation's largest security firms, Wackenhut Services Incorporated. On April 1, 1981, Wackenhut entered into a joint venture with Cabazon Security Corporation Inc. The joint venture was terminated effective October 1, 1984.

Contrary to the sinister motives ascribed to this business deal by rumormongers far and wide, the joint venture agreement document leaves no doubt as to its intent. Just as Armtec Defense Products Inc., an armaments manufacturer in Coachella, California, is in business to make money, so was Cabazon Security Corporation Inc.—only through security, not major armaments. And why would a large firm like Wackenhut consider associating with a small Indian tribe? The "edge" would have increased their profits by a wide margin.

Section 2 of the agreement, headed "Nature of the Joint Venture," read in part:

The *dominant and paramount purpose* of the Joint Venture *is to qualify for*, bid on and obtain government *guard service contracts*, at both the prime and subcontract level, *which accord preference to small business concerns which are owned and controlled by socially and economically disadvantaged individuals.* (Emphasis added.)

And to underscore this intent, Section 26 of the agreement, "Duration of Joint Venture," provided:

This Joint Venture shall remain in effect for so long as Cabazon Security continues in the security guard and/or related protective-services business and *qualifies for preferences as a small business concern owned and controlled by socially and economically disadvantaged individuals.* (Emphasis added.)

Under the terms of the agreement, Cabazon Security's share of profits and losses was to be 51 percent, and it was required to provide 51 percent of the working capital. The Tribe, as always, insisted on control of its destiny. Section 122 provided in part, that:

Consistent with the majority interest of Cabazon Security in this Joint Venture, *all management and daily business operations* of Joint Venture client contracts *will be under the general charge of and controlled by the Cabazon Security representative.* (Emphasis added.)

The Tribe, Dr. Nichols, and the Wackenhut point man A. Robert Frye, were understandably optimistic regarding future prospects for this new venture. What, they must have asked themselves, could prevent their winning federal contracts for guard and security services worth many millions of dollars? Wackenhut had listed in its 1979 Annual Report 14 international offices, 92 domestic offices, 6 domestic subsidiary corporations, $148,217,000 in revenues with an after-taxes net of $3,258,000 and 20,000 employees. It boasted "security operations at the National Aeronautics and Space Administration's John F. Kennedy Space Center, the Department of Energy's Nevada Test Site where underground atomic testing is carried out, and the 800-mile trans-Alaska oil pipeline from Pruhoe Bay to Valdez [Alaska]."

Wackenhut also reported to its stockholders on two other major U.S. government contracts, brought about by "WSI's outstanding performance record." Both were for security services. According to the report, "one [contract] covered six strategic petroleum-reserve sites operated by the Department of Energy in underground salt caverns along the Texas-Louisiana Gulf Coast; the other covers the period of construction of the Department of Energy's Gas Centrifuge Enrichment Plant, expected to be the most advanced uranium-enrichment plant in the world, at Piketon, Ohio."

Wackenhut was a big company, providing security services around the world, including a $24 million contract with the Saudi Arabian government. But John Hussar of *The Desert Sun* in Palm Springs, California, obviously unaware of this fact, made a mountain out of a molehill for the Cabazons when he alerted the public to a finder's fee sought by Dr. Nichols for putting Wackenhut in the running for "the development of a security system for the palace of a Saudi prince." To the average reader, not an international businessperson, dealings with the Saudis today may seem a mysterious, dramatic and/or bizarre event. But, in the '70s and '80s, any businessperson with international connections or even past contacts "knew" or knew of someone who "knew" of a deal with someone "important" associated with the Saudi government.

The Saudi oil dollars were flowing. And, as any journalist with vision or knowledge beyond the sand dunes knew, in those years there seemed to be hundreds, if not thousands, of young men in American large cities claiming to be Saudi princes. And since there are, in reality, hundreds of Saudi princes, American businessmen were inclined to believe most of those who claimed to be a prince. With oil dollars flowing, an American businessperson might just strike it rich. The results were often humorous or strange or even hilarious; sometimes American businesspeople were fleeced out of many thousands of dollars by tricksters posing as Saudi princes. During this period of free-flowing oil dollars, many Nigerians and other nationalities also fleeced these greedy and careless Americans out of their money.

Every businessperson in America understands the concept of a finder's fee, as should every journalist. It simply means that the finder of a business opportunity or contact for someone gets paid for the "finding," in accordance with the agreement made with the person or firm searching for that opportunity or contact. Often the fee is only 2 percent, but 2 percent of something is better than 100 percent of nothing.

In this context, it is questionable why Hussar made an issue out of trying to earn a finder's fee for putting someone identified as a Saudi prince (who later turned out to be bogus) in touch with a security firm. Research would have revealed that Wackenhut, the Cabazon security-firm partner Hussar and other "journalists" became so concerned with, was not the firm Dr. Nichols turned to for a finder's fee; it was Intersect, which was not in business with the Cabazons in any way at that time. Either Hussar and other "journalists" who later used his articles as their reality base were ignorant of the facts, which means they had not completely researched their stories, or they chose to withhold this information from their readers.

A more interesting true story might have been the following:

Robert Frye was initially employed by Wackenhut in 1968 as its director of physical security and, two years later, was elected a corporate vice president for contracts management. The February-March 1981 edition of the corporate publication *Wackenhut Pipeline* chronicled Frye's then recent ascent to the presidency of Wackenhut's subsidiary, Wackenhut Services Inc., which was responsible for all government contracts. This subsidiary would be the Tribe's partner in the joint venture, not the parent Wackenhut itself. Before joining Wackenhut, Frye had been director of security for Trans World Airlines; chief of security and law enforcement for Pan American World Airways; industrial security specialist, Assistant Section Chiefs, Provost Marshall Branch for the Air Force Missile Test Center/ Patrick Air Force Base; and special agent for the FBI for seven years.

To the uninitiated in the area of minority contracting, it would seem that a team made up of Wackenhut, the parent; Wackenhut Services Inc., the subsidiary; Bob Frye; the Cabazons; and their resource developer, Dr. John Nichols, could only be overwhelmingly successful in securing many substantial government contracts. However, the uninitiated would make the mistake of not factoring in the corroding and sabotaging impact of racism and favoritism on decisions made by non-minority Americans on possible contracts going to minority Americans.

During the Reagan years, whenever the President was quoted as saying he didn't have a racist bone in his body, many agreed; but those who had closely followed his political career would counter that he was right—the racism was not in his bones but in the very marrow of his bones. The same was true for many non-minority Americans who occupied positions of authority in government contracting. As a result, few qualified minority firms won financially significant contracts, regardless of the language of the law.

It should be noted that the Directorate of Small and Disadvantaged Business Utilization, Office of the Secretary of Defense, publishes a book titled *Subcontracting Opportunities with DoD* [Department of Defense] *Major Prime Contractors*. The Foreword of that publication reads, in part:

> This publication exclusively addresses the defense subcontracting opportunities market. The DoD encourages small business and small disadvantaged business to enter the defense subcontracting market. By entering the market, goods and services flow to strengthen national security and the defense industrial base.
>
> *The DoD requires major prime contractors and subcontractors* receiving contracts valued over $500,000 ($1 million for construction) *to develop plans and goals for subcontracting with small business and small disadvantaged business.* This requirement generates a significant subcontracting opportunity market. In FY 1990, for example, DoD prime contractors awarded $54.7 billion in subcontracts of which $21.5 billion (or 39.3%) was awarded to small business firms. (Emphasis added.)

Listed in this publication are major defense contractors and multi-national corporations such as General Electric, Boeing, B.F. Goodrich Aerospace, Unisys Corporation and Rockwell International Corporation as well as smaller firms. *For California alone there are 273 firms listed.* Among them is Peter Zokosky's old Coachella firm, Armtec Defense Products Co.

Within a month after executing their Joint Venture Agreement, the Tribe and Wackenhut Services were already in high gear. In a May 11, 1981, letter (over the signature of Tribal Chairman Art Welmas) to every local Congressperson and California's two U.S. Senators (the late Senator Hayakawa and former Senator

Alan Cranston), the Joint Venture's composition and reason for being were clearly spelled out and the officials' assistance sought. Once again, the scatter-gun approach was employed. Here, in part, is how they said they thought the Senators and Congresspersons could best help them:

President Reagan has indicated that he favors a shift away from using tax dollars for security protection in military and government installations and agencies. This has given us, as private industry, the impetus to pursue to the fullest extent the opportunity to bid on government service contracts.

We need your help in reaching the appropriate bid lists which are distributed from the various governmental agencies and departments. We wish to be included on the following bid lists . . .

The letter listed 37 departments and agencies of the federal government, ranging from Agriculture to the U.S. Postal Service. It was as if someone simply copied a pre-existing list from some source, wanting to make certain no possible opportunity would be overlooked.

While that letter was being circulated in offices on Capitol Hill, representatives of the Joint Venture had already begun to hit the road to develop business possibilities. But although the Joint Venture Agreement said its "activities and engagements shall be limited to the United States which shall be deemed to mean the States, its territories and possessions, the Commonwealth of Puerto Rico, the Trust Territories of the Pacific Islands, and the District of Columbia," the Cabazon Security representatives' early actions demonstrated a much wider geographical interest as well as interests beyond "guard services" and "other protective services." Their actions revealed a geographical interest in the Western Hemisphere, and a business interest in any Defense Department-related contract possible. As further documentation shows, this broadened interest had been inspired by the husband of the mayor of Indio and former president of Armtec, Peter Zokosky, who had approached Cabazon Security about going into competition with Armtec. The following Wackenhut interoffice memorandum describes the relationship:

WACKENHUT
INTER-OFFICE MEMORANDUM
TO: R.E. Chasen, S & S Group
DATE: May 25, 1981
FROM: A.R. Frye
AREA: WSI
SUBJECT: Trip Report (May 11-22, 1981)

During the above period, the writer traveled to New Jersey, Indiana and Washington, D.C., accompanied by Dr. John Nichols, Administrator for the Cabazon Indians. The threefold purpose of the trip was as follows:

1: To explore the apparent potential for the Cabazon-WSI Joint Venture to enter into the manufacture of 120mm. combustible cartridge cases; and other related armament activities—using Cabazon land as the site for such actions.

2: To contact appropriate U.S. Government agencies in Washington, D.C., with a view to insuring the Joint Venture is placed on pertinent Bidder's Lists re security services involving small business, socially disadvantaged firms, and set-asides for Indian firms.

3: To contact the appropriate U.S. Government agencies associated with the possible export of items on the Munitions List (specifically the night vision goggles), as well as to contact several recommended attorneys who are experienced in processing of requests for export licenses, etc.

Re Item (1)

During this part of the trip we were also accompanied by Peter Zokosky, the former president of Armtec Defense Products, Inc., Coachella, Calif. . . . He has indicated an interest in working with the Joint Venture in this regard.

Based upon Zokosky's prior business relationship with Army personnel at the Pickitinny Arsenal, we spent a considerable amount of time on May 12 & 13 at the Arsenal (U.S. Army Armament Research & Development Command, Large Caliber Weapon Systems Laboratory, Dover, N.J. 07901—"ARRADCOM").

Personnel contacted at the Arsenal included Mr. R. Scott Westley, Army Project Officer and Dr. Harry D. Fair, Chief, Propulsion Technology, Applied Sciences Division, as well as Ken Russell, Project Officer. Predicated upon these contacts, the following potential activities merit consideration as business to be initiated by the Joint Venture:

- Construction of a facility for the manufacture of 120mm. combustible cartridge cases for sale to the U.S. Army, under Army contracts; with sales also to NATO, especially to the Federal Republic of Germany, who are adopting the use of such cases in their Leopard tanks. *(The obvious key to any such endeavor is Zokosky. He is reportedly one of only 6-7 personnel in the world who have had any significant experience in the development and manufacture of the slurry process involved in combustible cartridge cases. He is under a present non-compete agreement with Armtec, his former company, until August 1981. Armtec is the present sole source supplier of 120mm. combustible cartridge cases to the U.S. Govt. Zokosky is also serving as a consultant to the British Govt.)*
  It should be noted that several key ingredients necessary for the successful manufacture of such cases are available through the use of land on the Cabazon Reservation in Calif., namely, an arid climate, a large quantity of water, remote location, available work force, closeness to major transportation routes, and lack of opposition by adjacent governing bodies and "irate citizens" over the siting of such a facility.
- Developing a companion facility on the reservation for the complete assembly of shell casings, to include the assembly of propellants, war heads, fuses, etc.; as well as an R&D facility for the development of new combustible cartridge cases for other weapons systems.
- Use of adjacent Indian tribal lands as a location for a large caliber weapons range test site. . . .
- Potential use of a test firing range for the U.S. Government on the Santa Rosa Mountain. (During our discussions with Dr. Fair at the Pickitinny Arsenal, he indicated the Govt. was interested in locating a site near the main power grid on the West Coast, which was also at an elevation of at least 8000 feet for possible

> testing of the railgun. These requirements are met on the Santa Rosa mountain—under the control of the Santa Rosa Indians. . . . Note attached *Time Magazine* article of 12/1/80 on the railgun.)

On May 13, 1981, we also met with a former Army associate of Zokosky's, Mr. Victor Guadagno, Vice President, Flinchbaugh Products, Product Development Center, Wharton, N.J., a Division of General Defense Corp. This Flinchbaugh facility manufactures warheads and related items under Army contracts for the 105/120/155mm. projectiles. Guadagno advised that since he retired as a Colonel from the Pickitinny Arsenal in 1978 and was placed in charge of the Flinchbaugh effort at Wharton, he has increased the business from an annual volume of under $300,000 to more than $3 million in 1980, with an anticipated volume of $6 million in 1981, at an expected profit margin of 10%. Guadagno said that Flinchbaugh would be most interested in forming some kind of joint venture relationship with Cabazon-WSI regarding the production of warheads, etc.; and that he would be personally interested in working for the Cabazon-WSI Joint Venture in developing such a production capability.

On May 14, 1981, we met with personnel at the Indiana Army Ammunition Plant, Charlestown, Ind. This is a GOCO plant operated under Army contract by ICI Americas Inc., and currently employs some 1,500 workers. Per a recent news release, ICI Americas Inc. was awarded a $60 million contract by the Army to so operate this facility—although the contract period was not specified.

We were afforded the opportunity of being escorted on a tour of the loading operations at the plant involving production of bag charges for 155mm. shells. It was apparent that this facility is very labor intensive; uses production methods that are highly automated; and continues to use the Government plant originally built for World War I. During our discussions with the Chief Buyer, Mr. Fred L. Marquis, he advised that he was aware that a Canadian munitions plant, which was involved in the production of propellants for both the Canadian and U.S. Governments, was having some sort of financial difficulties with the Canadian Government, and was sought to be purchased by several international firms, including Welland Chemicals, SNPE, and Muden Machine. The name of this Canadian firm is Valleyfield Chemical Products Corp., P.O. Box 5520, Valleyfield, Quebec, Canada J65 4V9; and the plant is located in Valleyfield, near Montreal. Mr. Marquis advised that due to a desire by the U.S. Army authorities that ICI Americas Inc. overhead costs in operating the GOCO plant should be reduced by foreign military sales or other foreign commercial sales, ICI Americas Inc. was interested in whether the Cabazon-WSI Joint Venture might be interested in becoming involved in a marketing arrangement with ICI Americas Inc. to handle foreign sales. We advised we would probably be so interested and would accordingly respond to them shortly.

On May 15–21, in several discussions with officials of the Valleyfield Chemical Products Corp. and a representative of the Canadian Munitions Board, it was ascertained that the Valleyfield plant was in fact under receivership by the Canadian Government due to the default on a Canadian Government loan; that the default was primarily due to a judgmental error of the first order in not meeting a loan repayment schedule solely in order to not have an adverse appearing quarterly P&L statement, which prompted the Canadian Government to take over the plant under receivership; that the plant had an estimated capital value of about $18 million, but due to an anomaly in the Canadian law applicable to this instance, purchasers could bid to take over the plant for only some $6 million; and that it was the expressed desire of pertinent Canadian officials that the takeover be accomplished solely by Canadian interests without any foreign representation. Moreover, should there not be any qualifying parties, the Canadian Government was prepared to nationalize the plant in order to continue with the production of propellants under Canadian and U.S. Government contracts.

Through personal contacts of Dr. John Nichols with Barry Zuckerman and Charles F. Agar, both Canadian citizens, who are involved in a Canadian firm called Mineral Resources International Limited, as well as both being involved in Canadian financial institutions, it was ascertained that they are interested in the possibility of acquiring this plant, using their own financial capabilities. Dr. Nichols envisions that the role of the Cabazon-WSI Joint Venture, should the Zuckerman-Agar group be successful in so purchasing this plant, would be to serve as the foreign marketing representative for the plant; to have this group possibly finance the establishment of the casing/loading facility on the Cabazon Reservation; and to have the capability to conduct R&D for the group in the armament industry. (It is to be noted that the Cabazon Indians have also set up a Joint Venture with Mineral Resources International Limited wherein this Joint Venture will conduct oil and gas exploration on Indian lands throughout the U.S. This entity is under the aegis of the Cabazon Oil and Gas Company [no longer in business].)

A meeting has been set up in Ottawa, Canada at 9:00 a.m., May 26, 1981, involving Dr. Nichols, Frank Agar, F. Thornburg, the writer, and members of the Canadian Munitions Board re this matter. The Cabazon-WSI Joint Venture will not be involved in any manner of capital investment in this Valleyfield plant. [Note: This remained the position of the Cabazon-WSI Joint Venture. Unfortunately, various journalists including Jonathan Littman, then with the *San Francisco Chronicle,* would allege otherwise. Littman, who confided to a member of a Washington, D.C.-based public relations firm that his series on the Tribe almost won him a Pulitzer Prize, wrote in the first of his three-part series that "the Cabazons and Wackenhut made a formal proposal to purchase Valleyfield Chemical of Valleyfield, Quebec, in 1981. . . . The proposal, backed by Canadian investors and a Canadian senator, was rejected in June 1981 because the government wanted Canadian management of the firm."]

Re Item (2):

While in Washington, D.C., personal contact was made with the offices of Senators Hayakawa and Cranston of California; the Bureau of Indian Affairs; the Department of Commerce; and the General Services Administration. Follow-up will be made with other appropriate agencies by Robert Meskunis (sp), for and on behalf of the Cabazon-WSI Joint Venture, to ensure the J-V is placed on bidder's list, etc. . . .

Re Item (3):

Through arrangements made between Senator Hayakawa's office and the Department of State, we were able to have an appointment on May 18, 1981, with Mr. Jos. P. Smaldone, Chief, Arms Licensing Division, Office of Munitions Control (PM/MC), U.S. Department of State. We were thoroughly briefed about the general aspects of the International Traffic in Arms Regulations [ITAR]; the fact that all items contained on the Munitions List under the ITAR are processed by his office when approval is sought to export such items from the U.S. to a non-barred country (only communist bloc countries are so barred by the ITAR, as well as present shipments to Iran-Iraq due to their war); and were provided with a copy of the pertinent ITAR and other explanatory data in the form of MC Letters. Mr. Smaldone confirmed that the night vision goggles are items set forth under Category XIIa of the munitions list, which required approval by his office for export; and that the prerequisite for obtaining any such license was to file an Application for Registration. He also advised that his office coordinated with the Department of Defense on the granting of any license to permanently export any munitions list item; and that all other items which are not set forth on the Munitions List are handled by the Department of Commerce re approval to export.

Meetings were subsequently held with several attorneys in the Washington area who were recommended to Dr. Nichols as being eminently qualified to handle the processing of the Cabazon-WSI Joint Venture Application of Registration with the Department of State; the subsequent processing of application/licenses for the export of night vision goggles to foreign buyers; and the possible utilization of the Joint Venture in other business opportunities involving clients of these attorneys, as well as representing the Joint Venture on specific projects of significant magnitude, such as the establishment of the Army test sites on the Cabazon lands, etc. These attorneys are Mr. William M. Briggs, 910 Seventeenth St., N.W., Washington, D.C. 20006, and Mr. Glade R. Flake, 5530 Wisconsin Ave., Washington, DC 20015.

RECOMMENDATIONS: (Immediate Near-Term Only)

1. Predicated upon discussions with Dr. Nichols, and the obvious need to bring in revenue to the Cabazon-WSI Joint Venture at the earliest possible date, it is highly desirous that the sale of the projected amount of 300 night vision goggles to Guatemala be expedited. To facilitate these transactions, it is necessary to:

- File an application for registration by the Joint Venture with the Department of State. This registration will cost $350 for a three year period.
- Firm up the deal between the Joint Venture and John Vanderwerker, President of Intersect Corporation, Irvine, Calif., who has the apparent exclusive rights for foreign marketing with the Litton Electron Tube Division in third world countries; also most important is to ensure a firm arrangement is working out with Litton on behalf of Intersect/Joint Venture re pass through of warranties. (This firming up of the arrangements with Vanderwerker and Litton should occur in meetings in Tempe, Ariz. within the next 2–3 weeks.)
- Obtain letters of commitment from the Guatemalan representative on the order for 300 goggles; and after the Registration is approved by the State Department, and pending approval by the State Dept. on the license approval, contractually obtain up-front moneys which will permit the ordering of the modular facilities for use in assembling the goggles on the Cabazon Reservation.
- The processing of the registration and license application will necessitate an agreement in working out with one of the above mentioned attorneys, ostensibly Mr. Glade Flake, who has indicated he would be initially willing to so assist on an hourly basis.

2. *It is crucial for any anticipated involvement of the Joint Venture in the manufacture/assembly of combustible cartridge cases and loading of shells, etc. to have the talents of Peter Zokosky as the Joint Venture representative in charge of these activities. Peter Zokosky has considerable personal wealth and is highly thought of by those persons whom we met at the Arsenals. We will hopefully be able to secure his services on the basis of equity participation. He will be instrumental in the planning for and obtaining Government contracts, based upon unsolicited proposals.* (Emphasis added.)

When Dr. Nichols was interviewed, he was asked how the relationship with Wackenhut came about. According to him, establishing that contact was a source of pride. Because of the uncertainty of adequate income to meet the increasing expenses of the Tribe, he was pushed to concentrate on seeking new business opportunities. He described the hookup with Wackenhut this way:

When I was told to go out and look for new business, that's what I did. Wackenhut—I was very proud of this and the way that came about—Mr. Wackenhut's mother was a friend of a guy named Charles Emmert, and Emmert was a friend of Mike Riconosciuto's father, Marshal Riconosciuto. He was also a friend of Beryl Barber and Beryl Barber had reputedly developed a lot of the hardware for the AWAC's airplane. This Charles Emmert was the head of a group calling itself something like "We Won't Pay Income Tax." They refused to pay income tax because of wars and all that stuff, and he [Emmert] just wouldn't pay it. So of course the federal government was really hot on his tail. But he was also a conservative.

Apparently Emmert was also a friend of a fellow named Pat Moriarity who owned Red Devil Fireworks Company. Moriarity, allegedly a former CIA agent who had worked overseas and in Northern Japan, was an acquaintance of Robert Meskunas who knew me. Meskunas supposedly told some of them I was a social worker who often successfully treated people with severe mental and emotional problems, citing for example my work in Kentucky and Michigan. Apparently they had been discussing Mike Riconosciuto.

So what happened, Charles Emmert called me and said, "Look, I have a problem. We have a genius by the name of Michael Riconosciuto." He said Michael had shot down an RCA satellite in Mozambique where he had gone when he had gotten mad at RCA. Now Mike was hanging around the Stanford Research Institute and he knew all the scientists there. Mike had lived with Janis Joplin in the past and it was stated he was a cook for the Hell's Angels for making amphetamines. I said, "He sounds pretty sick to me."

Emmert felt I could help get Mike cleaned up for Wackenhut. Emmert felt Wackenhut would like to have him mentally and emotionally straight to use his genius. I went to Pinole, California, accompanied by Peter Zokosky and my wife and his wife. Pinole was the site of Hercules Powder Company which had been owned by Dupont. It had been sold, and Michael's father had gotten control of this mammoth, mammoth plant. His son Mike was manufacturing amphetamines, apparently unknown by his dad. Mike wanted to hire me. He brought with him to the meeting $100,000 in street money. He was disheveled, dirty looking, and smelled like he needed a bath. He said, "I would like to work with Wackenhut," as Emmert had said Wackenhut could use him. Zokosky still thought he really was a genius. Zokosky had been president of Armtec, which made caseless ammunition that was used in the Vietnam War. They made artillery ammunition out of nitrocellulose, with a metal cap and a traditional nose on each shell. The case, when fired, would disintegrate. After disintegration, only the bottom of the shell would be left. Before this invention, the entire hot shell would be left, burning the legs of the soldiers. Zokosky had been president of this company which was the sole source for these shells, located in Coachella.

Zokosky, Riconosciuto, Bob Frye and myself went to two U.S. Arsenals, one was Dover Arsenal in New Jersey, and I forgot the name of the second in Indiana. We sat there with the absolute top brass in the United States in military physics talking about particle beams.

Riconosciuto held his own all the way through. I didn't know a particle beam from a sunbeam. I gave Wackenhut a lot of help with Mike because he was sent to me. That's how we met Riconosciuto. The bottom line was Riconosciuto was nuts. He brought with him a young man named Victor. They said they were running teenage prostitutes to service L.A.

cops. They brought some of their prostitutes with them. Mike said he owned that business. Of course, he had all this money from manufacturing and selling drugs. He had been busted, because to escape detection he had built an under-the-water laboratory to make drugs. This way the lab couldn't be detected by Seattle Police helicopters. The guy is the closest to, if you ever read comic books, [Lex] Luthor in Superman. He is one of the most evil people I ever met. My diagnosis was he suffered from a combination character defect and was a sociopath.

The bottom line was that Nichols, according to those who introduced him and the Tribe to Wackenhut, gave Wackenhut what it wanted—an attempt by Nichols to treat Riconosciuto to make him more functional—and Wackenhut gave Nichols what he wanted, a tribal joint venture business relationship. As events would prove, it was not a good bargain for either.

In October, the Joint Venture submitted bids for two security guard service contracts. On October 12, 1981, it responded to the government's Request for Proposal (RFP) for security support services for the Johnson Space Center (JSC) in Houston, Texas. Its bid document outlined the services to be provided in its General Scope of Work section. The Joint Venture proposed:

To respond to all Security Support Services requirements of this RFP by providing on a twenty-four hour, seven day a week basis, a uniformed and armed security guard force, and other qualified personnel, for security functions at JSC including, but not limited to: the safeguarding of data and property against unauthorized access, loss, theft or damage; the investigation of incidents relating to unauthorized access; the periodic checking of classified material repositories to ensure the proper safeguarding of classified material, on a frequency as prescribed . . . conducting escorts of classified shipments and other designated material/vehicles/personnel . . . providing required responses to security emergencies and other disaster preparedness events; providing extensive security support for the operational phase of the Shuttle Transportation System . . . and issuing and maintaining pertinent orders and instructions, as well as prompt reports, required for all such security functions.

In accomplishing these requirements, the Joint Venture will provide a senior shift supervisor on a continuous basis to maintain contact with the NASA-JSC Security Office, and will also provide competent management and other security personnel who are properly trained in the fields of police science, law enforcement and security techniques such as:

- Industrial security
- JSC badge and identification systems
- Criminal and general investigation
- Plant protection and area control
- Traffic systems and controls
- Use of firearms and other special law enforcement and security . . . equipment, communications, vehicles and alarm systems
- Criminal and general investigation
- Plant protection and area control
- Safeguarding classified information
- Elementary first aid and fire protection.

The bid price was $7,960,651 plus profit of $634,358 for a total of $8,595,009. The second bid, submitted on October 27, 1981, was to provide security guard service for the Hawthorne Army Ammunition Plant in Hawthorne, Nevada. The bid price submitted was for $1,770,983, including a profit of $99,500.

The Joint Venture won neither contract and over the next 18 to 24 months would experience the same failure. It would file an application for certification under the Small Business Administration's (SBA) 8(a) Program for minority-controlled firms. But, in a March 7, 1983, letter from the SBA, the Joint Venture was informed that its application could not "be processed at this time since contract support is not available to meet your firm's business plan projections."

Chairman Welmas was assured that the Joint Venture's application would be "kept in file in the San Francisco District Office (SFDO) for a six-month period only, to determine if there is a sufficient increase in the volume of requirements offered to warrant further processing of your application. Should sufficient contract support be identified, SFDO will issue you a business plan application to determine personal and business eligibility." Although the official letter of termination of the Joint Venture was sent to Cabazon Security Corporation on June 6, 1984, a letter dated August 29, 1983, almost a year earlier, used the language "in view of the *effective termination* of the Cabazon Indian Security-WSI Joint Venture." It is probable that this 8(a) rejection was the final straw that disaffected the top brass at Wackenhut of the continued belief in the "edge" they had sought.

The handling of two bids in the fall of 1982 must have alerted Wackenhut and the Cabazons to the real world of government contracting involving firms known to be minority-owned firms. In mid 1982, the Joint Venture responded to Invitation for Bids to provide Fire Protection services, Naval Air Station, Corpus Christi, Texas, and similar services for Naval Air Station, Pensacola, Florida. Although low bidder on each contract, the Joint Venture was awarded neither.

The following brief chronology of events prepared by Tribal Attorney Glenn Feldman tells the story. Throughout, the Joint Venture is referred to as CIS/WSI (Cabazon Indian Security/Wackenhut Services, Inc.). The chronology was prepared as part of an appeal to the SBA's Size Appeals Board by the Joint Venture from the adverse ruling by the SBA that CIS/WSI was "not an eligible small business concern for purposes of the two contracts in question." The finding by the Regional Administrator of SBA's Region IX stated the obvious, that "each solicitation was a total small business set-aside," which required a bidder to show "its average annual receipts for its preceding three (3) fiscal years do not exceed $4.5 million." Feldman's chronology read in part:

The Corpus Christi solicitation was issued on June 23, 1982. CIS/WSI submitted its bid thereon July 27, 1982. The Pensacola solicitation was issued on June 28, 1982, and CIS/WSI's bid was submitted on August 10, 1982.

The Corpus Christi bid opening occurred on August 4, 1982. On August 6, a representative of CIS/WSI was advised by telephone that it was the apparent low bidder, but that the bid appeared to include an "obvious error." On August 9, 1982, CIS/WSI telexed the contracting officer advising that as a result of the error, it was withdrawing from the Corpus Christi solicitation, which was followed by a letter to that effect of the same date. On August 18th, CIS/WSI received a letter from the contracting officer dated August 12, 1982, authorizing the withdrawal. On September 7, 1982, the Department of the Navy canceled the Corpus Christi solicitation in its entirety. As of that date, then, CIS/WSI regarded the Corpus Christi matter as moot and of no further concern.

The bids in response to the Pensacola solicitation were opened on August 12, 1982. Several days later, CIS/WSI was telephonically advised that it was not the apparent low bidder on that contract, but that its bid was second lowest.

It was in this context, then, that CIS/WSI received a letter, dated September 21, 1982, from Mr. Robert S. Burnside, Assistant District Director for Procurement Assistance, Small Business Administration, San Diego, California. That letter asked CIS/WSI to complete and return SBA form 355 in connection with the Corpus Christi solicitation. Significantly, however, that letter failed to advise CIS/WSI that a size protest had been initiated against it with respect to the Corpus Christi solicitation (the letter stated only that the SBA "has been asked to determine your business status . . ."; the letter wholly failed to mention the Pensacola solicitation or the fact a protest had been instituted against it with respect to Pensacola and failed to enclose a copy of either protest.

Having withdrawn its Corpus Christi bid, and knowing that the solicitation had been canceled, CIS/WSI responded by letter dated October 6, 1982, advising Mr. Burnside that it had withdrawn its bid with respect to the Corpus Christi solicitation.

CIS/WSI heard nothing further from SBA until October 20, 1982, when it received Dale Rettig's letter of October 14th, enclosing the adverse size determination of October 13th and advising it of its right to appeal. It was at that time that CIS/WSI learned for the first time a) that it had become the apparent low bidder of the Pensacola solicitation, b) that a protest had been filed against it with respect to Pensacola at least two months earlier, and c) that it had been determined to be other than a small business with respect to the Pensacola contract. CIS/WSI has still not been provided a copy of the size protest ostensibly filed against it by an entity identified only as "Consolidated Fire Protection Organization." However, pursuant to 13CFR ss121.3-5(a), the protest must have been filed by August 19, 1982, to have been timely. It is, therefore, inexplicable why the SBA's letter of September 21, 1982, made no reference to the Pensacola solicitation or the Pensacola protest.

As a result of these actions, Feldman's appeal of the Regional Administrator's finding concluded that the SBA "violated its own regulations in making the size determination with respect to CIS/WSI." Feldman wrote, in part:

The size determination appealed from indicated that a size protest on the Corpus Christi solicitation was initiated by the contracting officer, while a protest on the Pensacola solicitation was filed by an entity identified only as "Consolidated Fire Protection Organization, Naval Air Station, Pensacola, Florida." The manner in which these protests were processed and the resulting size determination violated SBA regulations in at least the following respects:

The SBA wholly failed to notify CIS/WSI of the protest initiated with regard to the Pensacola solicitation. The requirement is clear and unambiguous. That section requires the applicable regulation of SBA that following receipt of a size protest, the SBA "shall also advise the protested bidder or offeror of the receipt of the protest . . . ." The SBA violated this regulation in failing to notify CIS/WSI of the protest filed on the Pensacola solicitation, which had to have been filed no later than August 19, 1982, to be timely.

The SBA failed to provide CIS/WSI with a copy of the Pensacola protest. The second requirement of the applicable regulation is equally clear: The SBA "shall forward to the protested bidder or offeror a copy of the protest. . . ." The SBA has totally failed to comply with this basic requirement and, to date, CIS/WSI has still not been furnished with a copy of the protest ostensibly filed by the "Consolidated Fire Protection Organization." It is a basic element of due process that a party against whom charges have been made ought to be able to see the charges in order to prepare its response. As a result of the SBA's failure to observe its own procedural regulations, CIS/WSI has been deprived of this opportunity.

The SBA failed to provide CIS/WSI with a copy of the Corpus Christi protest initiated by the contracting officer. Again, the violation by SBA of its own regulations has deprived CIS/WSI of the opportunity to review and respond to the allegations made against it.

The SBA failed to notify CIS/WSI of the receipt of the Corpus Christi protest. The September 21, 1982, letter of Robert S. Burnside failed to advise that a size protest had been lodged against it by the contracting officer for the Corpus Christi solicitation. Rather, the letter merely stated that "The Small Business Administration has been asked to determine your business status. . . ." In no way can this language be construed to comply with the regulatory requirement that SBA "advise the protested bidder . . . of the receipt of the protest. . . ."

In the instant matter, SBA's regulatory violations have been both substantial and prejudicial to the appellant herein. By failing to notify CIS/WSI of the protest filed against it with respect to the Pensacola solicitation, by failing to advise the appellant that its failure to respond to what was then a moot protest with respect to the Corpus Christi solicitation might affect its ability to receive the Pensacola contract, and by failing to provide CIS/WSI with copies of either protest so that it could adequately defend itself, actions render the size determination void and invalid with respect to the Pensacola solicitation. As a result, this Board should reverse the decision of the Regional Administrator and direct that the contract resulting from the Pensacola solicitation be awarded to CIS/WSI forthwith.

Feldman then proceeded to make his case that CIS/WSI was, in fact, an "independent small business concern controlled by Cabazon Indian Security Corporation" which "should be certified as eligible to bid on similar future contracts":

As previously demonstrated, SBA's flagrant violation of its procedural regulations requires a holding that the size determination appealed from is void with regard to the Pensacola procurement. Recognizing, however, that an adverse ruling from the Board might preclude CIS/WSI from bidding on similar future solicitations, it is herein demonstrated that the determination that CIS/WSI is not an eligible small business concern for purposes of such other contracts is erroneous and should be reversed by the Board.

CIS/WSI is a joint business venture, created in April, 1981, by and between Cabazon Indian Security Corporation, a small business venture chartered and wholly owned by the Cabazon Band of Mission Indians, and Wackenhut Services, Inc. The joint venture operated pursuant to a written joint venture agreement, a copy of which is appended to the completed copy of SBA form 355 for CIS/WSI, which is attached hereto.

The sole basis for the determination by the Region IX Administrator that CIS/WSI is not an eligible small business concern appears to be an improper and unwarranted interpretation of 13 CFR ss 121.3-2(a)9vii(9c), which provides, in pertinent part:

Concerns bidding on a particular procurement or property sale as joint ventures are considered as affiliated and controlling or having the power to control each other with regard to the performance of the contract.

The Regional Administrator apparently believed that this regulation constitutes a conclusive presumption that any joint venture between a small business concern and a large business must, by definition, result in a finding that the joint venture is affiliated with the larger business and is, therefore, ineligible as a small business concern. Under general principles of law, the precedents of this Board and the specific facts of this case, however, such a conclusion is unwarranted and the size determination with respect to CIS/WSI should be reversed on appeal.

The regulation with respect to joint ventures creates only a rebuttable presumption with respect to affiliation. The operative language of the regulation—that parties to a joint venture "are considered as being affiliated"—was not intended to create, and should not be interpreted as creating, a conclusive presumption as to the matter of affiliation. Instead, it must be viewed as establishing only a rebuttable presumption, which may be overcome by evidence to the contrary.

The agreement between Cabazon Security and Wackenhut Services clearly places the control and management of the joint venture's activities for contract services on Cabazon, and negates any inference that the venture's activities can be controlled by Wackenhut. The CIS/WSI joint venture is neither a sham enterprise nor an "apple." Rather, it represents a serious and substantial effort by an American Indian Tribe to create, maintain and succeed with a rather unique business enterprise; an enterprise that will create jobs and revenues for an economically disadvantaged population. . . .

This conclusion is buttressed by other provisions of the agreement. Thus, for example, under Paragraph 7, the principal office of the joint venture is located on the Cabazon Indian Reservation in Indio, California, thousands of miles from the Florida headquarters of Wackenhut. Under Paragraph 17(a), the books of account for the joint venture are to be kept in the office of the Cabazon Reservation. Finally, pursuant to Paragraph 9, Cabazon is required to furnish the majority of the working capital for the joint venture's activities.

These factors clearly require a finding by the Board that the activities of CIS/WSI are not controlled or subject to control by Wackenhut and that, as a result, the adverse size determination by the Region IX Administrator was erroneous and should be reversed.

A reversal by this Board would be consistent with Minority Small Business/Capital Ownership Development Standard Operating Procedures, which specifically authorize joint ventures between minority small business concerns and large businesses for the purpose of performing federal contracts under the 8(a) program. The Minority Small Business and Capital Ownership Development Standard Operating Procedures Manual, at Chapter 6, S.O.P.49(a), provides:

An 8(a) concern may enter into a Joint Venture Agreement with another approved 8(a) concern *or with a nondisadvantaged concern, large or small,* for the purpose of performing a specific 8(a) contract.

Under 13 CFR ss124.1-1(c)(1), a "minority small business concern," in order to meet 8(a) eligibility requirements, must also meet the regulatory definition of "small business concern" as set forth in 13 CFR Part 121. It is, thus, apparent that there is nothing inconsistent or regulatorily improper in a joint venture between a small business concern (as all 8(a) concerns must be) and a large business performing a contract awarded under a small business set aside program. While the procurement in question was not issued under the SBA 8(a) program, there is no reason, in law or logic, to disallow the CIS/WSI joint venture when the SBA's own procedures clearly contemplate and authorize such arrangements. This is particularly true where, as here, the joint venture agreement specifically vests control of the venture with the small business concern.

For all of the reasons set forth above, CIS/WSI respectfully requests that the Size Appeals Board find the size determination of the Region IX Administrator void with respect to the Pensacola solicitation, erroneous as to all other similar solicitations, reverse the determination of ineligibility as regards CIS/WSI, and direct that the contract under the Pensacola solicitation bc awarded to CIS/WSI forthwith. (Emphasis added.)

Feldman's appeal was contained in a letter dated October 27, 1982. In a memorandum dated June 29, 1983—*more than eight months later*—sent by certified mail, return receipt requested, the SBA's Attorney Advisor Michael F. Kinkead transmitted the Size Appeals Board's findings to Dale Rettig, Regional Counsel, Region IX, with a copy to Feldman. In the legalese familiar to most minority firms seeking government contracts, Kinkead advised:

The Board found that in arriving at the subject size determination your [Rettig's] office did not have available for examination an executed SBA Form 355, and that the contents of the Joint Venture Agreement between CIS/WSI were never examined.

In light of this, the Board took no action in this appeal, and directed that the matter be remanded to your office for reconsideration.

Accordingly, we are enclosing your file, together with copies of materials subsequently received by this office, including the material submitted by the appellant's attorney, for your examination.

It was a "stellar performance" by government officials who seemed to be grossly incompetent functionaries and/or racist gate watchers, determined to block the economic progress of minorities, even those acting in concert with well-connected majority firms. Although the Tribe had won a victory of sorts, there was little to celebrate. The contract had already been let to another firm in the eight-month period it took to decide the appeal. Although it was low bidder, it had been "fast-shuffled" out of a contract. The Tribe and Wackenhut knew their relationship—begun with great hope on both sides—was now on a downslide to nothingness. The end was only a matter of time, just a formality.

A lazy, misinformed press and its "investigative" reporters would, in later years, try mightily to make this Joint Venture out to be something sinister and foreboding. But in the final analysis, it was simply the story, in part, of a politically well-connected majority-owned firm trying to use a minority-owned firm to get an "edge" in competition for government contracts with other majority-owned firms.

The Zokosky connection was apparently his attempt to compete with his old armaments firm, Armtec, by offering the government a second source of combustible cartridge cases at a competitive price. The attempt did not succeed, and today Armtec continues business, just a few miles down the road from the Cabazon Reservation.

The other part of the story is Wackehut's attempt to clean up on the "cheap" a person it viewed as a valuable "weirdo genius," by quietly using the services of Dr. Nichols, a professional social worker. This issue would haunt the Tribe for years to come, as that "weirdo genius" would continue successfully manipulating the press and police even from inside his prison cell.

Wackenhut was far from the only large firm the Tribe approached in its economic development thrust. The lesson had been learned early that joint venturing made sense as long as one did not give up control. Looking back at the Wackenhut joint venture experience, John Paul told an interviewer:

We were smart enough to realize there was an opportunity when they approached us. They are big in the security industry, provide major security services and, in fact, what this company (CIS/WSI) was set up to do was to go after security services. . . . The Tribe would benefit. . . . In fact, Wackenhut today provides security for the Nevada test site.

Out of our relationship with Wackenhut we also met somebody named Peter Zokosky who was then a principal of Armtec, which is a company that's been here for many years . . . for decades in the defense industry, that just happened to make weapons that our troops shoot in places like Iran. But such companies exist in this country and they are legitimate businesses. Why is it "wronger" for an Indian tribe to consider getting into businesses of this nature than it would be for a non-Indian entrepreneur or group?

Why did it fall apart? For a variety of reasons. I think Wackenhut was willing to spend a minimum amount of money; they funded some contracts, they put some proposals in writing; they were willing to fund some office expenses, etc.; but once they saw that it wasn't going to be a slam dunk, it wasn't really the "edge" that they saw to get the contracts, they pretty much pulled out of it.

Some of the players that they brought to the table and some of the players we brought to the table then saw that maybe there's an opportunity here to develop some manufacturing plants on the reservation. And manufacturing plants, incidentally, made woody cellulose shells. It didn't make any difference what they made. The point was manufacturing. It really was never put together—a lot of discussion with nothing really coming of it.

There were a variety of meetings with Litton, with Night Vision. We also met with this Robert Booth Nichols, the guy you read about in the press now, who approached us and said, "I manufacture machine guns." Nothing ever came out of it. Not one thing ever got built, produced, manufactured, ordered, sent, nothing, not one thing. And yet there is this appearance that we had this armed empire.

There was also this monoclonal production system that, in fact, developed out of our relationship with Wackenhut. Wackenhut is in the business of looking at these types of projects; the same reason we attracted Colmac [bio-mass electric power plant located on the Cabazon Reservation]. What kills these types of projects isn't that they are not viable business enterprises, in fact most of them are. It is that local communities with a conditional-use permit process kill these things. The issue is that the local city typically gets nervous or the county supervisor is afraid he/she won't get reelected; whereas that environment didn't exist here. The tribal government was more sure of itself and was willing to consider "controversial" projects, but not unsafe projects.

There is another reason Dad was looking at this monoclonal project, and it was kind of a weird reason, to be honest with you, and had to do with my Mom's death. (This is the project the press used to accuse us of being involved in germ warfare.) Some of the technology that applied to this cloning of biological agents was being applied to cancer research. So Dad, Dad was grasping at straws; he just wanted to look at anything that might save Mom's life. He had the ability to talk to people in this industry and there was always his hope that there was some miracle drug cure for Mom's cancer. It's hard to relate those two. You really have to look at what this monoclonal project was.

What was the project? We were not considering creating biological agents here. We were considering *creating an antidote for biological agents*. That's a big goddamn difference.

During Desert Storm, we and the whole country sat there and watched as every person going there was provided this stuff. Every soldier over there had a supply of this stuff in the event of germ warfare. Would it have been different or horrible if we manufactured this stuff on our reservation and sold it to the U.S. government? Of course it never came to happen.

Last, but not least, Wackenhut never ponied up. Wackenhut, I think, evaluated it and looked at it. The political instability here at the Tribe . . . had a lot to do with their saying we are not going to proceed [with them], meaning the dissident tribal group. They just said, they didn't know the long-range political structure of the Tribe. We were in a lot of litigation over gambling, and I think Wackenhut ultimately decided they were not going to proceed on that basis, and it just fell apart.

Other such projects that grew out of the Wackenhut connection and involved the defense industry also eventually fell apart; the relationship with Intersect Corporation is one example. Intersect is another security firm. It was referred to in a letter to the Staff Director of the U.S. Senate's Select Committee on Indian Affairs from Art Welmas and Dr. Nichols on behalf of the Tribe's security corporation and its oil and gas corporation.

During the early 1980s the Cabazons learned from a Government Accounting Office (GAO) report that oil and gas being pumped on many reservations were, in fact, being stolen by the American government and other private oil companies. Millions of dollars were being lost to tribes by various methods of sophisticated theft and poor security. The Cabazons, not wanting to miss what appeared to be an opportunity, a role in search of a hero, wrote the Committee's Staff Director to offer its security services and to get his direction. The letter advised that the Tribe was, in addition to its joint venture with Wackenhut, "involved with Intersect Corporation which is headed by John Van Dewerker, who is former head of Central Research for the Central Intelligence Agency."

As is explored more fully in Chapter 5, the Tribe's involvement in assisting in the demonstration of night vision equipment would attract the attention of ambitious, overly imaginative reporters. It was the Tribe's relationship with Intersect that would make the equipment available. In an April 9, 1981, "To Whom It May Concern" letter, R. Barry Ashby, Intersect's Vice President and Director, wrote the following:

This letter serves as evidence that Dr. John P. Nichols is authorized to convey and use two items of night vision equipment in his possession. These items are the model M 802 night vision goggle and the model M 841 night vision pocketscope. This equipment is for demonstration purpose and none other, as has been authorized by the manufacturer (Litton Industries), the sales representative (INTERSECT Corporation), and the United States government licensing agent (Department of State), to be in the care of Dr. Nichols.

A year earlier, Intersect provided a draft proposal and briefing booklet for Integrated Security Systems through Dr. Nichols for the United Arab Shipment Company of Jeddah, Saudi Arabia. The systems were proposals, ostensibly, for a Saudi palace. Dr. Nichols would later report to the Tribe that they had been misled about getting the Saudi contract.

During this period of optimism that federal contracts were probable, the Tribe—secure in its control of the CIS/WSI Joint Venture—placed Peter Zokosky on CIS's Board of Directors, making him President and Security Officer, and Robert Frye Vice President. It was an attempt to maximize whatever clout these persons may have had in the defense agencies. The payoff was small, but there was a payoff.

The CIS/WSI joint venture, with Wackenhut as its patron and Zokosky as its president, sought and secured Department of Defense security clearance from the Defense Investigative Service (DIS). In a letter dated April 14, 1982, the DIS advised CIS/WSI:

In response to a request by Wackenhut Services, Inc., 3280 Ponce De Leon Blvd., Coral Gables, FL 33134, and subject to your approval, this office will initiate action to determine the eligibility of your facility for a Department of Defense security clearance.

This office is the Government cognizant security office for your facility; however, for ease of operation, the initial security survey of your facility and all necessary follow-up security inspections will be performed by the Santa Ana Field Office of this region.

Accompanying the letter was an attachment listing 24 questions and document requests to which CIS/WSI was required to respond.

In a December 8, 1982, letter addressed to Zokosky as CIS/WSI's president, the DIS gave this progress report:

I acknowledge receipt of the Standard Practice Procedure submitted in connection with handling of classified material by your facility. It has been reviewed and has been found to be consistent with applicable requirements of the Industrial Security Manual.

Upon receipt of your facility security clearance from our headquarters, you will be eligible for access to classified material through the level of Secret but will not be able to store same at your facility since you do not presently possess an approved storage container.

Finally, in a July 29, 1983, letter, DIS gave CIS/WSI the good news in standard government language. It stated "reference is made to our earlier correspondence regarding the eligibility of your facility for a Department of Defense security clearance. I am pleased to advise that the necessary processing has been completed and a security clearance at the SECRET level is hereby granted your facility." It was good news in the limited sense that an important government agency accorded CIS/WSI another level of legitimacy and credibility. Yet CIS/WSI could not toot its horn publicly, for the letter also stated that CIS/WSI could not use its newly won security clearance "for advertising or promotional purposes, nor may this letter be reproduced in any form except for the necessary records of your organization." It was a win without an award or reward, except the achievement of the win itself. It gained CIS/WSI and the Tribe not one penny, not one contract, not one job. (Although such clearance would seem to indicate conclusively that no criminal involvement—organized or unorganized—surfaced during the investigation, the press seemed to continue to miss the point.)

LAND ALLOTMENT AND BLOOD QUANTUM

In the early 1980s, the unity of the Tribe in the face of the war being waged against their efforts was seriously threatened. There were several reasons for this internal strain, but one was the lingering influence of the Dawes Allotment Act passed by Congress in 1887. Senator Abourezk briefly commented on the impact of the Act in his book *Advise and Dissent*:

> The Act took the land out of tribal control and allotted each Indian adult 160 acres of land to be held in trust by the government. Because the land could not be sold, with the passing of each generation, ownership of the allotted quarter section had to be shared by all the heirs of the original allottee. As generations passed, an individual share of 1/256th of a quarter of land was not uncommon. . . . The Allotment Act was intended to "civilize" the Indians and to get their land out of common, tribal ownership and into the hands of white men.

This would prove a major stumbling block to the tribal unity of the Cabazons. The records and documents of the Tribe would seem to support the view that tribal members of the Alvarez family, the Callaways, and former Chairman Benitez took the Allotment Act view, while the two Welmas families and the James family took the more traditional view that the land should be viewed as tribal land, and improvements to and products from the land belonged equally to the tribal members. The Welmas/James families also believed members should be paid salaries only if they work. This difference in philosophy would become an increasingly serious problem and a public relations nightmare.

An example of this difference in philosophy occurred in 1982 when John James and Art Welmas offered to sell their personal allotments. Their allotments were offered only to the Tribe to be purchased only by the Tribe and placed in trust for the Tribe. Leroy Alvarez and his daughter, Linda, placed their allotted land on the general real-estate market, did not offer it to the Tribe, and did not seek tribal sanction. The Alvarez land sale was potentially very traumatic because it could have meant permanent loss of the access road to the tribal cemetery. Just prior to adjournment of the August 24, 1982, Business Committee meeting, Art Welmas "spoke of the good of tribal sovereignty and tribal heritage. He indicated that Leroy Alvarez and Linda Streeter [-Dukic] had sold their birthright by selling their land."

Another issue dividing tribal members was the issue of blood quantum, or what percentage of Indian blood was required for membership. There has been at least a 30-year separation of views on this issue, with the Alvarez faction voting to lower the blood-quantum requirement to one-eighth percent Indian and the Welmas-James faction voting to retain the one-quarter percent requirement.

The earliest tribal records the author could find that officially discussed this issue were the tribal minutes of May 6, 1967, when the Council voted to keep the blood quantum requirement at one-quarter percent. What apparently triggered this vote was a letter, dated November 14, 1966, from the area director of the Bureau of Indian Affairs. The letter was in response to a submittal from BIA's Riverside Area Field Office requesting that the area director review and take appropriate action on "certain documents relating to a revision of the Cabazon Band's membership roll to bring it current as of October 8, 1966." Among the documents submitted were enrollment applications for Bridgette Marie Swanson—daughter of Linda Lee Alvarez Swanson [Streeter-Dukic], granddaughter of Leroy Alvarez and niece of Fred Alvarez—and for Brenda Allison James, daughter of John James. The area director concluded:

> With reference to the two applicants whose names you approved as additions to the roll, we regret that it has not been possible for us to concur in the decisions of the Business Committee. The enclosed copies of our letters of rejection are self-explanatory. As stated in the letter written to Mrs. Swanson, her daughter does not possess sufficient Indian blood to qualify for membership. Regarding the other applicant, our letter addressed to Mr. John A. James explains that our rejection is based on the fact that the application was not filed within the time period prescribed in the enrollment ordinance.
>
> It appears that the Business Committee overlooked the ninety-day filing period stipulated in the ordinance or had regarded it unnecessary to comply with those requirements. We would recommend that the ordinance be amended by deleting the language which requires applications to be filed within the ninety-day period. If the General Council is agreeable to making such a change in the enrollment provisions, we have the authority to approve the amended ordinance. In the event the document is to be amended, we also suggest that thought be given to placing language in the ordinance to provide that the roll be brought current annually. This might be a more practical procedure for making certain that the roll is kept current.
>
> If the ordinance is amended, it will be possible to enroll Brenda James after the amended ordinance receives approval. In connection with the question relating to degree of Indian blood for Linda Lee Swanson, the membership roll should be corrected to show her Indian

blood as three-eighths degree instead of one-half as presently shown. The same correction should be made for Linda's brother, Alfred M. Alvarez.

Attached to the area director's letter to the Tribe were separate letters addressed directly to Linda Lee Swanson and John Alexander James, dated November 10, 1966. These were more detailed letters of rejection. The rejection of James's daughter was temporary and correctable simply by amendment of the Ordinance requiring application for membership to "be filed within ninety (90) days after the date of birth." The rejection of Linda Alvarez Swanson's daughter was more permanent, correctable only if the tribe lowered its Indian-blood-quantum requirement. The letter to Linda Alvarez Swanson [Streeter-Dukic] read, in part:

We have reviewed the enrollment application you filed on July 20, 1966, requesting membership for your daughter, Bridgette Marie Swanson, born July 7, 1966. According to the information given on the application, Bridgette Marie derives her 1/4 degree Indian blood from you, her father being non-Indian. Also, the application shows that your 1/2 degree Indian blood is computed on the basis that your father, Leroy J. Alvarez, possessed 1/2 degree Indian blood and your mother, Phyllis M. Alvarez, is also 1/2 degree Indian. The application did not include any information to identify the name of your mother's tribe or reservation affiliation. There was no evidence that the Business Committee had made any verification of the degree of Indian blood claimed for your mother. Such verification is important when determining membership eligibility of your daughter. For this reason we made a search of records in this office with the hope of finding evidence to support the Indian blood percentages claimed for your mother and yourself.

Your mother made application for enrollment as a California Indian but did not qualify under the law dated May 24, 1950. However, from the information given on your mother's application, also information relating to the enrollment of members of her family, we find that Mrs. Alvarez, whose maiden name was Snell, inherits her Indian blood only from the maternal side of her family. From our records we have identified your mother's Indian ancestors. On the basis of Indian blood percentages shown in the records of your mother's ancestors, her Indian blood is computed as follows:

- Robert Lowry 1/2 degree Maidu, Maternal grandfather of Phyllis M. Alvarez
- Edna Lowry 1/2 degree Pit River, Maternal grandmother of Phyllis M. Alvarez
- Viola (Lowry) Snell Crume 1/2 degree, Mother of Phyllis M. (Maidu and Pit River) Alvarez
- Phyllis M. (Snell) Alvarez 1/4 degree total Indian Blood (1/8 Maidu and 1/8 Pit River)

Since the evidence of record supports 1/4 degree Indian blood for your mother instead of the 1/2 degree claimed on the enrollment application for your daughter, the percentage of Indian blood you derive from your mother would be 1/8. Therefore, we must disallow your claim of possessing 1/2 degree Indian blood. The 1/8 degree derived from your mother, when added with the 1/4 degree derived from your father, establishes your total Indian blood to be 3/8 degree. This means that your daughter can inherit only 3/16 degree Indian blood from you. Regrettably, it becomes necessary for us to disapprove your daughter's application for the reason that she does not meet the minimum 1/4 degree total Indian blood as required for membership with the Cabazon Band. The provisions set forth in the Band's Articles of Association, referring to Subsection A.(2) of the membership article, read:

> Descendants of those persons listed on the roll approved by the Deputy Commissioner of Indian Affairs on January 26, 1962, regardless of whether the ancestor on that roll is living or deceased, providing such descendants possess one-fourth or more degree Indian blood.

After the May 6, 1967, vote to keep the blood quantum at one-quarter percent, two more attempts would be made in 1967 to lower the quantum requirement, pushed principally by Leroy Alvarez. At the Tribe's September meeting, the minutes relate that "a motion was made to take a vote again on the degree of blood to allow new members in the tribe. A vote is to be taken at the next meeting to clear it up again."

Following that meeting, two "Special Meetings" were held in October and in November. Only in minutes of the latter meeting of November 29, 1967, is there any indication the issue was discussed. The minutes relate "the vote on the degree of blood was discussed at this time, the tribe will vote on the subject when the next meeting is to be held (December 16, 1967)."

In a hand-written letter to John James, dated November 29, 1967, Leroy Alvarez made his case for lowering the blood quantum requirement. He wrote, in part:

> As you know from our last general meeting we voted to adopt Bridgette into the tribe and was approved by the members.
>
> The members agreed for adoption so I can't see why we can't lower to 1/8 as she is very close to 1/4. This also will help you and Joe in the future years with your grandchildren.
>
> We have ample land for allotment since Amelia did not put her children in our band.
>
> You know your dad would see to this and for his grandchildren as you and Joe. Just think what would happen if you, Joe, Willie, and Remiejo were wiped out in a car accident.
>
> These 40 or 50 year leases would lay dormant and we would have to depend on say Linda, Fred, Joe's son—your daughter.
>
> With these things in mind I would be 91—never make it. Linda 71, Fred 69, Joe's son 57 maybe go to war?—your girl 53 or so. These wars are no help to our male heirs, as we are getting old very fast. These children are not going to marry Indian blood. This is not all I can think of but I have talked to lots of people of all walks of life and they think like I do and more so; we inherited this, so we shall think of our heirs. This was given to us free and left to us. Answer me on this.

To this day, the Tribe has consistently held its position and has retained the one-quarter requirement. Just as consistently, the internal opposition, led on this issue by Linda Alvarez Swanson Streeter-Dukic and her father Leroy, has pushed for quantum lowering. Although her original battle was fought to get her daughter Bridgette in, much of the battle in recent years has involved her daughter Michelle.

The Tribe has used its financial resources to help finance Michelle's college education, but it has declined to lower its quantum membership requirements.

FRED ALVAREZ'S DEATH

The Alvarez family lived almost 400 miles north of the reservation, in the Truckee area near Lake Tahoe, California. Leroy, the father, had kept up his interest in tribal matters during the '60s and '70s by traveling to the reservation area once or twice a year to meetings and by keeping in touch with then tribal Secretary-Treasurer John James by letter and telephone.

Alvarez's son Fred was a standout athlete and became an All-State wrestler at Lassen High School in Susanville, CA, played football at the University of Utah, and did a brief stint at professional football with the Calgary Stampeders of Canada. According to friends on the reservation, Fred himself said he lost his football ring during his college years for dealing drugs to teammates and got kicked off the Stampeders for the same thing. According to those who knew him, Fred, at 6 feet tall and weighing about 250 pounds, with long straight black hair and eyes, and tattoos on his arms and body, made a striking figure on or off his Harley-Davidson motorcycle. Unfortunately, according to these same associates, Fred had no moral center.

During the first six months of 1981, the behavior of Fred Alvarez became more intensely negative and occasionally disruptive to Tribal business. As reported in the January minutes, Fred reported he had an argument with the Tribe's casino manager. Apparently, Fred's dress, or lack thereof, had been strongly objected to by the manager. According to the minutes:

> Fred Alvarez stated that he had an argument with Rocco Zangari at the casino on New Year's Eve regarding Fred's clothing attire and Rocco's attitude toward it. John Paul Nichols stated that the business needs to appeal to wealthy card players, often older women, and all those connected with the casino should act accordingly. Art Welmas stressed the importance of all persons behaving properly in order to increase and help business. He indicated that Rocco should have been more tactful in the matter in dealing with Fred, and that Fred should dress properly in a place of tribal business.

Once again, as the Tribe had done many times previously, Fred had been placated as they took care of their business.

In March, it had become clear that Fred was planning to go down a road paralleling the path being taken by the Tribe—an individually owned casino. The March 5 and April 29 minutes tell the story in part. The March 5 minutes report:

> John Nichols Sr. reported that Fred Alvarez had approached him regarding developing Cabazon Allotment 3, interest in which is held by Leroy Alvarez, William Callaway, Amelia Callaway, Leroy Segundo, Alana Mae Segundo, Belinda Sue Segundo and Dorothy Segundo.

Dr. Nichols indicated that Fred had plans to open a bar, a gambling room, entertainment palace, etc. It was pointed out that the Cabazon Gambling Ordinance allows just one license and only to the Band in 5 years and that a liquor license can only be issued to the Band according to the liquor ordinance.

It was suggested that any change in ordinances by the General Council be delayed until after the Casino court case in order not to change the legal position and ramifications of the present situation. Motion was made by Sam Welmas, seconded by John James and passed unanimously to hold the next General Council meeting late in June.

Motion was made by Fred Alvarez, seconded by John James and passed unanimously to approve effective utilization of Allotment 3, keeping in mind the legal ramifications and the best interests of the Cabazon Band. Glenn Feldman was to be contacted regarding planned development.

The April 29 minutes read:

Dr. John Nichols stated that Fred Alvarez had approached him concerning Fred's opening a bar and gaming place on allotment #3, Cabazon Indian Reservation. He said Fred wants licensure on individually owned land. Dr. Nichols said the attorney has stated the ordinances would need amending regarding tribal liquor and gambling licenses.

Fred Alvarez moved for Business Committee permission to be able to begin clearing the allotted land pending General Council approval, stating he has the financing available. The motion died for lack of a second. Art Welmas said he would have voted no because Fred Alvarez has not supported the tribe in its tribal efforts to establish other businesses.

On June 6, 1981, the General Council meeting was held. Items on the agenda included hearings on charges against Joe Benitez and election of officers. But, from a reading of the minutes, it is clear that the Alvarez faction came with an agenda of its own. Reporters from the *Indio Daily News* attended but were asked to leave "as their presence had not been authorized by the Tribe."

The first motion made was by Fred to change the order of the agenda, putting new business first. The motion lost by a vote of 13 to 3 and the official agenda was approved. After Benitez explained his unreadiness to proceed and his request for a continuance, his hearing was continued until the next meeting.

Motion was then made by Fred and seconded by his father to "strike the election of officers from the agenda." The motion was voted down. Joe Benitez then suggested "that the office of secretary-treasurer be divided and that two persons be elected." The tribal attorney advised that prior approval from the BIA would be needed for such a change. The election of officers then proceeded in accordance with the agenda. The Nominating Committee presented its nominees and nominations were accepted from the floor. The minutes record the votes, as follows:

The vote was held by secret ballot and counted by Glenn Feldman, tribal attorney. Nominations and votes for Secretary-Treasurer as follows:

John James (incumbent) 11
Leroy Alvarez 3
Amelia Giff 2
Abstention 1

Nominations and votes for Second Vice Chairman as follows:

Amelia Giff 6
Charles Welmas 10
Abstention 1

Nominations and votes for First Vice Chairman as follows:

Fred Alvarez (incumbent) 7
Brenda James 10

Nominations and votes for Tribal Chairman as follows:

Arthur Welmas (incumbent) 10
Linda Streeter [-Dukic] 1
Floyd Welmas 3
Leroy Alvarez 3

Elected tribal officers for four years are Arthur Welmas, tribal chairman; Brenda James, 1st vice chairman; Charles Welmas, 2nd vice chairman; John James, secretary-treasurer. Arthur Welmas stated that he would do his best for the Tribe for the next four years.

Fred Alvarez made a motion, seconded by Joe Benitez, that the Council go into executive session at this time. Motion defeated by 7 for, 9 against, and 0 abstentions.

It was not a very good meeting for the Alvarez/Joe Benitez faction. In addition to their other losses, Fred had been voted out of office as a tribal officer. His sister Linda would later say that he had been an "insider." What she and Fred could never seem to understand was that the majority of the tribe defined an "insider" as a member who worked on behalf of the whole tribe, not selfishly on behalf of him/herself alone or of one family alone.

Just prior to adjournment of the meeting, Fred would make his last Tribal meeting motion. The minutes report:

Fred Alvarez moved for General Council permission for a gambling permit and liquor license for use on his property. He asked for tribal sanction of a casino and sanction of division of allotted private property. The motion died for lack of a second.

Art Welmas and John James suggested that Dr. Nichols talk with Fred Alvarez regarding liquor licensing.

It is instructive to note that neither his father nor his sister seconded Fred's motion. In less than a month Fred would be dead, and his death still lingers and hovers like a terrible cloud over the Cabazons, a cloud produced by their press enemies at the *Daily News* especially.

At some point during the six months prior to Fred's reelection defeat, the Alvarez/Joe Benitez alliance was formed, and this new faction began a disinformation campaign to sabotage the efforts of the Tribe. After Fred's death, newspaper articles and reporters revealed he and others of this alliance had been to local newspapers and elsewhere making charges of mismanagement of tribal resources. The Nichols family was accused of stealing from the Tribe and defrauding them of their money and resources. What the outside world did not know was that the Tribe itself was always in control and tracked casino earnings daily. In the early days, the security officer that accompanied the daily deposit to the bank was Bruce James, who was the first tribal member trained by the Department of Interior in law enforcement and was appointed by the Tribe to chair its Committee on Reservation Law Enforcement and Fire Protection.

As will be discussed more fully in Chapter 5, the local press had its own agenda and had no interest in learning or publishing the truth. With few exceptions, non-local press found it easier to repeat and embellish the lies, half-truths and distortions published locally.

At some point in time, between an unknown evening hour on June 29, 1981, and "prior to midnight on June 30, 1981," Fred Alvarez and two companions were murdered. An investigator from the Riverside County Coroner's Office, Robert L. Drake, filed this report on the murder:

MULTIPLE DEATHS WERE INVOLVED IN THIS INCIDENT. This summary covers investigation and details of the deaths of the following listed deceased:

ALFRED M. ALVAREZ FND 7-1-81#47344
RALPH ARTHUR BOGER FND 7-1-81#47345
PATRICIA ROBERTA CASTRO FND 7-1-81#47346

I was contacted by telephone at 7:34 a.m. on July 1, 1981, by the Riverside County Sheriff's Office in Indio. I was told of a triple homicide at 35-040 Bob Hope Drive, in the rural area of Rancho Mirage. I arrived at that location at 8:08 a.m., where I was met by Sheriff's Deputy Vaughn. Later Det. Mapula, Swearingen and Lasiter arrived. Others coming to the scene were Lt. Landy, Lt. Conroy, Inv. Burge and Garcia. The identification work was done by Sgt. Carlson and I.D. Technician Reyes (with Evelyn Raygor and Jerry Hopf) and Faye Springer and Thomas Abercrombe of the Department of Justice from Riverside.

The scene of this homicide is the backyard patio of the residence of Alvarez at 35-040 Bob Hope Drive. The three victims had been sitting in a semicircle. Castro had been sitting on a single bed facing south. Alvarez was sitting to her right on a wooden chair and Boger had been sitting to his right in a wooden chair facing north. They were discovered by friends of Alvarez, William Gallaway [Callaway] and Joe R. Benitez at about 6:40 a.m. on July 1, 1981. They in turn notified the Sheriff's Office. When found, Castro was lying back across the bed, head to the north (face up). Alvarez was still sitting, but slumped to the right while Boger was lying face down in the sand where he had fallen forward from his chair. All three were dressed and from the initial distant examination it appeared that all three had been shot in the head, and had been dead a number of hours.

When the identification work was completed, the bodies were removed to the Wiefels and Son Mortuary in Palm Springs, by attendants, H. Comstock, J. Albertson and the undersigned at 12:00 p.m. X-rays were ordered at 10:45 a.m. and done at 8:00 p.m. the same evening by Ken Carpenter of Bedside X-rays. The X-rays were secured for the use of the autopsy surgeon.

The post-mortem examinations were started at 3:50 p.m. on July 2, 1981, by Dr. Modglin, and his assistant Harold Thompson. Those present were: Sgt. Carlson, Det. Lasiter and I.D. Technician Jerry Hopf from the Sheriff's Office and Bill Edwards and Jack Albertson from the Mortuary and the undersigned. It was learned that each of the victims had been shot once in the head, *each from a different direction* (see autopsy protocols for details of each victim) with what appeared to be a .38 caliber weapon or weapons, since all three projectiles were recovered. It was estimated that the deaths occurred prior to midnight on June 30, 1981. The postmortems were completed at 6:23 p.m. on July 2, 1981.

On completion of the examinations, the bodies were released to the remaining families for final disposition. This information appears on the face page of each respective report, as does the next of kin in each case.

At the time of this writing no suspects have been apprehended. It is felt by the undersigned that *this crime was committed by more than one person*, since none of the victims had a chance to run from the area in which they sat. The investigation is continuing. (Emphasis added.)

The bodies were discovered by two members of the Alvarez/Joe Benitez faction who later told the press they and Fred were going to an appointment with Attorney Steve Rios. Rios is the attorney that represented Benitez in his hearing before the Tribe's General Council and Tribal Court. Within 24 hours after discovery of the bodies, Rios had suggested that his legal work with the Tribe and Fred's murder "may be related" and Benitez told the press "he was advised by his attorney not to discuss anything regarding the death." It was to be—as John Paul loved to say—"a slam dunk" press propaganda shot by the faction against the tribe.

Temperatures in Rancho Mirage, California, can rise as high as 120 degrees during the summer months. Because of the intense heat, some things could not be determined by the autopsy and lab reports. Several questions, however, are raised by both what is contained in and what is absent from the three Tissue Pathology reports. The report on Fred, performed by Bio-Laboratories Medical Group, Inc., F. Rene Modglin, Pathologist, M.D., found:

EXTERNAL EXAMINATION:

The 72 in. about 235 lb . . . body is of an adult brown skin male with: a 1/4 in. diameter round hole in the right preauricular skin. . . .

INTERNAL EXAMINATION:

A badly deformed lead metal object appearing to be a medium caliber bullet is found nestled in the fractured soft tissues of the left side of the jaw in association with the fractured maxilla and the absent teeth 19, 20 and 21.

The floor of the right middle fossa has two separate transverse nondisplaced linear fractures.

The brain literally flows from the cranial cavity. . . .

SIGNIFICANT NEGATIVE FINDING:

There are no intracranial metallic foreign bodies.

There is no fracture of the thyoid bone or thyroid cartilage.

There is no fractured rib or obvious laceration or perforation of the lining of the chest or abdominal cavity.

There is no hemorrhage into the stomach and there are no gastric contents.

There is no foreign body obstruction of the laryngotracheobronchial tree, pulmonary embolus, fractured rib.

There is no fracture of a long bone or laceration of the skin other than the wound in the right preauricular area.

COMMENTS:

The autopsy findings are interpreted as a death resulting from injuries to the brain and associated with hemorrhages due to gunshot basal skull fractures.

The gunshot resulting in death entered the right preauricular region and did not pass into the skull but passed apparently close enough to cause basilar skull fractures and then passed over into the left side to fracture the mandible and knock out three of the lower teeth and came to rest in the same area.

The fatal bullet passed from right to left, from above downward and from posterior to slightly anterior. Again, it did not enter the cranial cavity.

I did not engrave the bullet in any manner but it was recovered at about 16:30 and passed to ID Tech. Hopf.

X-rays were available for the autopsy but were left in the custody of Deputy Coroner Drake. . . .

There was no urine and the left plural cavity had a blood-like fluid with liquid fat on the surface.

Directions are with the body in the anatomic position.

Witnesses: Deputy Coroner Bob Drake; ID Tech. Hopf; Dt. Fred Lassiter; Sgt. Carlson, Harold Thompson.

ANATOMIC DIAGNOSIS:

MODERATE PUTREFACTIVE CHANGE OF BODY

SKULL FRACTURES

METALLIC FOREIGN BODY OF JAW

CAUSE OF DEATH: Brain injuries and hemorrhages, due to Gunshot basal skull fractures.

Pathologist,

Rene Modglin, M.D.

No lab work was done on Patricia Castro, and an explanation for not doing so was absent from the coroner's report. According to the report, no urine was found in either of the men's bodies and specimens were taken from the Pleural Fluid to determine whether barbituates and ethyl alcohol were present. In Fred's case, no barbituates were detected, but "Pleural Fluid Alcohol—0.14%" was present. For Ralph Boger, only "0.08% Pleural Fluid Alcohol" was found and no barbituates. This alcohol content—.08 percent—is the base used to determine driver intoxication in California. A private investigator, however, reported to the Tribe that he had seen a laboratory test which "showed Mr. Alvarez had a 125 count (RIA) of opiates in his blood stream at the time he died." This investigator also reported confidentially to the Tribe that law-enforcement personnel had told him confidentially that "law enforcement knows who one of the shooters was." According to this source of information, "one of the shooters, or *the* shooter, was an outlaw biker from the Idyllwild [California] area."

The circumstances surrounding Fred's death raise many questions. The report of Robert L. Drake of the Coroner's Office concluded that "more than one person" was responsible for the multiple killings. Drake also observed that "each of the victims had been shot once in the head, each from a different direction."

According to Drake's report, Fred and Patricia Castro were facing south while Boger was facing north when the killings took place. Thus, if they were conscious, they could see anyone approaching. Boger and Fred were seated facing each other and each was shot from above right and behind, while Castro, seated on the bed, was shot from below right and from the front.

If they were awake, persons unknown to them (such as paid hit men) could not have gotten close enough to them with guns in their hands, as such persons would have been seen, and the evidence does not support long-distance shooting or any attempt to flee.

Evidence would seem to support the notion that the killers were known to the victims and, perhaps, had been partying or otherwise socializing with them prior to the killings. It is possible that Fred was encouraged by his killers to get drunk in order to neturalize him as a physical force. Evidence supports his being drunk.

Evidence would seem to indicate that Fred and Boger were killed at approximately the same time, each by a separate shooter. It is possible that Castro had been lying on the bed and was shocked awake or into action by the other shootings. She possibly bolted into a sitting position before one of the killers dropped to a kneeling position and shot her, the impact of the bullet knocking her back onto the bed on her back as she was found. Or a third person shot her.

Finally, it seems strange to a layperson that no urine was found in the bodies of either male victim, that chemical tests usually performed on the urine had to be performed on tissues from the lungs, and that no tests seem to have been performed on Patricia Castro at all, according to the Coroner's Report.

Not long before he was killed, Fred revealed to Joann, Dr. Nichols and tribal members that Castro's husband was soon to be released from prison and had passed the word he was going to kill his wife's lover. Fred also told the Nicholses, without detail, that one of Fred's drug deals had gone bad and for this reason he was going to "lock down" the following weekend.

The world may never know how much truth was in Fred's assertions. All that is known is that Fred was dead within days of his conversation with the Nicholses. The authorities were fully apprised of the conversation, but it is still unknown to what extent these revelations were investigated.

The Tribe issued its own press release regarding Fred's murder. It read:

> The Cabazon Band of Mission Indians expresses its sorrow over the death of Alfred Alvarez, a member of the Band. His untimely death, along with those of Patricia Castro and Ralph Boger, are most unfortunate. We publicly express our condolences to the immediate family and friends of the three victims.
>
> Since the deaths did not occur on Federal land, the state of California, County of Riverside has jurisdiction. Mr. Ben Clark, the capable Sheriff of Riverside County has our full confidence in being able to solve these deaths. We as a tribe will help and cooperate in

any way we can with the Sheriff's office. The Cabazon Band of Mission Indians respects the American Judicial system and knows that justice will prevail.

We wish to state categorically that the unfortunate incident, which involved three victims only one of whom was a tribal member, was wholly unrelated to Cabazon Tribal business or the operation of our Tribal Casino. We are in possession of certain evidence which we have already turned over to the county Sheriff's office, which indicated that the murders may have been attributable to personal relationships between the victims and other persons unconnected in any way with the Cabazon Band.

It is unfortunate that Steven Rios, attorney for former Tribal Chairman Joseph Benitez, would use this tragedy in an effort to sow seeds of discord amongst our tribal members at this time. We think it is important for the record to clearly show that Mr. Benitez, in a recent Tribal proceeding, pleaded guilty to certain charges and was found guilty of other charges involving mismanagement of Tribal affairs and misappropriation of Tribal and Federal funds while he was Tribal Chairman.

For Mr. Rios and Mr. Benitez to now attempt to connect these senseless murders with the Cabazon Band is ridiculous and malicious. We are confident that when the case is solved, as it will be, and all the facts are disclosed their charges and innuendoes will be shown to be groundless.

Until that time, we would only ask that the press deal with this tragedy in a responsible and professional manner and not allow itself to be used by those with ulterior motives.

It was to no avail. The press was determined to make a martyr of Fred and no facts contrary to that intent were ever allowed to surface. And immediately following Fred's death, Leroy Alvarez and Linda Streeter-Dukic, Fred's father and sister, placed their Dawes Allotment Act allotted properties on the real estate market for sale.

Within little more than a month after Fred's murder—August 5, 1981—the City of Indio sent Indio police with a search warrant to the Reservation and Tribal Office. They removed truckloads of records, taking any and all documents they could find, although the warrant addressed itself only to mail-order records. The police had also invited the Alcoholic Beverage Commission to come along for the fun. Within a few short weeks, the City of Indio filed a petition asking the court to set aside its ruling that allowed the casino to remain open. Along with its petition, the City filed affidavits by Joe Benitez, Marc Benitez, Leroy Alvarez, Linda Streeter-Dukic and William Callaway in support of its closure petition. Later, it is understood the City paid these witnesses travel expenses to and from the court hearing in Los Angeles. The suspicion that the Alvarez/Joe Benitez faction was working hand in hand with the Tribe's enemies in government and the press was now a documented fact. But instead of crushing the tribal leadership and its supporters, it stiffened their resolve.

And part of what sustained them was their knowledge of Fred and themselves. In a recent interview, Brenda James Soulliere discussed her reactions to these events:

Author: What was yours and the Business Committee's reaction to Fred's murder?

Brenda: I was in shock for several days. Everyone else was too. I mean, we all had our little petty things with Fred. Fred was always real nice to me. I never had a problem with him. Fred was Fred. I mean . . . you know, he had some weird ideas. He had talked about having topless dancers and different things like that. I just thought . . . it's just one of those things. He's going to say one thing and do another. I was in shock when I heard about what happened to him. Everybody was in shock. I mean . . . everybody had their opinions about Fred, but that's about as far as it went. But no one wanted to see him get killed. I mean it's in all kinds of accusations that it's been tribal related. . . .

Author: How did the Committee react to Linda's accusation that it was related to the Tribe?

Brenda: That was weird. She's always been kind of weird . . . a nice-to-your-face but stabbing-you-in-the-back type of person. I've always been real leery about her. You want to trust her, but you . . . something deep down inside of you says that you can't. So, I've never really had a problem with her other than I wouldn't trust her. Just like Fred, just the kind of people that you can be around but you can't trust them with anything. But I didn't know either of them for that long . . . not really, not to really get to know somebody. You know what I mean? . . . Just kind of "hey, how are you doing" type of relationship.

Author: You must have had a double shock because not only is he blown away, but now his sister is suggesting that the Tribe somehow had something to do with it. This meeting of July 3rd is also your first as an elected officer. Do you remember your reaction? I notice you made the motion to issue a press release explaining the tribal position.

Brenda: I felt that there was . . . the Tribe was in no way capable of anything like that. I mean . . . just from the way I knew people . . . my dad. He's always been a talker, but would never . . . you know; he's a big teddy bear inside. So when Linda started accusing people, I was really surprised. You know, this is your own, this is your own dad, your own relatives, and you're accusing them of killing someone. It just really wasn't right. I thought we needed to say something about it too . . . that we couldn't just leave it there and just say, "Well here it is. We're going to let everybody run a stable and not stand up." You know . . . all you can do is stand up and say the truth and let it go.

Author: How was the pressure from the press?

Brenda: Oh, at that time, it was terrible. We had no media or public relations skills. People today are a lot more skeptical about the media. Back then, they were a little more dependent on it than they are now. So, basically what the media said was truth . . . [now] here's all these things that are plastered about the Tribe. I thought, "Wait a minute. This is not only not true, but everybody's going to think it is!" That was really a rough one to go through, sitting and just being talked about and having fingers pointed at you when you knew it wasn't right. So, I really got a lesson about the media. They don't always print the truth. I was upset that there was really nothing I could do about it. I was just thankful that I still lived in Banning, and the papers were down here. That was one thing that helped. We just basically had to wait and just see what would happen.

Author: Was television as bad as the newspapers?

Brenda: Later on it was. Not really at that time . . . I wasn't in this area, so I didn't really watch anything, the desert channels. I was never a TV person anyway, so I don't think I watched anything on TV.

Author: Were you getting a lot of questions from your friends about it.

Brenda: No, I didn't. My friends were up in Banning. I didn't really have friends down here except for the ones I worked with, and the ones that we worked with knew better.

> Linda has always had, from what I understand, a reputation for shooting her mouth off. So, basically, it was just another step in that direction. You kind of take it with a grain of salt.

When Charles Welmas was asked about Fred, he called him "a strange kind of guy. I don't exactly know how to explain him, other than he was just a little off beam."

Author: What do you think happened to Fred?
Charles: I just think he told his biker buddies some stuff that he had going on. I think they just got even with him.
Author: Over drugs?
Charles: Yes, drugs.

Mark Nichols, the Tribe's current CEO, shared his thoughts about Fred and Linda and a wide range of issues starting with when he arrived in the Coachella Valley. Mark was the first of the brothers to follow his parents from Florida to the Indio area in November 1978, traveling with his girlfriend Heidi Zinn. When he arrived, the joint offices of Pro Plan and the Tribe were in a motel. The offices were "really a couple of rooms that had been carved out of a motel," said Mark. "There was a radio station located there, a couple of other businesses, and a pool in the center of the courtyard. . . . Heidi and I rented an apartment which was adjoining two of the rooms at the motel adjoining the Tribal office."

Author: As an outsider in reviewing records, I saw some changes. For example, the emphasis on training the tribal members seemed to substantially increase when you became CEO.
Mark: It's very difficult to see that I suppose. Maybe it's easier for somebody to see from the outside. But I think there was always a commitment to training, but the major decisions were group decisions. I just think there was a much higher level of involvement across the board in all aspects of the business. I think it's a matter of approachability; I think it is also a matter of a more positive outlook and/or a belief that everything will come out right, to maybe encapsulate it in the word faith: faith in what we are doing and faith in the future; faith in God; and faith in the fact that we will receive what we need; and the willingness to have the faith to risk.
Author: And the faith to learn?
Mark: But to risk too. We have taken some significant risks. When I took over as CEO after the reorganization, we had huge debts. We had a business that was in a slump. The very last thing that had been done was everybody had been given an increase, so costs had gone through the roof and it's really a miracle that we survived through that period. There were other periods where we have seen some miracles, but that's the one that I am real familiar with. We went straight ahead; we didn't let it deter us.
Author: You also at one point decided to professionalize your security force.
Mark: Yes, it wasn't so much the effort of professionalizing the security force as it was

putting our money where our mouth was. We talked about being the Cabazon nation, but we weren't spending the money to be the Cabazon nation. So I felt that it was well worth the money, and the Tribe was willing to spend the money in basically creating a government—it was a council until about 1989—and today I think it really more emulates a government. There has been a transition that has occurred there, and it's because of the money that has been spent. We have basically taken services that we could have done outside and brought them inside at really an increased cost, but for the purposes of undergoing this psychological transition from being only a for-profit enterprise—which it still is somewhat—and budding into something bigger and broader. I think it's visible and perceivable by outsiders. I think it is reflected in the mentality of the tribal elected officials and the way they are approaching it. I think the decisions that are made are not how's it going to benefit me personally, but how is it going to totally benefit the organism, if you will.

The mission has even become broader than the tribe itself. It's really encompassed all the people that are working here. And I don't know that wasn't the case before, but I do know that the understanding and the commitment to it is much greater than it ever was.

Author: How does that relate to the opposition, and what is the motivation, in your view, of that opposition?

Mark: People generally have separate and unique perspectives, separate values, different motivations, just as we do, if you will, within the group that currently is the Council and their supporters and constituents. I'd like to think that some of the opposition has caught a little of the enthusiasm that we are involved in today, and I'd like to think of them, at least in part, as not the opposition but the underutilized resources, and as not necessarily being as opposed as they might have been at one time.

Author: I'm including in that the opposition outside of the current tribal membership.

Mark: Well, it's a pretty broad statement. Everybody wants nice things in their lives, and that's a big motivator. Sometimes something happens that is a little bit bigger and more meaningful, in terms of a commitment towards growth, creating jobs, and there is also something a little sexy about being outside the mainstream that's fun and what you can become committed to. You feel as if you are truly a pioneer in a sense. You get a little bit of that mystique there. I think that there has always been and always will be a great resistance towards any kind of change, because it is thought there are a limited number of resources out there; at least there is that perception. That's not always true. . . . So I think there is just a natural tendency to shut out growth and to keep that growth within your own entity. . . .

I think, and this has changed radically, but I don't think that tribal people were viewed by others as capable of handling their own affairs, not that they were ever really given the opportunity, and if you look at Sammy [Welmas] and if you look at Gene [Welmas], in those instances, they had really not wanted to. Yet, at the same time I think they came to recognize that the world was changing and that you could no longer be an island unto yourself, and as a matter of survival you better start participating in some manner, fashion, or form.

Even today when we go in to see Congressmen and Senators and you read the court documents and so forth, you will generally see the assumption that tribes cannot govern themselves, or certainly not honestly, and certainly not in a sophisticated manner.

So I think there is a real flawed assumption there, and I think that it is really based on the competition of economics. There's lack of understanding, ignorance; there's social, racial bias. There are a lot of dynamics out there at work. And then you have people that feel and see and can take something that is a little broader than immediate gratification and/or that have faith in something and you have those that, perhaps, don't have as much faith, and they are not necessarily willing to put it [immediate gratification] off and/or they don't have the faith in putting it off. That's probably the crux of what divides the Tribe, at least internally.

The broader dynamics of what I was just talking about, with regards to ignorant racism and economic competition, the very nature of capitalism, are all facets in the dispute internally as well as externally. They are intricately linked all the way down to the newspapers, or the media in general, and we are looking at developing a story. I am sure there are some conscientious people out there trying to get the truth out. But there again, they are operating often times from the premise of making a buck, making a story, making a name and having to compete in the economic reality of today.

Author: Are you now prepared to go from the general to the specific? For example, Linda and Fred. What motivation can we infer from your discussion?

Mark: Fred I knew much better than Linda. My association with Linda is limited to, for the most part, when she came back into the working environment.

Author: You hired her briefly?

Mark: Right, 1990 I guess was the time. With Fred, I knew him because in the early days I lived right next to the office, and he lived three doors up on the left, at least for a few months.

Fred didn't care about anybody but Fred. He was funny about it; he had a sense of humor. He was a very large fellow and he used that in his life. I think he was sort of a natural bully in terms of how big he was.

Author: Did you ever talk about his football days?

Mark: Very little. He talked about using drugs during football, and he talked about how they used to have jars of reds [in the locker room]. I think reds are typically downers, and they would have bowls of them. Coaches, Fred said, would literally set these things in the locker room and the different players would grab what they wanted out of them. That's how wide open that issue had been, according to Fred.

Author: College and pro.

Mark: I don't remember the distinction, but college comes to mind because he said he got kicked off the team eventually, because he tested positive and he used to complain, because he said it had been the very coaches themselves that had given them the drugs. In other words it was wide open, yet he got in trouble for it; and he felt that he had gotten a raw deal.

Author: Did he ever talk about something spectacular he did when he was a football player?

Mark: No, not at all. I had seen a couple of pictures. He didn't display them or anything. Fred was a free spirit in the sense that he and I both related to not wanting to necessarily buy into society's overall goals, but we parted when it came to our views on becoming wealthy. I think that was more important to him than it was to me, certainly at that time. He basically operated from the standpoint, "how am I going to end up?" His real mission was to make a lot of money, to not have to obey any rules, and to have a good time. Those were basically his motivating factors.

He was involved in dealing with stolen merchandise insofar as motorcycles were concerned, the sale of drugs, prostitution, stolen jewelry and other goods that he would have. He ran with the Hell's Angels and a group of independents that he had associations with out of Desert Hot Springs [California] as well as, I understand, up North from up in the Truckee area. But he really was more of an independent person. Loved tattoos. . . .

He had the biker mentality that women were possessions, and if he decided he was going to give his girl to somebody, that was it. I remember him talking about biker mamas and what they were and how they were basically slaves to the group.

Author: Were you surprised to find out that he had been meeting with City officials?

Mark: No, because there are a couple of things in common between Fred and Linda. I later discovered that Fred was perpetually stoned [not that Linda was]. That was what he lived and breathed, and he wasn't shy about it. He would walk into the office and roll a big joint [of marijuana]. It made no difference to him. He knew no bounds in terms of that stuff; he'd walk into the office in his underwear, whatever.

He also had an insatiable need to talk. He would love to just talk and talk and talk. His conversations would be disjointed; he'd switch from one subject to another, and he would make connections where others weren't bright enough to make them. Frankly, his sister does the same thing. She also can make connections and see a big picture that nobody else can see.

I recall having heard of him going in to see the mayor of Indio and telling the mayor of Indio, who was Regina Zokosky, Peter Zokosky's wife, that the Cabazon tribe could open its own embassy and was going to grow marijuana. Fred wanted to open up a biker bar. This is the bar he talked about often, where the bikers would drive down a ramp and then be served cocaine wine and smoke marijuana. The reason cocaine wine was going to be okay was because he researched this, he said, and the Popes used to drink cocaine wine. In fact, he said, a Pope used to hang a vial around his neck.

He never knew when to shut up. No, he never knew when not to talk and when he got lost between fiction and truth.

Now Linda is like Fred in many ways. Keep in mind I believe everybody at their core has the same amount of worth. She could make the most bizarre connections, and where with Fred, I think his particular motivation was financial gain—I am sure he had others, but that was very pronounced—with Linda, hers is also financial gain, but she appeared—and of course I knew her years later in a little different capacity—to have a real need to have power. Her motivating factor seemed to be more of an empowerment issue than anything else, and that's where I would draw the distinction, but they had very similar personalities.

If you look at Linda, basically everything she ever does is toward the end of seizing control, seizing power. She uses the death of her brother as the guise or the reason to show where her motivation is coming from. Just as when she was working with us over here, she was on a mission to determine how she eventually could become Chairperson and/or take over, whatever her deal was.

But she was willing to see whether or not she could make some dough out of it on the way, and when it became clear that she wasn't going to be just "bribed" off, and that's kind of what she was hoping for, in my opinion, when she asked for a brand new white Cadillac and a couple of other things. Oh, she came in one day and said, "I talked to John James, and I think I should have a brand new white Cadillac."

I went to John [James] about this and . . . he really wanted me to deal with the situation, and I did.

Well, then there's this whole issue of the Kitchens, which are part of this. John can talk to you a little about that, the fact that Leroy seems to belong to a slightly different Indian faction, a different group or faction within the Band that had some ties to the Mission Creek Indian Reservation that used to lie outside Desert Hot Springs. It was terminated. I know very little about it, other than there are a number of members who are called Kitchens who migrated to the Cahuilla Reservation up the mountain, a significantly large group of people. I think there are about 14 of them that were very close to Leroy and Linda and Fred.

Fred told me about several of the Kitchens that would become eligible for membership in this tribe if the quantum was lowered to one-eighth, in addition to Linda's children. So it's not a matter of one or two. That's a start. There would be a significant shift or potential, with several people applying for membership and then the entire dynamic power structure, if you will, would change under that scenario. But the motivation is they would gain control.

Author: In 1983 they all filed these depositions in Court opposing the Tribe continuing gaming. Let's say the Court had ruled in their favor. What would the gain be?

Mark: It's sort of like the Democrats and the Republicans. Somebody builds something and the next group comes in and tears it down. They are not always looking in terms of the overall good of the group, but the two competing agents are so strong that the health of the whole is overlooked. I think that they were willing to destroy at all costs the existing power structure, so that they would reverse the power. The other thing was, I think, without the gaming they could eliminate the economics and therefore make it collapse. I think that it wouldn't necessarily have collapsed; it would have been altered significantly. But, some how, some way, we would be involved in other things.

Fred, however, worked for Fred. If he could put a casino on his property, he would put a casino on his property. If he could put a nude dancing place, which he discussed, on his property, he would put nude dancing on his property. If he could put hazardous waste—I don't care what it was—he did not think in terms of the group. His mentality was "what's good for Fred is good for you." That's exactly what he went out and told the mayor of Indio or whomever he spoke to, including newspaper reporters.

Finally, John Paul Nichols recalled the murder of Fred as one of the limited number of events that could be labeled "catalytic."

John Paul: In 1981, Fred Alvarez was murdered in June. Fred lost the election the month before and was no longer a Tribal officer. He apparently, for whatever reason, was running around town and bad mouthing everybody, etc., and had gone to some local newspaper and said, "I fear for my life," or whatever the hell he said. To make a long story short, the next day, two days later, or a week later, he and two other people are murdered. . . . Immediate front-page headlines. We had zip to do with it. To this day there's this perception that we were involved. I'm in Austin, Texas, and people say to me, "You were involved in that, weren't you?" It's amazing.

Author: Give me your perspective. Why would Linda et al accuse unnamed persons associated with the Tribe of killing Fred?

John Paul: Let's look at the position Fred was in. Fred was a very mean, vibrant Indian. There is no other way of saying it. Fred, in my view, was paranoid. He was very, very power hungry. He had lost; the Tribe had voted him out, whenever the hell it was,

March, May, I don't even remember what the day was in '81. He wasn't even a Tribal officer anymore. There is this perception that he was a Tribal officer. He wasn't. That's when his sister said, "We've got problems." There was no Alvarez power base in 1981. It didn't exist.

So, Fred was an inconvenience at that point in time. There was this perception that Fred was an insider that somebody had to get because he knew everything, which was totally erroneous. He had no support to begin with. But honest to God, Fred was very verbal. If you met Linda Streeter [-Dukic], Linda Streeter is also very verbal. But, you can sit there until thc sun don't shine, and sooner or later people will listen to you. I hate to say this, but I'll use Adolf Hitler as an example, in the sense that you say enough things enough times and sooner or later someone goes, well, look at the history of these things! Jesus Christ, you read enough bullshit, you believe anything!

I don't know if it was the next day, anyway, I walked into the casino and right there in the newspaper machine and pasted on the thing "Man Foretold Own Death." I read that and go, "What?!" This is, like, the next day. Fred supposedly, or allegedly, had gone to the newspaper reporter the day before or two days before and just ranted and raved. It was taped, "I fear for my life." I'm sure this was a continuous conversation about a grand conspiracy that made perfect sense. From that point on, it was a hell of a newspaper story. Mafia. Hiding stuff. I mean that was it. Forget all the weapons bullshit that you read years later; that was all tacked on to the basic story. All that allegedly happened afterwards anyway. "Foretold" he was in danger, but didn't say who he was in danger from, of course.

In retrospect when I look at it, or what all really happened, I think I spent 10 minutes with the sheriff one time two days after the murder. Somebody asked me a couple of questions about "what do you think happened?" I've never talked to somebody in law enforcement once, before or after that. Never been asked one question. To my knowledge, nobody questioned Rocco Zangari, who according to the press is the bad guy here supposedly. Right? Right or wrong, I think maybe the Alvarez family had to blame someone. Grief is grief. I don't discount that, regardless of who Fred was. Family is family, and Linda somehow had to come to grips with that. I don't think she wanted to face it, and I don't think to this day she wants to face who her brother really was. I think personally he got knocked off—obviously he got knocked off—but to me it sounds like a drug deal or something of that nature and he had made an enemy somewhere down the line, and that's it.

Fred's been a catalyst around which a lot of other hate built. It's the hate built out of "I've got power." The issue is taking over the tribe. If the Nicholses left tomorrow, Joe Blow could be in this position and it would be the same issues.

Author: And the other thing is there's been one issue that's been consistent and that was trying to get tribal membership for Linda's daughter since 1966.

John Paul: Why do you think?

Author: Power?

John Paul: Power. That's the name of the game.

BANKRUPTCY

In its October 21, 1981, meeting a report was given to the Tribe on the October 5 Federal Court hearing on the casino. Art Welmas reported that "turncoats Joe

Benitez, Leroy Alvarez, Willie Callaway, Marc Benitez, and Linda Streeter [-Dukic] had sat with Police Chief Cross and other City of Indio representatives" at the hearing. The judge ruled in the Tribe's favor, allowing the casino to remain open. One requirement of the court, to submit an audit, would cost the Tribe between "$10,000 to $15,000," money it could ill afford at the time.

While under these continuing attacks, the Tribe was forced, by events and limited cash flow, into filing for bankruptcy on behalf of Cabazon Indian Reservation Sales, the Smoke Shop. One of the Tribe's early established practices—placing each business under separate corporations—would prove its value. John Paul, who managed the businesses, talked about the bankruptcies and the reactions to them:

John Paul: There was a lot of confusion. The Tribe knew what it was doing; we knew what we were doing; but the outside always said, nah, nah, nah, it's a bunch of White guys in there who have some management contracts. Bankruptcy stuff is open to the public. So they look at the documents and say, "Wait a second, the Tribe owns the casino?" [Bankruptcy documents clearly answered the question.] None of us anticipated going to the United States Supreme Court in 1980, and the facts that went before the Court were perfect—100% tribe-owned business; we were employees. And I think those are the facts that needed to go before the Supreme Court.

Whether we were very bright in 1980 or it was an accident of fate, it ended up being right.

Author: Tell me about the bankruptcy, how you got through it.

John Paul: Which one?

Author: Talk about the first one first.

John Paul: The first one was really fairly simple. It was a situation where we had a legal right to do business, but we started out undercapitalized, really financed everything out of cash flow. We had $50,000 to start a business, and you spend that to buy the inventory. It was not like we had a lot of money here from Al Pearlman or anything. But, what we would find is much of our growth was confined to cash flow; every dime we had was tied up in inventory. When we built this building, we were going to pay the contractors out of cash flow. When the cash stopped, the cash stopped. Al wasn't willing to put any more money in, especially if the fact was that he was not going to be a partner in the gambling business. I don't blame him. At some point you say, okay, you take your lumps and that's it. It was the uniform way to do it, regardless of whether we built the casino, regardless of whether we liquidated the business.

The way to do it was to file bankruptcy, to allow a uniform means of administering the liquidation of the business . . . I think there was only seven or eight grand—seven or eight grand in a bankruptcy is peanuts, which eventually got paid. All the bankruptcy did in that case was delay the scenario a few months, because it [the debt] would go out [be passed on] to the principal of the corporation, including yours truly, and the tribal principals, for personal guarantees until we paid it one way or the other. But the issue was a $1.2 million—big number—tax liability that the State Board of Equalization, right or wrong, assessed. Keep in mind, the IRS doesn't care whether they are right or wrong; they just assess; and they assessed every tribal member known to man, whether they were minors, big guys, little guys, the assumption being that you owe us tax; we don't care what that law says.

Of course the bankruptcy court stayed that process, stayed any ability of theirs to attempt to enforce it. We took that issue out of the bankruptcy court and put it into the district court on the one issue of tax. The district court ruled in our favor, and the State Board of Equalization had no ability to collect these funds. The court ruled that, regardless, tribes don't owe tax and you can't pass it down to the tribal members. So the tribal members won, which left two people exposed—Dr. John Nichols and John Nichols, more specifically John Paul Nichols, because Dr. Nichols they knew didn't have two dimes to rub together anyway, and he wasn't involved in the business. Dad was on the tribal side, never had any responsibility in any of the enterprises; to this day has never had any responsibility in any of the enterprises with the exception of a short tenure at Bingo.

Then it got up to $1.6 million personal liability which created all sorts of problems, certainly tax problems, and it created a personal bankruptcy that I had to go through when I decided to protect myself. Somehow, when these guys were attaching everything I owned, it made me explain lots of things to lots of people everywhere I went to try and get credit, because it's unusual for somebody 24, 25 years old to have a $1.6 million tax liability.

How we won that case was we were on appeal and they were appealing against us and there was concern that we might not be able to get this thing reversed. As I liked to say, "Tell me where to send the check, I'll be happy to send it to you." But there was no way in hell they would ever get paid the money.

I remember one of the attorneys happened to go on safari to Africa—this is a true story, the lead attorney [for the prosecution] missed the filing deadline. So we walked into court two weeks later and said, your Honor Attorney XYZ missed the deadline. The judge said, "Attorney XYZ should have been here," and threw the whole thing out; that was it. A brother of the attorney lost his job over the issue because the State Board of Equalization hated our guts. We'd embarrassed them. It took many years afterward to get that stuff cleared off the record. You still had to get a release from the court, take it to TRW, but nonetheless, that was the end of the tax liability for all involved.

Author: How many years did it take for you to get that off?

John Paul: 1988; eight years later. There was one other issue in the cigarette problems, one other loose string. Keep in mind, we were playing what I like to call cops and robbers: We were these businesses that were "unusual" and the local police were trying to close us. When we went from being the good guys—fighting the tax authorities, selling cigarettes, selling booze, things that cops happen to smoke and drink a lot (they were some of our best customers, state police and local police)—and said we were going to go into gambling, we became bad guys. We went from you guys are nice little quiet Indians to now you are bad Indians, and you are bad Indians with bad White guys. It sounds simplistic, but that's sort of what happened when we said what we were going to do.

Some mail-order customers did not get their refunds; they were tied up in the bankruptcy. I think our list of creditors had [about] 1,500 mail-order guys that we owed varying amounts, $35 to $50, $400; hell, we listed them for the court. And we said that if we were going to liquidate $100,000, maybe they'd get 10 cents on the dollar. If I remember right, some of them got some distribution of some liquidated funds.

The Supreme Court ruled against the tribe in Washington state and subsequently ruled against the tribe in California; the one having to do with taxes on cigarettes which really impacted liquor also, the other one having to do with whether a liquor license would be required of a tribe in the State of California. I'm not saying that those decisions could have been better, but we didn't have the ability to join them because we were fighting everybody at that point in time; so we weren't even a party to those cases. In fact, they put us out of business. These cases gave the State the right to seize truckloads of cigarettes before they got here, at $50,000/$60,000 a truckload. So we essentially told Al [that due to the Colville decision] we had to close down—Chapter 7 Bankruptcy to a certain extent dissolved the relationship, not formally, but that was it. Al was part and party to that business.

What happened though, interestingly enough, we showed in all the bankruptcy papers we had hundreds of checks from customers; we had $200,000 worth of inventory; and [yet] we Chapter 7'd this business. We had bills; we had this huge tax obligation—the state said we owed them more than $6 million.

We transferred the money to another account and built this building. Well the building is here; we fixed it up; bought the cardroom furniture and all that; and showed it in the bankruptcy papers. That's it; that's what we did. In any other bankruptcy I know of they would have said, "you've got to pay what you owe back." Nobody said a word to us. We eventually paid all those creditors, but my point being if somebody said to us at that point in time, "you can't do it," that would have been it. We had no money. We would have liquidated everything, paid all the bills, and there wouldn't have been anything left. Instead, we didn't pay the bills. We took this warehouse, put drywall up, bought tables, bought chips, bought aprons for chip girls, bought cards, built a cage, put restrooms in, and we were in the cardroom business. That was it; that was how we got into this business. The point is, the last time I saw Al Pearlman was six months after we got in the cardroom business; he came in with Bill Blank. One time, he said, "How did you guys get into this business?" We had a discussion and I told him, Al, the Tribe does not perceive that you are involved in this business. In fact, the Tribe doesn't perceive me being part of management at this point in time. The Tribe perceives this as 100-percent-tribally owned, and I am an employee of the Tribe. He left friendly; we talked and said whatever; and I think he just wrote off his investment and that was it.

Author: If you had not filed bankruptcy, what would have happened?

John Paul: We had to file bankruptcy. If we didn't file bankruptcy, we were too exposed in myriad lawsuits. In fact, we had to file bankruptcy to stave off creditors to give us time to do what we had to do. We bought time from bankruptcy. In fact, everybody eventually got paid in that bankruptcy and in the Chapter 11 the casino got in . . . but it was a lesson learned.

The other reason we had to file bankruptcy was the tax obligation. We had to get rid of that tax obligation, and in fact had a major tax obligation. We didn't think we owed it, and the bankruptcy essentially disposed of that tax obligation.

Author: Would it be fair to say if you had not filed bankruptcy, you would have been wiped out?

John Paul: Absolutely, no question about it. In fact that brings up one other thing. The first thing the City of Indio tried to do was they raided us and in fact took all the mail-order business records claiming [in City court] that we had defrauded all the mail-order customers. . . . So we went and tried to quash the search order and do all these good things . . . hiring a local attorney who was a guy we found out years later was accused of ripping off all the trust funds—but you live and learn.

Bad publicity, notoriety, but the police gave us those boxes back three months later saying, "Sorry, we were wrong." In other words, it was just ludicrous, unbelievable. I think we used that bankruptcy as any enterprise should. No different than what Texaco does, or Continental. It certainly was much more important to us. We could have done it another way. We could have said, screw you; we're Indians, and we're not going to pay. But we didn't think that was the right way. Because that, in the long run, would have hurt the Tribe far more than the bankruptcy. Instead, we went through the formal process; filed bankruptcy. We could have said we are sovereign; we have immunity; we don't owe you a dime; see ya. But we wanted to make certain there was not going to be any potential risk to individual tribal members and wanted to deal with the issue in an orderly, systematic fashion.

TRAP AND SKEET RANGE AND BINGO

While court cases were being heard and bankruptcy was being filed, the casino was still in operation. Equally important, new business opportunities were being planned and pursued. One such business was the Cabazon Trap and Skeet Range.

The following is the first report made to the Business Committee on this newly proposed venture. It is interesting to note that the report tells of a meeting held with Indio's then City Manager Phil Hawes. Hawes was a major enemy of the Tribe. The City of Indio has what is known as a weak-mayor form of government. The mayor is only one of five council persons, elected by a majority vote of his/her colleagues and not by all the city's voters. The Council hires a City manager to run things, and Hawes ran things in Indio for decades.

The fights against the Tribe were all conducted by Hawes. It was Hawes who authorized funds for the long legal battle against the Tribe and it was Hawes's police that were directed to raid Tribal offices and businesses. Yet, as this report spells out, the Tribe chose to do things "by the book," even knowing they were dealing with an enemy. In fact, upon hearing of the Tribe's dealings with Hawes regarding their planned Trap and Skeet Range, a member of the Council warned tribal representatives that City officials were racists and their enemies.

According to Tribal Business Committee minutes, "On Tuesday, August 18, we began our first meeting with Phil Hawes (Indio City Manager). We briefly discussed the components as to how to set up a trap and skeet range. Mr. Hawes gave us the name of more important gentlemen who would take more of a personal interest in the range." Said Jimmy Hughes, a security guard for the Cabazon Band who had prepared the initial trap-and-skeet report:

Bryce Hadley of Indio Pipe and Steel Supply was contacted next. On Thursday morning, August 20, I met with Bryce at his office to discuss what would be needed to set up a range. First, approximately 20 acres of land, which we have, would be needed for parking, club house and range. The club house, which would have to be at least 1,200 square feet, would cater to the needs of the shooters, including the sale of ammunition and targets, hot dogs, hamburgers, soda and beer. The sale of ammunition, equipment and food would bring in a small profit. The profit, of course, would increase as the range grows with increased numbers of customers. The club house is important as a gathering place for the shooters. We would sell shotguns and accessories in the club house. A licensed person is required to sell the guns. The sale of guns would increase the profit, as well. Parking, of course, is a necessity including approximately three extra acres for RV parking as many of the trap shooters travel in campers and stay two and three days at a time. If the range is constructed near the Casino area, additional business could be brought into the existing Casino restaurant.

On Friday, August 21, I met with Jim Kelly of Rancho Mirage. Jim is an engineer and lawyer. He is also one of the head people of the Palm Springs Airport, being its former director. Jim will be very important to us since he will donate his time and expertise in setting up the range. Jim also has many contacts who will be glad to help us.

Following the above meeting, Jim made an appointment to meet Mark Nichols and myself on August 22 in order to inspect the old range on 58th Street and inspect the Cabazon land.

The afternoon of August 22, I went to the Redlands Trap and Skeet range and met with the owner, Gerald Eubanks. Gerald has a very nice range and was happy to hear we were going to start a range in Indio. He offered assistance in building our range. Gerald has an impressive range which includes parking for cars, RV parking, a club house and a gunsmithing shop. Gerald said it would cost approximately $8,000 to build just one trap house which includes the cement house, the throwing machine, cemented area and grass behind the trap house.

August 23, Mark Nichols and myself met with Jim Kelly at the Casino. From there, we went out and looked at the land, picking out an area that would be in Section 19 behind the Casino and far enough removed so that shots could not be heard, yet close enough for shooters to utilize the Casino and restaurant. Jim then took Mark and myself out to the old range by Cahuilla Lake, which gave us a pretty good idea of what we would need for a start up. The range has 4 skeet houses and 8 trap houses which is a good beginning set up for us.

I met with Ray Howard, a friend of Jim Kelly's who is an architect. I took Ray out to see the land we would probably use. He thought it was a good choice. . . .

I talked on the phone with Beryl Barber from Santa Rosa, CA. Beryl is a member of the N.R.A. [National Rifle Association] and owns his own business. He is most knowledgeable in the trap and skeet field. It will probably be most important for all of us to meet with Beryl. He also sent me data and information on trap and skeet ranges, including what it is all about. Beryl will be flying in with two other gentlemen on September 9 to meet with us and discuss further the needs of our range.

Within eight months after this report, the Trap and Skeet Range would open for business.

By August 1982, the Tribe would also enter into a Joint Venture between the tribe and a California corporation, Bingo Palace Inc. The Agreement stipulated "the dominant and paramount purpose of the Joint Venture is to construct and operate a profit-making Bingo Facility. Such facility shall comply with all laws and ordinances of the Cabazon Band of Mission Indians."

The Tribe, as in the joint venture with Wackenhut, held 51 percent interest, with Bingo Palace holding 49 percent. Initial capitalization called for Bingo Palace to provide $130,000 for the "construction, outfitting and early operation" of the joint venture. The Tribe provided "initial acreage, approximately 20 acres valued at approximately $15,000/acre. Under no circumstances, however, will Bingo, Inc. receive or obtain any interest in or to such land. . . ." Finally, the Agreement provided that "the total amount expended (of the initial capital advanced by Bingo, Inc.) shall be repaid to Bingo, Inc. prior to the distribution of any profits hereunder."

In April 1982, Dr. Nichols would report on the necessity of securing security clearance from the government for certain government contracts and on the fact that security clearance was in process. At that same meeting, it was announced that Peter Zokosky was preparing an unsolicited proposal to be submitted to the government "regarding armaments manufacturing on Section 6, to be submitted under the Joint Venture" with Wackenhut. His proposal was to establish a second source for the 120mm. combustible case for the M-1 Battle Tank. It called for an investment of $24 million, with a yearly sales projection of $32 million.

Although the Trap and Skeet Range business would not last and Zokosky's unsolicited proposal would not fly, Zokosky and Jimmy Hughes would prove to be would-be asps in the Tribe's bosom. Both would be implicated in an obvious attempted takeover of the Tribe's Casino, in concert with developer Wayne Reeder, the principal behind Bingo Palace Inc.

OTHER DEATHS

Undoubtedly adding to the unsavory and unsubstantiated rumors circulating at the time, Fred Alvarez's death by murder was the third significant death within the Tribe in a six-month period. Floyd (Eugene) Welmas died on November 19, 1980, and his brother Samuel died on April 4, 1981. Both Floyd and Samuel, affectionately called Gene and Sammy, had become strong supporters of the path being pursued by the Tribe's leadership. Both spent many hours either at the Smoke Shop or the tribal offices. Both deaths were from severe, cumulative health problems.

Gene and Mark Nichols became warm associates, as did Mark and Gene's children. One, Gene's daughter Virginia, became Mark's wife and mother of their daughter. Mark spoke about both Gene and Sammy:

Author: I would like to know your impressions. Tell me about Eugene Welmas.

Mark: The thing with Gene is, he was about as Indian as you could get. I had experience with Indians before coming here because my father had worked with them over a period of years—Indians in other countries and so forth. Gene was about as Indian as you could get in terms of his mannerisms, his sense of humor, his perspective. There is something that I find very difficult to describe when I look at a Hispanic person, which is basically an Indian that speaks Spanish in a sense, and an Indian. There is a transition there that is kind of hard to describe, but it is very clear. It is just a whole sense of identification and so forth. Gene had a great sense of humor, had a lot of depth. He was a very bright man, but had some problems, claimed to speak five different dialects. I know for a fact that he spoke at least three well—Indian dialects—he spoke his mother's, his father's, and had some familiarity with Chemehuevi. He was very knowledgeable about the desert, having been brought up in a very traditional manner. When I say traditional, that's not the right word. He was just a lot closer to the old source having known the languages and been on the reservations and really, by choice, elected to stay dropped out and never really wanted to change in his heart like some Indians.

Some Indians had gotten involved in more of a political spectrum. Some of his friends had gone into the Army and had bought into more of the Westernization. Some really went full fledged into the non-Indian community for a length of time, but Gene and Sammy never quite made that transition. In some people's eyes that might have been looked on as lazy and all those other kinds of things that would be associated with laziness. Clearly they had some of those traits, like all humans do. . . . Alcohol was a problem. But they, in fact, had not made that transition and really were Indians in a purer sense than most. That is how I perceived it.

Author: Where was Gene living?

Mark: When I first came out, he was still staying out in Banning. He owned a house out there on Cherry Street, as I recall. His wife Beverly, my mother-in-law, still owns it; she has renters there now. . . . He sold his 40 acres down in Section 6 and used that money to buy this home up in the city [of Banning]. Because of his alcoholism, he was having problems at that time, but I think he was living up there. At one time there was employment here and he was working on the plantation project. He started, at least during the week nights, living on Section 6 in a trailer we had down there. In fact, for a while he used to sleep under a tree immediately across the parking lot from this building. There were three cots out there, and Gene, [and his sons] Floyd and Charles used to sleep out there.

Gene loved the outdoors. The work he did was always gardening and horticulture, things of that nature; he just really loved the outdoors. He knew a lot about plants, and we would go on walks and, unfortunately, I don't remember much of it, but he would show me which plants you use if you were dying of thirst. He showed me that you could eat clay if you had nothing else to eat. He told me about something that I always remembered—hunting by following flies, something that I never would have considered, and being able to distinguish between different types of insects and, thereby, get an idea as to what might be in the vicinity. He really had some marvelous skills in the outdoor area.

Author: He had how many children?

Mark: Gene was married to Beverly Toro, and he had a daughter named Beverly, a son named Floyd, a son named Charles, a daughter named Virginia (my wife), and his wife had another daughter by the name of Shirley by a previous relationship. There was also another child that died. Gene had a brother named Harry that died prior to my coming out, I believe, prior to my parents coming out. He had been part of a fairly large family, as I recall. I think there were five kids or so. One of them died from a rattlesnake bite; I remember him telling me about that. He had been bitten twice himself, but survived them.

Author: Tell me about Sammy. Is that what they called him?

Mark: Yes, Sammy was more quiet than Gene. Gene tended to be a little more outspoken person, whereas Sammy generally was very, very quiet. He was the kind of person you could spend time with, be with, and not have to talk.

Author: Were they blood brothers?

Mark: Yes, they were blood brothers. Sammy, of course, was much shorter and always had a lot of skin problems, some medical problems that always seemed to crop up. He had a kidney problem, which I think ultimately killed him. He had health problems for a long time. He didn't do things to hurt people, but he never quite picked up any of the pieces as he went along; he wasn't very disciplined. He loved to visit his friends and go to powwows, and he networked a lot with the singers and other spiritual leaders and elders in the Indian community throughout the mountains—Palm Springs as well as in Morongo.

Author: Was he a singer?

Mark: Sammy was a singer in the sense that he knew how to sing and he had his own rattles. He had possession of—kind of the icon of the tribe—a set of rattles made out of turtle shells which, as I understand it, are now in the possession of Biff Andreas who is the principal singer for the Agua Calientes, and at some point, if we ever get a museum, that would be very nice to get back. That was Sammy's icon. He was definitely a singer in Indian spirituality as well, as I understand it.

I don't know that any particular person is that much more spiritual than another in terms of tribal spiritual leadership, but rather it is something everyone [in the Tribe] achieves with a certain amount of depth and understanding in their lives. It is part and parcel of that understanding, of the connectedness of life in general in man, but [instead of spiritual leadership] perhaps what happens . . . is they develop specific [spiritual] skills in areas. So Sam, for example, was a singer and Gene was an herb person, where Ruby Modesto, who was very close to both of them, was a soul healer and David was an herb healer. The Indian inner circle is holy, but people have different skills in different areas, if that makes any sense.

Author: What did Gene die of?

Mark: As I understand, he had kind of a combination cardiac arrest and overall system failure that had been brought upon him, or which he brought upon himself, by excessive alcohol.

Author: And Sam went about five months later?

Mark: It was a great loss for Sammy to have Gene go, because if there was anybody he could identify very closely with here, it was Gene. There was an affinity towards Art [Welmas] because he tended to be a little more Indian than John [James] in the traditional sense, but not near the same relationship as Sam had with Gene.

So I think there was a void in Sammy's life, but he also had complicated medical problems that related to his kidneys. Again, alcoholism, particularly coupled with diabetes in his case, was very, very pronounced. I think he would drink, but he wasn't the same kind of drinker as Gene. Sammy abused alcohol and didn't take care of himself. I think he ate more banana splits than he drank liquor. It was definitely the sugar in both because he was doing both, but not heavy on the drinking. Diabetes basically killed Sammy. . . .

Author: Did Sammy have family?

Mark: Sammy's only family was Gene and the Welmas family for the most part. Harry, who was the other brother, had died. He, I believe, felt some affinity towards Art Welmas's family and probably more so for Art's wife, because she kind of served as a pillar of stability. . . .

> For a lot of tribal people in this area, the Army had been their first and only experience out of the area. There is an Indian fellow that I went to visit up in the mountains that Sammy knew, and I can't remember what his name was, but he lived up outside of Pala at the edge of town—the name Ernest comes to mind—names oftentimes are very unimportant to me; I remember faces. He was a fellow about 40 and he wore his hair long, a black mane that went back—what you would see in the movies—well built. He was wearing these little cut-off shorts and he lived in this hut that had no electricity, no water to it. In fact, he had a couple of stools and several ammo boxes.
>
> That guy went to Vietnam and said to hell with this. He had come back and completely shut himself off from integration and society at large, because if that was what it meant to be part of society at large he had absolutely no desire.
>
> Those were the kinds of people that Sammy knew and visited. There was Uncle Frank; there were these people that he would go up into the hills and see; and those were the people that he would identify with.
>
> Part of Sam's problem, too, was he was an extremely small, ill person. His health wasn't good, so he couldn't work with his body much. It wouldn't have been very productive for him.

Later in the interview, Mark mused that "people who drink want to have some reason to drink. . . . Gene drank because he killed a lot of people in Korea; he would tell you that. He would break down. He would say that he had killed women and children and whole families in Korea. He said he had come off the reservation and gone into the army; they shipped him off to Korea; and his big experience was to go out and kill people for something he didn't understand . . . and that was his reason."

Within less than 18 months after Gene's death, his son Floyd (Jim) Jr. took his own life. When he died in April 1982, the young turks in the Tribe were assuming more and more influence, and he was a part of that youth movement. Floyd has been described as "a tall, well-mannered, well-built, good-looking, intelligent person," who had "lots of girlfriends and lots of opportunities." As a "jock," however, he had also acquired the macho drinking habit. When asked about Floyd, Mark became pensive before responding:

> Floyd was a very good baseball player, had been in the army and honorably discharged. . . . He had a lot of potential in the sports area, a lot of trophies. They were very prominently displayed in his house. His parents were very proud, particularly his mother who has been a softball fan and sports enthusiast all her life. That was a very important thing for her and conversely for him. When he lost the arm, which apparently resulted from a slip in the shower, I don't know if you discussed that or not, but he was taking a shower and he slipped and he severed the arm. I had been under the impression that he was treated by Federal Indian Health doctors, but I was set straight on that a couple of days ago by my wife. Apparently he was at Banning Memorial Hospital, which did not necessarily have the latest and best level of care. But, in any case, they amputated the arm, and he never quite got over that—it was a full amputation. . . . It was his pitching, his main arm.
>
> So, he went through a couple of professional alcohol treatment programs as I recall.

He had gone over to the Methodist Medical Center in Des Moines, Iowa, one of the first tribal members that went over, and seemed to successfully defeat it, but he didn't have the support system around him that he should have. Some people close to him didn't understand how being Indian can sometimes be a little confusing in a certain way. You don't necessarily feel comfortable with somebody else changing, so you don't think you have the support there [to change either]. In fact, if anything, it would have been the opposite for him; he would have had some actually pulling him back into that former lifestyle.

Because he had tasted the freedom of not being under the spell of chemicals, he had a lot of emotional problems. He was torn between his old self or that other thing and what he was trying to become. Some persons close to him were not necessarily a support, and it wasn't their fault, it was just that they were part of that illness.

His relationships were also problems. When you are in relationships and go off and [get sober] then come back, that creates stress, because they have to change or you have to separate from each other. It was a whole combination of things: low self-esteem, loss of the arm and alienation which ultimately ended up in the suicide. He and his brother Charles spent quite a bit of time at our apartment. They would go down and together frequent the bars or whatever in town, sometimes getting into trouble. When I heard that he died, I really cried a tremendous amount. I hadn't realized how close we had become until he died.

Within a little over a year after Floyd's suicide, another tragic death would shake the tribe and the Nichols family. Joann Nichols, wife of Dr. Nichols and tribal administrator, died in early June 1983.

By the time of her death, a symbiosis of sorts had taken place between the Tribe's majority leadership and the Nichols family. It was as if there were "two tribes" working extremely hard together in a cooperative and mutually beneficial union. Joann had been important in the forging of that "two tribes" symbiosis. And she would suffer a debilitating, long and painful illness before dying what loved ones felt was a senseless death.

At the time of her death, her oldest child, Philip Leslie, was about 31 years old. Philip was a philosophy major in college and a Vietnam-era veteran. He had given up his own paint contracting business in Florida, after staying behind to handle the sale of his parents' home, and relocated to Indio in June 1979, four years earlier. He described his reaction to his mother's death this way:

Philip: We all deal with grief differently. . . . The problem is not with dying, but how the person dies. Where there is no dignity in death, it eats everyone up worse than the cancer does. The incompetency of our law enforcement people pales before the incompetency of our medical profession. John F. Kennedy Hospital [in Indio] is the worst sight I have ever seen, and I have seen hospitals in Third World countries. . . .

She [his mother] was in pain for several years and they treated her for I think everything, and I think it took years before they took a chest X-ray to determine she had lung cancer. She went to the UCLA oncology thing. She went through chemo and all that. She didn't die from cancer; that was in remission. She ended up dying from pneumonia. But what actually killed her was a doctor at JFK Emergency, a very influential one now at JFK, who was new because they always put the new ones in emergency, and she was weak. He collapsed her lung, basically through inexperience and incompetence as far as I was concerned.

Author: You mean he accidentally . . . ?

Philip: Right, he freaked. And then he did a tracheotomy, which he never should have done, and that basically regulated her. She did survive but spent the rest of her life on a lung machine because her lungs were going to petrify, and she was not ever able to verbalize again because of her tracheotomy. I'm not going to say the doctor's name right now; we didn't sue him, at least we haven't yet, but I always ask if he's on duty. When I ended up there in August 1992, the first thing I asked was if he was still in emergency, because if he was he wasn't treating me. But watching the pain and suffering is what tears the family [up], and back then is what I like to call the insane years.

When you are going through major grief and things like that . . . alcohol and drugs are not the problems; they are symptomatic of the problem. I was brought up as the eldest . . . I was responsible for my family. It took me many years to forgive myself for letting my mother die. That was my insanity, that I should have been able to fix it. I took full blame. I was God. I finally had to say, I'm not God—if there is one or not, I have no idea—I'm not. It took me a long time to forgive myself, to find out it was okay to do that, but again we all deal with grief differently. I didn't have the time to deal with it when she died, so I self-mitigated by coke (freezing), but I continued doing my job. Somebody had to be there. I never left the reservation, literally for years. I had no social life.

My mother's death devastated my father. That was his best friend, his mate, his bedrock of reality. My father was a dreamer. He never did things to make money. He did things out of principle because somebody needed help.

I finally cried for my mother almost five years after her death. I've been to her grave once. Eventually I'll go back and apologize, but that will come in time. I still go through grieving processes.

John Paul, the next oldest child, was 29 years old at his mother's death. When he was asked, nine years after, what her loss had meant he responded:

I was thinking earlier today—I worked out this morning—that we've been 10 years on this Indian reservation—actually our family has been here for 13 years now. These stories I'm telling you are not the stories of a typical guy that runs a hotel somewhere. In that sense it's exciting. I told you about the tension and stress and all that.

But this place has taken a huge toll on our family. In fact, it's not the same family that arrived here in 1979. It just isn't. I have to tell you, we've been through a catharsis where there's evidence that exists, somewhat catalytic [brought into focus] around the death of Mother, but even before and after, that you can't live in this crazy environment, work as a family and expect the family to not suffer as a result. In fact, I think it's a very high price to pay. I have had the luxury, and it is a luxury, to step out. I had to step out, because when you are in the midst of this, it makes perfect sense. But in fact, it is not a normal environment. It is not necessarily a healthy environment. It's not a business that lends itself to a healthy environment. It is an inherently and politically unstable environment. It's always the majority, but it is politically unstable nonetheless.

So, I think there's been a lot of family damage, even prior to my mother's death. I think the businesses involved here—liquor, cigarettes, lounge, gambling, all the tension associated with this place, bad publicity, the reputation of the family—can help to create family damage. We look at these newspaper attacks and say it doesn't hurt, but it does hurt. We're blemished whether I like it or not. I hired a maintenance guy that works for me in Amarillo [Texas], and he thinks I'm a mafia guy, which is absurd. I joke about that, but in fact it's a blemish. This business is a tough business to be in. It can hurt a lot of people. It's very much a 'company-store' type business in terms of its employees, especially. There is a detrimental side to gambling.

When Mom passed away, a variety of things happened. One, all of us kids were going through a family tragedy. I was an addict; Phil was an addict; Bob was an addict; Mark satisfies his addiction by using food—[although] I think he has self-actualized himself [now]. And Mom, because of her cancer, was a morphine addict for the last year, year and a half of her life. Dad sometimes doesn't face that.

We were all sitting there running this business by the seat of our pants, sober enough to survive but certainly not doing nearly the job that we could have been doing—nothing I wouldn't say in front of the tribal members because several of the tribal members went through treatment after us, too. All of us, the whole tribe, were dysfunctional, if you want to look at it from that perspective.

But as a family, we were a bunch of sick puppies, and Mom died. All of us went through a whole catharsis. My biggest catharsis was when Mom came to my wedding. She was dying in front of me, but I was so blitzed out of the world, I got married and went on a honeymoon for a month. I came back a day before she died and she writes on her blackboard, 'I waited for you.' Talk about a son and what it feels like. She dies the next day and I had been sitting around Europe, extending my vacation. Of course my reaction to that was to get f—ed up for the next year.

Mom's death in one sense created a catharsis to allow, if you will, the legacies of her children to have developed. Many of us, our biggest regret in life was the fact that Mom wasn't alive to see us at least on the path to recovery, which was altered for me by finishing an MBA, having a daughter—family. Life may not be so exciting, but I'm sure a much happier individual and I think I'm a more productive individual in the long run, which resulted in Mark being very successful in his work. I think he's enjoying what he's doing. With Bob, I think he's kind of more content. Children—all this—I think would have been great for Joann to see, but it was not to be.

When Joann died, a relationship for Dr. Nichols that spanned 38 years or more came to an end. Theirs had been a union that books need to be written about. After going together for five or so years, she and John eloped and were married after getting their license in Chicago. The clerk at that time, who kept their license out of the book for a few days so the press wouldn't publish it, was none other than the future Mayor Richard Daley.

An advisor to royalty once told his charge that those who became successful at making a mark on life "owed nothing to fortune but the opportunity which gave them matter to be shaped into what form they thought fit; without the opportunity, their abilities would have been wasted and without their abilities, the opportunity would have come in vain." In John and Joann, there seemed to be a real marriage of ability and opportunity. Most things and people they touched changed many lives and communities for the better.

Joann's death would have a lingering and devastating impact on her husband's purpose and balance. In an interview in 1992, Nichols talked about Joann with difficulty:

Dr. Nichols: Joann was a healer, but strong. She would always give a straight answer, like Mark. When we were working together it worked out very well, because she would keep things running; and she would always handle the press; she always gave straight answers. I was always wondering, "Where are they coming from? When do we go to trial?" I'd say this. I was conditioned from the Labor Movement.

In '83 we had all these people that stepped in, like Harold Gibbons from the Teamsters; he was already living here. He had come down. We needed some things delivered, picked up. I had friends from the carpenter's union, all these people around that would be—not visible, but there—to help. As I said, we had help from Israelis and Arabs because we weren't discriminating and we weren't selling our souls to any of these people. In '83, we had gone through the cigarette thing. We were mounting gaming.

The biggest thing that I was doing was getting every book there was on Indian history and researching every aspect of gaming. Philip eventually took that over during Joann's illness. Philip was able to get everything refocused on the study. I had come up with the wrong material and Philip was able to get the focus.

Author: When did Joann go into the hospital? Was it February?

Dr. Nichols: Well, she actually first went in [in] January. Then she got out. Then she was in again. She was here for the Tribal meeting in January. She had been in the hospital [briefly] in December, but she had gotten out and gone to that meeting. We actually held some meetings when she was in the hospital. It wasn't supposed to be that way, but I was there—maybe John James wanted to find something out or Art. They came down there, and the next thing we knew we had a quorum.

Author: Did she have cancer of the lung?

Dr. Nichols: She had cancer of the lungs from smoking. When I was doing training, she had smoked Kents; she smoked sometimes up to five packs a day, not all the way down; she just smoked a few puffs off each. She would never use a partially smoked cigarette. My father would always crumble up one and he would re-roll it. Of course, he died of emphysema from smoking. Joann read some early articles on the possibility of cancer so she just gave it up. That was eight years prior to her dying. I was having a training course in New Orleans. She said, "Don't you notice anything different?" I said, "No," and I kept looking at her. Well, she hadn't smoked for two days. I hadn't noticed. . . .

They did get her cancer arrested. She got pneumonia. How long she would have lasted I don't know; but after radiation, often times you become so frail and weak that a wind can blow you away. It's a lot like people with AIDS. They've lost the ability for their immune system to function. The whole thing was, I felt so helpless and hopeless. And I would call Bishop Chavez in Chile, and he had 8,500 Pentecostals praying in the streets down there. I hadn't been there for a while. I met these guys from Germany and had selenium and we tried that. I tried everything.

Author: How did you take it? How did you deal with it?

Dr. Nichols: Her death?

Author: Yes.

Dr. Nichols: Poorly. We were married 33 years and I had gone with her five years prior to that. Whatever I did, I always talked it over with her. It was always a collective decision. We may have argued, but when we went to bed, we compromised one way or the other. There I was, I didn't have anybody to share with and your children are something else. They all wanted to share with me. They all wanted to help me.

Author: It's a different level.

Dr. Nichols: I just couldn't do it. It's a different thing. And I couldn't pick one over the other. Bob [the youngest son] came back to live with me. His mother also made him go on the road to take a gig in Las Vegas, and he'd been nursing her all along, so she dies without him. She said, "We owe this to his career." It's so amazing to me how she functioned. The lung specialist did the tracheotomy, so she couldn't speak and she lost her power to live. Speech is so important to most people and especially if you can't write because you don't have the strength.

She was misdiagnosed. Eighteen months we had been seeking a diagnosis, but no one ever gave her an X-ray for 18 months. They felt she had something with a tooth, one here, back there, and it wasn't that and they sent her to neurologists and all these things, and no one took an X-ray. As a result, all of us now get X-rays in our family. You would think that is standard operating procedure, but it sure wasn't in her case.

Joann was very good at evaluating people's intents. She knew what people you could trust, what people not to trust. When the time came to go, to move on, she knew that. I never went against her advice on these things. The biggest thing is she was always able to see in me, when I was reaching out to some poor, unfortunate person, that often times I was reaching out for self-destruction. And that, she had the ability to do, and nobody else.

My kids certainly told me, but I would resent what my children were saying to me. It's wrong, but I could not accept what they were saying.

Author: They're going to tell their old man what to do?

Dr. Nichols: Right, it was a bad thing. And the Indians, on the other hand, a lot of them are very sort of mystical and they always felt that her ghost was present. The older guys at that time wanted to name a building after her, something like this. We never did that. I often thought about a clinic, because she was a nurse—I would name a clinic Joann Nichols Clinic or something like that. I gave some money, not much, but you can build a church in Chile for $3,000, so I gave some of the money I had to build a church in her name in a small community.

When I went down to Chile with Dr. Hulsizer a few years later, I went down and saw it. It was way up in the mountains, a clean little chapel, and there's a little cornerstone that has her name there.

Author: People don't know that, do they?

Dr. Nichols: No, they don't. I'm unable to talk to my kids about it.

Author: They don't know it?

Dr. Nichols: No, I never told them . . . I don't tell my children everything.

Author: Don't you think they need to know?

Dr. Nichols: Well, I'd rather they find out from someone else, because some are always worried that I am going to manipulate them. I just learned there are some things I'm better off not to say. What I do is I just do things.

Author: Where is the church located?

Dr. Nichols: It's outside of Curico. It's a wooded pine forest area. I liked Bishop Chavez; he

> subsequently died. He'd kept all these little churches going, and again I'm not a Pentecostal. It could have been a mosque for that matter, but the idea is it gave people something better to think about. The thing that I learned about Pentecostals in Chile and early churches to begin with is that you'd have a society which is made up of many drunkards, whores, petty thieves and other miscreants. They then became Christians. Maybe before they became Christians they were spending 60 percent of their income on liquor, on women, etc. They join a church and give 10 percent of their money to a church, maybe another 5 percent to the pastor, and they begin saving money. I had to learn that in a society with a lot of pathology, you need to have a volunteer structure for goodness.
>
> I knew Bishop Chavez, and he was enjoyable, someone I cared about. I told you about all those people he had praying for Joann. I suppose right now I would be as prone to try and raise money, as I did in the past, for something for him, but I've always had these other priorities since then. That's why when people talk to me about a second marriage or something, it's hard to think of marriage if you have a ghost in your soul.
>
> I think there are many animals that mate for once in their life. I think that a lot of people in our society nowadays don't even bother to mate; they sleep together. They may even get married, but there's no love, no binding; there's nothing to build on.

DR. NICHOLS'S ARREST AND CONVICTION

Within 18 months after Joann's death, Dr. Nichols would, as he said, "reach out for self-destruction" and there was no one there to warn him or pull him back. Twelve months earlier he became involved with a young female addict and convinced himself he could "save her."

Dr. Nichols also convinced himself he could, alone, pull off another big "victory," and at the same time entrap some dope pushers and send them to prison. He began to routinely tape-record almost all conversations on his telephone and in his house. He bought a little micro recorder that could be easily carried in his shirt pocket undetected. As the plan unfolded in his mind, Nichols would occasionally call members of the Indio Police Department.

In fact, on January 16, 1985—the day before his arrest—just before he was himself caught in the trap set for him by police using some addict-pusher informants, Nichols called the police to let them know where he was going.

The result of this "reaching out for destruction" was his arrest and conviction, under a no-contest plea, for murder solicitation. It would be humorous if it were not so tragic that the police would have to use Nichols's tape recording of the transaction because theirs was not so clear. He had not only reached out for destruction, he had delivered himself into the hands of the enemy that had been trying to destroy him and the success of the Tribe for many years.

The press and everyone close who had observed his behavior during this period referred to the young lady as his girlfriend, adding to his public embarrassment through their belief he had been "an old fool." They of course could not know, and Dr. Nichols's often macho front would not allow him to reveal, his long-time impotence. This condition was the result of his serious diabetes and the smashing of his penis during torture by terrorists in South America years before.

His son, John Paul, was perceptive, although partially wrong, in his evaluation of what his arrest for that specific crime meant in public terms:

He could have been arrested for gambling; he could have been arrested for child molestation; he could have been arrested for trying to shoot George Bush, anything but what he was arrested for. All that did was give credence to the myth. In fact to this day, that myth, those two independent acts (the fact that something happened to Fred Alvarez in 1981 that I believe had to do with the fact that Fred was a drug dealer, and then my dad's actions, which had zip relationship—totally independent—had no connection or causal relation at all) have been twisted to this day.

And in fact, there is confusion from anybody that I talk to that isn't intimately aware of the fact of what those two incidents were. So no, Dad was convicted of "X" in 1985 by the court of public opinion or certainly by the media. But unfortunately, the media dictates public opinion. Polls don't dictate the media, the media drives the polls, unfortunately. That's just the way it works. So once the media convicted him, from that point on we were so embattled, it became much harder.

The question is often asked, why didn't Nichols fight the case in court instead of plead no contest? The short and long answer is the same—money. Dr. Nichols had accumulated no personal savings of any consequence. Use of tribal funds of any kind was simply not an option. So, in effect, he delivered himself completely into the hands of the enemy. Although charged with five counts of solicitation, he pleaded no contest to only two counts.

While Nichols languished in the Indio City Jail, the court ordered a psychiatric evaluation of him, which was performed by Morton L. Kurland, M.D., Diplomat, American Board of Psychiatry & Neurology. Dr. Kurland was Chief, Section on Psychiatry, Eisenhower Medical Center. Here, in part, is his report:

CONFIDENTIAL PSYCHIATRIC REPORT

JOHN PHILLIP (sic.) NICHOLS

Dr. John Phillip (sic.) Nichols is a 60-year-old white male, social work[er] and religious education entrepreneur. He received his degrees in social work, and over a number of years worked in this field, as well as in the areas of religious education, religious planning, and activities associated with both social, religious and political groups around the United States and, to some extent, in Latin America. . . .

Most recently, Dr. Nichols was charged with several felonies relating to the alleged solicitation to commit murder of a number of individuals in the Indio area. . . .

Dr. Nichols is a smallish, somewhat chubby, white-haired individual, who looks somewhat older than his stated age and, in fact, does not appear to be in good physical health, although he does appear to be neat and clean in appearance. He was verbal and cooperative. . . .

He did not, however, show any gross evidence of an organic impairment in that he was oriented to time, place and person, and showed no evidence of gross confusion, loss of immediate recall, or other indications that he was, in fact, unable to understand what was going on around him or to deal with the specifics of the life situation in which he found himself. Rather, he attempted to act comfortable and relaxed and, in a somewhat inappropriate manner, indicated that he enjoyed being in jail because it gave him an opportunity to help others and, of course, he was able to counsel some of the other men with whom he came in contact in his imprisonment.

He showed no evidence of gross loss of touch with reality, and understood why I was there to see him, what my role was, and indicated a willingness to talk with me and to get me to understand his life situation. His thought processes, as noted above, were not loosened, but were tangential. That is, the ideas that he related were connected to each other, but they frequently did not relate to specific answers to questions. There was no evidence of inappropriateness of his emotional tone or affect, and he was generally appropriate in terms of the situations which we discussed, creating either sadness when we talked about the death of his wife, or humor when he talked about some of the incidents which had occurred to him in past years in connection with his various contacts with political figures over the years.

There was no evidence of blocked thinking or inability to make choices due to ambivalent thoughts. He did not demonstrate any indication that he was hallucinating nor that he was delusional nor that he had any specific psychotic thought processes.

He did appear to be depressed, and described a history consistent with depression, and showed a mild dysphoric mood during the interview. This was especially notable when he talked about the death of his wife and the fact that she had died of lung cancer as a patient at Eisenhower Medical Center in the previous year. Apparently, she had gone through a long and uncomfortable illness, and the relation of this particular problem was painful to him. In addition to this, he was uncomfortable and unhappy in describing some of his difficulties with his children who had pulled away from him, who had been less interested in his life and activities since the death of his wife and their mother. He also reported that two of his sons were A.A. members and said, "That's a lot to do with this," meaning his present difficulties were related to his concern about his children being substance abusers and his need to do something about this. Much of his discussion was related to his feeling that he had to do things about social problems in which he found himself and in which he discovered his children. He indicated that he was very concerned about people who sold drugs to his children and later sold them to his friend Anna. All of these events and people were discussed with a kind of sadness and unhappiness. . . .

In regard to the specific crime for which he was charged, he told me that in fact he was trying to trap others and that he never intended to kill anyone. He said that his goal was to uncover and unmask the drug trafficking; problem in the Coachella Valley. He specifically was concerned because his ward, a young woman named Anna Marie Vallespir, was using drugs and was being enslaved by heroin by drug dealers. His main interest was to unmask the drug dealers whom he said were being protected by the local police in exchange for their being their informants. . . .

Information obtained from his children indicates that he has not taken care of himself adequately with the diabetes and, in fact, in recent years, was not taking care of it well in terms of physical injuries. He burned his feet on one occasion while walking barefoot on hot blacktop during the past summer, and did not get treatment for them. Since most diabetics have very poor circulation and especially poor to the extremities, his feet burns did not heal, and the sons showed me pictures of his feet taken sometime last summer when after several weeks, he had not received treatment. They took pictures of them in order to demonstrate to him graphically how he was not taking care of himself adequately. He finally had to have four operations for skin grafts on his left foot after his children insisted on this treatment. This work was done by Dr. Vincent Forshand, at Eisenhower Medical Center.

DIAGNOSTIC IMPRESSION: It is my impression that Dr. Nichols suffers, at the very least from a cyclothymic personality. He may well have had a manic-depressive disorder most of his life, although at this point in his life, he appears to be burned out from the extremes of manic-depressive thinking, and now shows cyclothymic qualities, that is, a more mild form of ups and downs. At the time when I saw him, he seemed to be in a depressive mood, and probably had been for some time. It may well be, however, that during the alleged crimes he was in an upswing, thinking that he could save Anna Marie Vallespir and, in some way, also save other drug addicts from the evil practices of the drug dealers. Either this, or he may have felt that he was going to uncover plotting in the police department, somehow reveal the deals that were made with heroin purveyors, and "clean up" the Coachella Valley. In either event, he seemed to have been in at least a hypomanic phase of thinking.

It would be very consistent with his background and history that his diabetic arterial disorders can contribute to the underlying personality problems to create a situation in which he was exercising extremely poor judgment, grandiose thinking, and very poor reality testing in dealing with the issues which led to his arrest. *It is important to note that at this time of his arrest, he himself had been taking tape recordings of the proceedings which the police were recording at the same time. Apparently, Dr. Nichols had the feeling that he was going to use these tapes in some way to prove his case, that is, of police involvement in nefarious activities.* Whether this is realistic or not in terms of legal processes, it does indicate some rather bizarre thinking on his part and a real lack of good reality testing in general.

DISCUSSION:

Since Dr. Nichols has pleaded no contest to several of the charges against him, the real problem that is faced by the Court and society is how to handle this case.

While no excuse for the crimes themselves exists in his medical history and family background, as well as his emotional status, there is I think considerable mitigation involved in understanding the circumstances involved. . . .

In the light of these circumstances, I would respectfully suggest the following in the light of his age and physical condition:

1. State prison confinement would be of no value to this individual, nor would it, I feel, be of any value to society. He would gain nothing, and the example set by sending an aged and ailing individual to state prison would be lost upon young offenders who tend to deprecate age, education and background in the first place.

2. Dr. Nichols is not now dangerous to himself nor to others, in my opinion. The likelihood of his carrying out any plans or plots against other people is minimal, as is indicated in this abortive effort to take vigilante justice into his own hands and, in some way, right the wrongs of what he regarded as a drug dealing society. It would appear that he has, in fact, "learned his lesson" in terms of his present situation, and the likelihood of his repeating this seems to be minimal.

3. Since Dr. Nichols is bilingual and still retains a significant amount of his verbal and intellectual talent, despite the problems involved in his diabetes and aging, he still has something to offer society. He continues to have a drive to help others, and in his bilingual capacity, probably could perform significant community service to many of the underprivileged in our society locally.

It is further important to note that if probation were, in fact, granted to this individual, it would be very important to insist upon his having very careful and regular medical supervision, as he has not in the past been careful to follow up and keep in touch with his physician. In addition, it would probably be very useful to him and to society as well to have him followed in a directive kind of psychotherapy where a competent psychologist or psychiatrist could talk to him about his feelings, and possibly help him to channel his need to contribute to society and to fight against drug addiction in more realistic and productive channels. (Emphasis added.)

Dr. Nichols was later sent through the prison system to its institution in Chino, California, for further evaluation. There, the staff psychologist concluded that "he maintains a hostile, self-righteous stance. . . . The Subject's behavior is comprehended within the personality framework of sociopathy and manic propensity. His tending toward grandiosity and his sense of self-entitlement contribute to a behavioral pattern of living by his own rules, rather than respecting established social order. The Subject is viewed as representing a substantial danger for similar offense." And the Correctional Counselor, after a 45-minute interview, concluded that he "possibly feels he was above reproach . . . showed no remorse . . . and his lack of accepting his participation would further ingrain his belief of being "above the law."

Finally, the Correctional Administrator, in his letter and report to Judge Noah Ned Jamin, stated that his staff viewed Dr. Nichols "as a shrewd and dangerous manipulator who very evasively avoids responsibility for this very serious crime. Although he apparently has an abundance of community resources and has maintained an arrest free lifestyle, the dangerous threat that he presents to the community should he choose to reoffend contraindicates community supervision."

But neither the Correctional Administrator nor his staff were being fully honest with the judge. At no place in the official record is the judge advised of the influence on Chino's staff of Geraldo Rivera's *20/20* TV segment on the Cabazons' Bingo Palace. A dispassionate reading of the record shows the staff's concern about public reaction should they recommend non-incarceration.

On May 28, 1985, Dr. Nichols wrote the judge. His letter clearly anticipated the negative consequences that would flow from the Diagnostic Evaluation Report from Chino's staff and tried to place it in another perspective. In describing his processing upon arrival at Chino, he wrote:

When I was at the end of the line the sergeant recognized my name and I was taken to a special area which I found out by asking people next to me that this was where you were classified for protective custody.

I was interviewed by a sergeant who stated *20/20* was going to be shown that night for they had called the prison and he wanted to know if I planned to call a press conference while I was there and create a lot of pressure on the institution. He did not focus on why I was incarcerated or on what the charges were but on Bingo. I said I wasn't here to make any waves; just here for the diagnostic evaluation.

I asked why I would need protective custody since I had made a plea of nolo contendere and rested on the facts. He initially brought to my attention that friends of the alleged victims could be housed in the general population and I stated I could understand their feelings and there might not be time for a dialogue in the case of a stabbing.

Since there was a knifing in the hall just before I met the sergeant the reality of the situation was very apparent. Then I was taken and lodged in Palm Hall, which is protective custody.

April 5, 1985, I was moved from the third tier to the first tier at Palm Hall. During the move the two escorting officers told me I was primarily there for Bingo crimes.

Mental Achievement Tests on April 18, 1985

At approximately 5:00 P.M., at time of early evening meal, five of the new arrivals including myself were put in individual cells that were partially lighted.

A fellow inmate who, I discovered by questioning him, had no background in testing or evaluating psychological instruments give [gave] us minimal explanations of what we were taking and told us to ignore certain sections in the Army Alpha Test. We were given the California Short Form Maturity Test, the Army Alpha Classification, a Draw-A-Person test and asked to fill out a Background Information Sheet, and an explanation of why we were there and given a chance to write our version of what happened to cause us to have been arrested.

Before each of the tests I told the inmate administering the tests that I had laser treatments on my eyes and asked if I could be placed in a normally lighted area. I was told this was impossible. I completed the California Short Form Maturity Test, but had to guess at what half of the questions called for since I was unable to read them. I was only able to do one half of the Army Alpha General Classification Test because I could not see it to finish it.

I was not able to complete my version of what had happened when my maladaptive behavior had occurred.

I attached and signed a one page piece of scrap paper with my complaints about the test and further stated my reading glasses were broken and this created an additional handicap. I further requested a psychiatric exam plus a request for counseling and evaluation by a psychiatrist.

April 9, 1985—Met with Internal Classification Committee for Palm Hall

I spent 20 minutes with a classification committee headed by Mr. R. E. Pacheco, Corrections Administrator but the committee spokesperson was Lori Meyers, Correction Counselor I, the Lieutenant for Palm Hall, the Day Shift Sergeant Rodriques and several other people who were not identified to me. I was introduced as the person *20/20* had just had a television program about, a great deal of newspaper publicity, etc. By this point, I was getting to feel I had become a Bingo criminal. I was then questioned on why I felt I needed protective custody. I told the story of being pulled out of the line and then having been told by two other Indio residents, admitted heroin dealers and users who were in Palm Hall for protective custody, that my life was in danger. [One of them] had told me this before in the Indio Jail. What they said seemed logical, so I stated for the length of time of the diagnostic evaluation this seemed to be the right approach. I then returned to my cell. . . .

April 11, 1985

That night the sergeant asked me how much I had skimmed from Bingo. He said he felt I was a nice guy, but he wouldn't give me a dime of his money. He kept refocusing on Bingo. I asked how long the observation period would take. He said in my case three weeks but no longer than six weeks. I asked if I would see the psychiatrist and got no reply.

April 12, 1985

In the evening the sergeant brought me to the Lieutenant's Office. He wanted to know what Drug and Alcohol Program I had worked with and how much federal grant monies I had skimmed off their programs, plus more comments on Bingo. I offered to have my attorney to send my Resume, my current job description which outlined my public health responsibilities and some newspaper clippings other than what they had that told the other side of the story plus my medical records from the Indio Jail. . . .

April 22, 1985

Had an interview with two psychologists, a Mrs. Howell and a Raymond Scallen, PhD. The focus of the interview centered on Bingo and they made inquiries concerning my son John Paul's wages and one employment period of my life from a 1969–1973 when I was employed in mental health. They had a confidential file of xerox copies of newspaper article clippings, police reports and a probation report.

I complained to them about tests that were given to me on April 8th and told them how dark it was. They both stated we got to get that straightened out because it happened before and they talked about rescheduling me for new tests. Mrs. Howell agreed my IQ level due to the conditions under which I was tested would be low. During the interview when they discovered Dr. Jones's and Dr. Kurlan's [sp] reports and my resume were at Chino, they cut the interview short to look at these materials. They subsequently used the negative but not any positive portions of Jones's psychological report in preparing their findings. I would like to point out that I did not pick Dr. Kurland as the court appointed him to examine me.

During the interview, Mrs. Howell focused on my employment between 1968–1973 saying she was interested in the type of clinician I was. I explained I was functioning as an administrator-community organizer type of social worker not as a caseworker because I was back in the USA at this point primarily to get my Doctorate in Religious Education and had planned to return overseas to the mission field. . . .

April 25, 1985, Interview with Ms. Lori Meyers

Had forty-five minute interview with Ms. Lori Meyers. I asked her to read my memo to Mrs. Howell and stated I would send one to her the following morning to expand on any unanswered questions since I respond better in writing than orally.

I tried to concentrate in this interview to explain my wife had been the administrator of the Cabazon tribe while a lot of my time efforts were involved with many other groups both overseas and in the USA like the National Center for Community Action for I was not solely working with the Cabazons. Ms. Meyers' report is in error for it is my son John Paul Nichols who is the Projects Director and Business Manager of the Cabazons. I discussed my work with street gangs in New York, alcohol and drug programs with the labor movement in various parts of the country and how one does acquire enemies if you expose drug pushers.

I stated to her what I had written in my letter to you, that I do feel remorse about what happened, for the dangers I created to the life and limbs of others, and for the erroneous publicity created for the victims, etc. I stated what I did was wrong and would never do anything like this again. . . .

I was told by fellow inmates that a newspaper photographs [photographer] was allowed to come in to take a photo of an empty cell in the unit were [where] I was lodged. The reporter spoke to several of the inmates, one of whom came up the next day to identify himself as "a fellow hit man" and he proceeded to report his story that could have put my life at risk. I was told by one guard the Attorney General has sent someone to Chino to ask about my case. . . .

Your honor, the reason I plead nolo contendere was because I accepted the fact that it would be treated as a plea of guilty, but I rested on the facts as presented by the arresting officers without attempting to defend my actions. As stated in my earlier letter to you, I know what I did was wrong and could have been life threatening to the persons targeted.

I never used as a defense the fact that I was approached originally by the police informants with the idea, as my purpose was other than to solicit for murder. Whatever my intent was is immaterial for the end result could have been disastrous for the people involved and I understand this and am very remorseful for it. There are no excuses and whatever you will decide is the terms of my sentence I will accept and begin to meet whatever terms and conditions you have imposed.

If I can perform community service, I will carry out the responsibility in as professional a manner as possible or if you sent me to County Jail or to a state prison, I will be a model prisoner and I will live with the probation and parole terms.

Dr. Nichols ended his letter to the court with a direct "shot across the bow" at Chino's staff psychologist:

If my behavioral patterns truly "is [are] comprehended within the personality framework of sociopathy and manic propensity" I should be given an indefinite commitment to a state mental hospital which would be equipped to deal with me and isolate me from the mainstream of society until cured.

Nichols was sentenced to a four-year prison term and served approximately 24 months. In December of 1992 and early in 1993, Dr. Nichols had two major operations. His left leg was amputated below the knee because of infection and complications from his diabetic condition and, a few weeks later, he successfully underwent double bypass heart surgery.

THE CABAZON DECISION

On March 3, 1983, the Cabazon Bingo Palace opened for business. This time the Riverside County Sheriff closed it down, the Tribe went to court, and on May 6, 1983, Judge Waters issued a preliminary injunction against the county. He also imposed a bond of $50,000 on the Tribe.

Two years later, after thwarting an attempted takeover by Wayne Reeder, Peter Zokosky, John Patrick McGuire and Jimmy Hughes—which later devolved into charges by Reeder of threats on Reeder's life by Hughes and counter-charges by Hughes—the Tribe was hit by the *20/20* Geraldo Rivera TV report (which aired while Dr. Nichols was in Chino) that gave national coverage to distortions of reality. As a result, the Tribe would suffer terrible public credibility problems until February 25, 1987.

On that day the U.S. Supreme Court ruled that high-stakes Bingo and other gaming on Indian reservations could not be regulated by state and local governments, if state law allows such forms of gaming by anyone. That decision became known all over the nation as the "Cabazon Decision." The Tribe that had fought for seven years—and four for Bingo—had finally been vindicated. As John Paul was quoted as saying in a *Desert Sun* news article the next day, "We are fairly famous in Indian country." In a 1992 interview, John Paul said:

> When we won the Supreme Court decision, we all of a sudden were legitimatized. We were legitimatized in the view of Indian tribes nationwide. We, all of a sudden, became a political force in and of itself because the Cabazon Decision became the law of the land, if you will; and so, this small little tribe of 25 members, voting members, all of a sudden had the influence of 25,000 members. We became, in fact, one of the most influential tribes in the nation. It was an amazing turnaround from going to tribal meetings before that decision to going to tribal meetings after that decision. It was almost like being ostracized and then treated overly with respect, if you will.

Art Welmas asserted, "We knew all along we have sovereign rights. It's the last thing we have on the reservation. I'm sure Indians want a piece of the American dream. It [the decision] is going to help us economically—so we can provide employment, health care and day care for our people."

A few weeks prior to the decision, Congressional Committee staff led by Congressmen and Senators from Arizona, Montana, Nevada and South Dakota were rushing to beat the Court to the punch. After the decision, Senators John Melcher (D-MT) and Tom Daschle (D-SD) predicted congressional action. Daschle was quoted in a Gannett News Service article the day after the decision to the effect that "there is going to have to be some regulation of the process." But Suzan Shawn Harjo, executive director of the National Congress of American Indians, told the press she hoped the decision meant congressional legislation was "dead. . . . I have historic inhibitions dating back to the Little Big Horn about Indian victories and what happened afterwards. Indians can't win too big without some attempt at retribution."

It was not long in coming. The Indian Gaming Regulatory Act was passed by Congress and signed into law on October 17, 1988. Senator Daniel K. Inouye (D-HI) became Chairman of the Senate Committee on Indian Affairs in January 1987. In a March 19, 1993, meeting with representatives of Indian tribal governments involved in gaming, Inouye said, "All hell broke loose," when the Supreme Court issued its Cabazon Decision. "The opponents of Indian gaming were joined in full force by the states who painted ominous pictures of impending doom if the Supreme Court ruling were allowed to stand." Inouye said the Congress felt that:

If states and tribes were going to have some interaction in the area of gaming, it had to be premised on the basis of their status as equal sovereigns. . . . And so, the notion of tribal-state compacts were proposed, whereby tribes and states would sit down together on a sovereign-to-sovereign government basis. . . . But, let us be clear about this. Even before the bill was signed into law, it became known as the "Nevada Bill." More specifically, Las Vegas interests were boasting that they deserved the credit for the provisions of the Indian Gaming Regulatory Act. The act was not then, nor has it ever been viewed, as the bill that the Indians would have wanted. Nor was it ever the committee's bill. . . .

Five years later, although expressed in different terms, the states are still seeking what they sought in 1988—namely, *they want the Congress to overturn the Supreme Court's ruling in Cabazon*—and to reverse two hundred years of federal jurisprudence which has consistently held that unless Congress expressly authorizes it, state laws do not apply on Indian lands. (Emphasis added.)

Thus, an old battle has been joined around the issue of Indian gaming. It is a battle unworthy of elected officials in a democracy, as our nation approaches the 21st century. The unworthiness is reflected in the insane statement made by Arizona's governor in 1992, when Indians resisted a raid on their gaming facilities. He assured the people and, especially the Indians, that they had no need to worry; he would make sure those who had no income or jobs as a result of closing down their facility would be able to get on welfare. This strange and seemingly racist solution was hardly a happy alternative to economic independence. Yet, even he signed a compact with Arizona tribes.

But, perhaps, the unworthiness is best exemplified by many California officials—state and local—who waged, and are still waging, a disinformation campaign while accepting campaign funds from Nevada gaming interests. In 1985 California Deputy Attorney General Rudolf Corona told a U.S. House of Representatives Interior Committee, "This state has definitely established organized crime links with some of the Indian gambling operations which are currently operating." In that same protected testimony—you can't sue someone for what they say in testimony before a congressional committee—Corona alleged "the most dramatic example of organized crime involvement is that posed in the Cabazon tribal gambling operation."

Mr. Corona and his bosses were and had been in court opposing Cabazon gaming, yet not once did his office give evidence in support of his charge where it could have been effective. The problem for the Attorney General and the Governor was the same—there was no evidence of such involvement, and in court, under oath, they would have been required to produce evidence. So, without evidence, they chose a path of dishonor, knowing the Tribe would be smeared by the press reporting Corona's protected words.

This path of dishonor was not missed by the Court, which specifically noted that the State did not allege any organized crime involvement with either the Cabazon or the Morongo tribes, both of which were plaintiffs. But, as the state knew, the Tribe's public relations would be damaged. (Later Corona would lift from the public bankruptcy documents the loan papers filed by John Paul. These papers showed the wife of Tom Marson, a noted crime figure, had loaned $50,000 to the Tribe in 1981 and had been paid back with interest, or a total of $62,500. This then became his "proof." What was never told was that Leo Durocher arranged the $50,000 loan for John Paul, who signed a personal note on behalf of the tribe, although the loan was paid back in full out of earnings from the Casino at the rate of $6,250 per month.)

In a later meeting attended by John James, Art Welmas, John Paul Nichols, Glenn Feldman and others, Corona opened the meeting by asserting, "We wear the white hats and you wear the black hats. And I don't take directions from the federal government." Since the meeting had been called to clarify the state's position regarding tribal gaming, the tribal members came close to walking out of the meeting, angered by remarks that, at the most charitably, could be called insensitive.

One year later, in a case involving the Muscogee Creek Nation of Oklahoma, the Supreme Court let stand a circuit-court ruling that granted an exemption from state sales taxes to high-stakes Bingo games run by Indian tribes. The state wanted the tribes to be forced to charge, collect and send sales taxes to the state on Bingo players. In an Associated Press report of June 28, 1988, the Appeals Court was quoted as ruling that "Patrons do not travel onto Creek lands to play bingo in order to avoid sales taxes. . . . Creek Nation bingo does not undermine the state economy or tax base. The state is not losing tax revenues it would otherwise obtain from sales made outside of tribal boundaries."

In a *Desert Sun* article, Art Welmas was quoted as hailing the decision as a great victory. "I'm glad of their decision. . . . The state has never quit trying to tax us in many different ways. . . . But we don't get anything from the state—no road improvements or help. If we did, I wouldn't mind paying taxes."

Claiming legitimate "credit" for the language in the Indian Gaming Regulatory Act (language that would allow states to take dishonorable actions if they chose), Nevada gaming interests decided to take other steps to block the growth of Indian gaming. According to a July 1992 article published in *O'Dwyers's PR Services*, a monthly public relations industry publication authored by Kevin McCauley:

> The Machiavellian side of PR is again on public display with the "outing" of a third major strategic plan by a PR firm—this one prepared by Burson-Marsteller for a group called "Coalition to Protect Communities and States' Rights". . . . Members include horse-racing and casino interests whose immediate goal was to block a potential competitor in Adelanto, California. Had Adelanto gained approval, *Indian reservations* (but not other sponsors) *would have been able to open casinos across California* . . . a big threat to Las Vegas interests. . . . The proposal to open a casino near Nevada quickly lost steam and died but not before Burson-Marsteller, working for the Coalition, had drawn up a 14-page strategic plan to defeat it. (Emphasis added.)

It is perhaps of interest to note that a son of Bing Crosby, who grew up with

Indian Gaming Commission Chairman Tony Hope, son of comedian Bob Hope, was the Burson-Marsteller person placed in charge of this disinformation campaign. It is also of interest that the office of this effort was in the same building occupied by the Indian Gaming Commission in Washington, D.C. In an editorial in the same *O'Dwyers*'s issue, the publication was pointedly critical of so-called coalitions that are really only "front groups with lofty sounding names formed to do the dirty work of a single company or industry." It then focused in like a laser beam on the Nevada gaming industries' new "coalition," charging:

> Others hide behind coalitions and use them to hammer potential competitors. For example, The Nevada Resort Association [NRA] a member of the Coalition to Protect Community & States' Rights, a Burson-Marsteller client, piously argues that approval of gambling casinos on Indian reservations in California would unleash a lot of social ills—drugs, prostitution and assorted crimes—on local communities.
>
> At the same time, two NRA members—Circus Circus Enterprises and Hilton Hotels—are lobbying furiously for approval of a gambling complex in Chicago. Does this mean NRA worries about a gambling-related crime wave spilling into Nevada from bordering California, and that gambling thugs are okay in faraway Chicago? Or, more likely, does the NRA fear Californians may choose to lose their money at casinos closer to home?

It seems noteworthy that Nevada has legal prostitution, yet gaming interests and Nevada's elected officials, the latter using tax revenues from prostitution, have the gall to include prostitution in their fear campaigns in other states. By early 1993, the backlash from the exposure of this Burson-Marsteller plan for the Nevada Resort Association resulted in a *public* turnaround by the NRA. Its new stance? It was no longer going to oppose Indian gaming. In fact, several members of NRA—including Circus Circus and Hilton—contacted tribes in and outside of California to discuss joint ventures with the tribes.

It is emphasized here that this was the *public* stance of NRA. But in politics it is always wise "to follow the money." For example, one Washington lobbyist told the author that "Nevada's U.S. Senator Reid felt he had been left hanging on a limb by this new public NRA stance on gaming." If Reid really said that and felt abandoned, it certainly did not curtail his efforts to try to eliminate Senator Inouye's committee—his colleagues stopped that—and it did not stop his attempt to overturn the Cabazon Decision or to pass legislation calling for a moratorium on expansion of Indian gaming. Nor has NRA's changed public position affected the negative actions by California's Governor or Attorney General. "Follow the money," seems the best approach that tribes can take to protect their interests.

TRIBAL SAFETY

Security is extremely important for a cash business such as a casino. The Cabazons early on recognized the need to develop an in-house professional public safety force. It began, however, with security guards. But in 1985 that changed.

In September 1992, Bruce James talked about his beginning role in tribal public safety:

Author: I read in the minutes that you have a couple of real keen interests. One is law enforcement. The other is in military history, and guns related to that. How did that come about?

Bruce: I think, at least as far as military history and guns and things, my father might have been a big influence on that because that kind of thing was always around the house, and I learned to shoot at a really early age.

Author: When and how did you decide to pursue a career in law enforcement?

Bruce: Well, I don't know if I actually decided to pursue it. At the time I got into it, the Administrator at the time, John Paul Nichols, more or less shanghaied me into the Indian Police Academy. I wasn't really thrilled with it at the time, but you know, looking back on it, it's the one thing that's changed my life. You know, I think I took a drink *once* after I got out. I haven't had a drink since.

Author: Looking at you now, I would never think that you ever had a problem with drinking.

Bruce: Well, I did at one time. You know, some people would get drunk once in a while. I'd look for an excuse, and anything that sounded like a reason to get drunk, I'd do it—two, three times a week sometimes.

Author: How did John Paul shanghai you?

Bruce: Well, he called me in the office, and said he recognized my interest in the direction of law enforcement. So we hunted around and got the paperwork going for me to attend the Indian Police Academy . . . the initial paperwork, involving a physical and everything—that started in March of 1985, and I did not know that I had been accepted for a class beginning in September of that year until the middle of August. So, they kind of let me know at the last minute that I had been accepted. I got up there in September for that class. . . .

Author: Where was this being held?

Bruce: It was in a place about 30 miles north of Tucson on I-10. It's an area that the federal government leases from this company for a Federal Law Enforcement Training Center. It's not just an Indian Police Academy, but there's quite a few government agencies that have training going on there. . . .

I was there for three and a half months. They've since expanded it. It's up to about four, four and a half months now; I'm not really sure about it. Based on some input some of these earlier classes had, they've expanded the curriculum. It was in a state of confusion when I went there because the Academy had been at Brigham City, Utah. For whatever reason, they had just a class or two before, then moved it to the Arizona facility. So, they were still getting some bugs out.

Author: Well, what was the experience like for three and half months?

Bruce: It squared me away . . . I went there with the attitude that this is my last shot to be anything in my life. At the time I was 24 years old. I wasn't qualified to be much of anything else. So, I went to the Academy with the attitude: keep my mouth shut, follow orders, you know, do what I'm told; be someplace I'm supposed to be—I'd get along fine. Which is exactly how it worked out.

Author: Was it a good experience?

Bruce: Yeah. It was very intense. There were a lot of classroom sessions, plus a lot of physical training. It was like rolling up Marine Corps boot camp and a semester of college into one. So, it was very, very intense.

Author: So, you had a full day of physical and classroom activities?

Bruce: Yeah. Most of the physical took place after supper, but most of the activity during the day was classroom, except for what you'd call practical exercises, which means they'd show you something, or demonstrate it. Then you actually performed, and you got graded on how well you did it.

Author: That was good experience?

Bruce: It definitely was. It changed my life.

Author: Were you the first member of the Tribe to go through it?

Bruce: Yeah. In the class they had Native Americans from all over the country—Mississippi, South Dakota, Wyoming, North Dakota, New Mexico, Arizona.

Author: You made some good contacts?

Bruce: Oh yeah. Everybody helped each other out. One of the superintendents at the graduation exercise commented about our class that nobody had flunked out for the very simple reason that classmates had put the fear of God into each other, telling each other, "You will not disgrace this class by flunking out!" Like, if someone was in danger of flunking, we would take him behind the classroom and inform him of what would happen if he did fail. Then, from then on, the guy would pass all his tests. Everybody helped each other. There were a few people who were (I guess you could actually call them) extra sharp on the book work and everything. There were some cadets that were marginal. They were within a few points of, say, flunking a test. They'd say, "You want this bad enough? After supper, meet me in the day room, and we'll go over the subjects on the test and everything." Near as I could tell, anybody that had a problem went.

Author: What you've described is a kind of unity that's so rare. Have you had that same kind of experience with other training since then?

Bruce: No, I haven't. I went into a supervisory course in February of 1990 at the same facility. There wasn't that type of esprit de corps, as you would say, that I had in basic training.

Author: So, you went out and got the training, and you came back.

Bruce: Well, I became basically the lone ranger, if you will—the only one the Tribe had qualified to perform those types of functions. I mean, we had security guards and people of that nature, but, as far as fully trained—I was the only one at the time.

Author: You were also a Code Enforcement Officer?

Bruce: Right.

Author: You now have a Department of Public Safety. How did that develop?

Bruce: Well, I had been an advocate of a Department of Public Safety for quite a while, and I figured we could have a more professional department, you know—higher training standards, a selection of officers—that kind of thing. I recommended that to the Project manager who was John Paul Nichols back then. It was not a priority item. There wasn't a real strong need for it at the time. Within the past couple of years, it's really come along. It's just like an explosion, if you will, of progress as far as a formalized department. Currently it's along the lines of a police department, and in my estimation, it would stack up quite favorably to any local agency as far as organization and quality of officers—that kind of thing.

Paul Hare would agree with Bruce James regarding the professionalism and quality of the members of his Department of Public Safety. In an extensive interview in April 1993, Paul described the department he heads, its mission, qualifications and problems in considerable detail:

Author: How did you become affiliated or associated with the Tribe? Give us kind of a historical perspective.

Paul: Well, after retiring from law enforcement with the City of Palm Springs, I opened a private investigation firm here in the Coachella Valley. In the course of doing private investigations, I was retained by the Tribe in approximately 1984 or 1985 to do a couple of employee-related investigations, and to do their background investigations. That's how I first met Dr. John and his sons, and now Mark and tribal members and Council.

We had discussions from time to time regarding creating a law-enforcement entity for the Tribe. Eventually, the Tribe became economically independent enough where they had the moneys to provide those services. At that point, I was asked to come on board and create a public safety entity which now comprises approximately 26 men who are all either former police officers and/or fire personnel.

We have three fire engines and one emergency response truck. We have four patrol cars, and we have actually three divisions. We have a security division, which takes care of the casino activities; we have a law enforcement division, which will eventually take care of the housing area to be developed and patrol the properties; and we have a fire department.

Author: I've heard that you have some ex-FBI agents and officers with various other law enforcement backgrounds.

Paul: Well, we've had an ex-Secret Service agent who was assigned to the Ford detail, and because of the intensive traveling he resigned his position with the Secret Service and came to work here. He worked here over a year, when he decided again to go back in federal service.

Author: That is the Presidential service?

Paul: Yes, sir.

Author: President Ford?

Paul: That's right. . . . I had a former chief of police working for me, Donald Chance, who used to be the chief in Beaumont, [Calif.]; we have several former lieutenants; former sergeants from all over California—from LAPD [Los Angeles Police Department] to the Los Angeles Sheriff's Office to Santa Monica PD to Santa Cruz PD—all over.

Author: In other words, you have a force which allows you the ability to check out the background of the folks who come to work at the casino, for example?

Paul: Well, we do backgrounds of those people that come to work here. We have a process where we have computer access to public information files that are available to us for that purpose, specifically criminal convictions, credit records, UCC [Uniform Commercial Code] filing, federal tax liens, state tax liens, to determine if a person has filed bankruptcy, what his financial picture looks like—and this is all public record. We do this specifically for those people who work in and around the casino. But, we have a three-class-type structure background.

For instance, Class 1 would be for those people engaged in housekeeping services: waiters and waitresses, those types of things—jobs that don't entail a whole lot of exposure.

Class 2 would be those people who are engaged as cashiers, casino dealers—people who handle money in our count room.

Class 3 is obviously management, top executive people, and that entails even a door knock, going to their former neighbors and employers to check out their backgrounds.

Author: The reason I ask the question is because of the negative press which says the Tribe is involved with organized crime.

Paul: It's ironic that you say that, because even the FBI in federal testimony in Congress disputed that fact. Certainly there has been an attempt here in the State of California, but that was caught before it even was actually created. I mean it was in the talk stages, and those folks were indicted in a hurry down in San Diego. And, as I understand, they have some convictions. But in today's time, gaming is a showcase and people are watching, and it must be very uncomfortable for organized crime to try to make inroads into the gaming profession because of that. And certainly here we are very cognizant of that fact, and we do these backgrounds as a matter of daily routine. We have had some people apply for work here that were less than desirable, and we've let them go because of that. But we do have access to those records. Any Indian tribe has access to those records. It is public record, and it's just a matter of knowing how to do it, obviously, and I don't see why that can't multiply throughout the industry.

Author: In other words, the message should be clear that you have a pretty clean operation?

Paul: Obvious to anyone but a fool! I'm sure they have to know that we are looking at these people and they'd have to know that we are trying to police ourselves. I don't think I'm saying that I would object to a State Gaming Commission. Certainly, their assistance would be very helpful, but at this point we have learned to police ourselves. I sort of look at the picture here as a child in the inception. In the 1980s (through trick or deceit or whatever term you would like to use) the Tribe, out of the generosity of its heart and in an attempt with the enthusiasm to go into this business, were duped by a couple of people—one, a renowned celebrity. But, once that was discovered (which as I understand was only a couple of months later), immediately they fired these gentlemen, and that should have given some indication to someone that they were trying to clean up their act.

And then the track record for the next 10 years has been absolutely whistle clean. So, there again, what else can you say? That stands for itself.

Author: I understand that the person you are obviously referring to—Rocco Zangari—had no conviction at the time that they discovered his alleged background?

Paul: That's true. However, those folks that oppose gaming have used this as a matter of negativity imposed on gaming. But that's public, and that's the media. We all know what that is.

Author: Right. Give us a panoramic view of your background in law enforcement.

Paul: I started in 1962 in Los Angeles with the Sheriff's Department. I got out of law enforcement for about four years, went back to college and got my degree and came back. My mother and father had retired here in Palm Springs and came back, and, while I was visiting, I decided I would like to go back into law enforcement in Palm Springs and work there until I retired. So, I've been in the valley for about 21 years now. I enjoy living here.

Author: So, you've got about 25 years in law enforcement?

Paul: Well, I had eight years in the Air Force; I was an air policeman. So, I guess you could say a little over 30.

Author: Let me ask you another question about press coverage. The Tribe had been smeared with the death of one of its former officers, Fred Alvarez. From a law-enforcement point of view, how do you think that situation was handled?

Paul: There was an inference, and I say inference because I never found anything to confirm the allegations, that Mr. Alvarez had some type of information which he had planned to review regarding some internal skimming of funds and/or embezzlement. There is purported to have been a tape made by a local reporter which no one has ever confirmed, and that tape, as far as I know, has never surfaced.

There was a former security officer for the Tribe who made some allegations which have never been corroborated. The investigation into Mr. Alvarez's death is today active and continuing. There has never been any arrest made. There have been innuendoes coming out of the local sheriff's office as to the suspect, etc. There have been rumors of a former district attorney's investigator being threatened because he was going to reveal the suspects. And all of this is bullshit—pardon the expression.

As an investigator having a background in law enforcement, I can tell you that some of the allegations were at best allegations, but I think they were libelous. I think if I had been Dr. Nichols, I would have considered getting an attorney and filing suit against the County. My motto is, put up or shut up, and to this point we are looking at, what—12 years after the homicide now—13 years. There's never been an arrest; there's never been any formal interviewing of Dr. Nichols; and, as I understand, the County now is very reluctant to reveal any of that investigation in any shape or form. However, I understand it because it is an ongoing investigation, and there is no statute of limitations on homicide. So, from where we sit, that could remain open for the next 100 years.

There have been, however, some indications by various people indicating that Mr. Alvarez was a heroin addict, that he had several dealings with unsavory people in the area regarding illicit drugs, and that he may have been mentally unstable at the time. The female who was also murdered at the time was a girlfriend, wife type, common-law, of a person who had just gotten out of prison, and it was my understanding that she was living with Mr. Alvarez, cohabitating with him in a residence.

At least if I was conducting an investigation, I certainly would want to be looking at this person. I don't think that ever happened, but the inference has always been atrocities were occurring over here on the Indian reservation. I think you are looking at the ignorance of some people in the community and perhaps I'm being kind, but that's bigotry at its finest; it's much easier to point a finger than to prove it. I think at this point, as an investigator, I would say either do it or get off the pot.

Author: The thing that struck me is I've heard all kinds of rumors that Fred was not only a user of drugs, but that he had marijuana shipped to him from Hawaii to a radio station here in Indio, and that he was a dealer. The thing that has puzzled me is I've never seen that in the press, in all the stories that I've read.

Paul: It doesn't fit. It doesn't fit the picture, and the name of the game is to sell newspapers. You never see in the paper where Fred used to come into the council meeting in his underwear—you never see that! You never see Fred suggesting digging a big hole out here and having a wine bar for all his biker friends so they can drive in and out of it. We sit here and laugh at that, but he was very serious about doing things like that. None of this type of conduct has ever come to view, and you wonder why. So, I'm asking the question also: Why hasn't the media revealed some of this other, bizarre behavior at best?

Author: Would you kind of give us a picture of where you see the Department of Public Safety in the future and its whole relationship to the State of California and the federal government, and that whole range of relationships.

Paul: The basis for my beliefs for the expansion of the Public Safety Department is very simple, and that is to provide a parity of law enforcement to the tribal members of this reservation, and specifically because we are developing a housing area that will contain 3,000 to 4,000 people—those being predominantly non-Indian persons. Historically, we are going to be creating problems that we do not have here at this point. We are now seeing an influx of gang activity on reservations that, heretofore, we haven't. Because of the entrepreneurial development of the Tribe, we are getting and dealing with 98 percent of persons who are non-Indian. Historically, tribes have developed a police or public safety entity to enforce rules and regulations on Indian tribal members. But, as I say, because of the entrepreneurial development, the entertainment that is being created on the reservation and the housing that is being created on the reservation, we now have those problems that are prevalent in the outside communities, here on the reservation.

The problem is, legally we have no way to enforce the California Penal Code on the reservation. In the state of California, the Attorney General believes that they [the State] have exclusive criminal jurisdiction on reservation property, which is exactly opposite from the [federal] solicitor general's opinion that Indian tribes have concurrent jurisdiction. Now, let's say we even have concurrent jurisdiction here; we still don't have the power to arrest non-Indian persons.

So, what I'm trying to do is to get the federal government to recognize members of our Public Safety Department as federal law enforcement officers, for the purpose of enforcing the California Penal Code in the housing area and on reservation properties, which will hopefully curtail and cancel any liability suits that could be filed against the Tribe.

Author: You have a special problem. Most people think that when you say reservation, you have this one big area with boundaries. But you don't have that.

Paul: That's true. We have three different parcels.

Author: Describe the problem.

Paul: We have three parcels of land separated by 13 miles. On the furthest property, which is in Mecca, we have a biomass cogeneration plant. It's being developed as an industrial park, and in the not-too-distant future we are going to have a lot of commercial business down there.

In the second parcel, it is an unincorporated island of reservation trust land in the middle of a city.

And the third parcel is where the gaming casino is. In the not-too-distant future, we will again have a recreational park; we'll have an expansion on our casino; we'll have a lake, an amphitheater, a ballpark, an amusement park, etc., etc.

But those problems relate to the problem of having to traverse county and city roads from one parcel to the other. If you are going to give your public safety officer the job of enforcing the rules and regulations on reservation property, you must give him the proper tools to do so. That includes a police car, a badge, a gun, a pair of handcuffs, a red light, a pair of spotlights, etc., etc.

Author: How do you deal with hot pursuits?

Paul: Well, I think . . .

Author: Even hot pursuit of a non-Indian.

Paul: I think that's a question that's being analyzed throughout the state because hot pursuits or any type of pursuit have at times caused tragic results. There again, we are looking at how a split-second judgment must take place, and that's a judgment that's given, and the responsibility, to a police officer: Do you shoot, or don't you shoot? Do you pursue or don't you pursue? And if you pursue, what do you pursue under; what set of rules do you have?

Author: Let me give you a for instance. Let's say a group of guys come here and decide they want to rob the casino and they snatch some money; they try to escape—these are non-Indians. What legally can your Public Safety people do?

Paul: Well, legally, we can do what any citizen can do.

Author: Citizen's arrest?

Paul: Yes sir. However, we have the equipment that an average citizen does not have. Specifically though, the best and most proven method is to observe and report, and that's what I trained my people to do is observe and report. And with the communications we have today, I think we can get these people apprehended in a very short time.

Author: But your emphasis is on prevention?

Paul: Absolutely. Of course. We are looking at protecting those people, some 500,000 visitors annually, who come out here to enjoy our gaming and our entrepreneurial and entertaining enterprises. We are providing a service, and that service is to provide protection for the family that comes here, their vehicle, their person, their belongings—and that's what we do. And we've been very successful at it.

Author: So, how do you solve the problem, for example the problem coming up of the housing development? What, in the best of all worlds, should be done?

Paul: Well, there is no doubt in my mind, and certainly no doubt in the tribal members' minds, that the qualifications of our Public Safety officers far exceed any federal standards and meet the highest standards of California. We feel that, obviously, this is an innovative mission that we are all taking. It has never happened in the State of California before. It has happened, however, in the State of Florida, State of Minnesota, State of Wisconsin, and it's now happening in the State of Washington . . . a cooperative agreement between law enforcement agencies to recognize the fact that Indian tribes have the right to law enforcement by their own means if they can afford it. In our case, the Tribe can afford it. It has made a budget for it.

We have hired people who are extremely qualified, and those people who are standing back looking with chagrin on their faces are those who are afraid of losing an ounce of power, when, in fact, what they are getting is a good neighbor. They are getting additional manpower in this time of budgetary overruns, manpower shortages. . . . It's going to get even worse. It's just a myriad of problems, but it's a reality in this day and age. California is in tough shape, and what we have here is . . . a professional Public Safety Department that is willing to enter into a mutual aid pact with our surrounding communities, and provide the additional manpower in the moment of emergencies.

We are still looked at as having association with that old cliché and the bigotry toward Indian reservations. And, in some cases, I find that the people we deal with would rather have us sitting by the railroad track selling our bowls. Unfortunately, that's as simplistic as I can get—but it's the truth.

Author: Describe your capability in terms of fires, in terms of medical emergencies.

Paul: As a matter of fact, we just found out recently that the BIA has no contract with any of the local fire services to provide for structure fires. That simply means that they do not have to respond on the reservation to a structure fire.

Author: Houses burn down, and they have no responsibility?

Paul: That's true.

Author: A building of any kind burns down?

Paul: That's true.

Author: But if a field is burning?

Paul: They will respond. Yes. It doesn't make much sense, does it? No. There is a contract in place wherein the federal government reimburses cities and counties for fighting wild fires, grass fires. There is no contract for structure fires, which has necessitated this Tribe provide its own fire engine.

We now have three fire trucks and one emergency response truck. One truck is only a 500-gallon pumper, which we are going to utilize for grass fires only. It's a four-wheel drive, and it was used by the United States Air Force. It has about 26,000 miles on it—runs like a champ. It's the type of truck that you can take into the brush lands without any problem of getting stuck or not getting there.

Our other trucks provide structure protection, and we want to use them as proactive vehicles. In other words, we want to be able to go out and inspect the various commercial enterprises and make sure that they are complying with the fire codes. We want to be able to know that we can attack a structure fire, be there first and get some water on it until we can get some help. And I think that's what we are looking at at this point.

The people who would be manning the truck have many years of fire experience, and in the case of Howard Hatch, he has over 12 years. We have another gentleman who retired from fire fighting after 22 years. The third gentleman has over 15 years of experience, so we have some real pros that are going to be handling and training the other Public Safety officers.

Thus, the term "Public Safety." We are going to intertwine those law-enforcement duties and the fire suppression, so that each officer is capable of doing the elementary duties of each job. As we grow, obviously those jobs and duties will be more complex, but we will always have these plans. We will always have one person who is a professional engineer firefighter on duty in the housing area at all times with the engine itself, and those people capable of backing up that particular engineer in the field should a fire occur.

Author: Is there any kind of certification that the BIA, Department of Interior could give your officers that you don't have now?

Paul: Well, we have discussed this with the Bureau of Indian Affairs and they seem to be handcuffed by the opinion of our [California] attorney general—and that is that they have exclusive criminal jurisdiction on the reservation. And so, whether they made us federal peace officers or not, it wouldn't do any good. I do not share that opinion.

Obviously, having gone back to Wisconsin and seeing what has happened with the Oneida Tribe, they are now all cross-deputized with the two local sheriff's departments. They help the sheriff's departments with their calls, they are out there in the field doing an active job, and everyone has a perfect marriage back there. The local sheriff even admits that he was bigoted to begin with, and had he not cut himself with a saw and needed medical emergency [care]—and that emergency [care] came from a tribal officer who was only minutes away and saved his life—he today may still have shared that same opinion. But the tribal police officer saved his life. He was there, and that is the reality of the situation. We are here; we are going to remain here, we are going to be as professional as possible—so look at us.

Author: So one route in this state, would it be cross-deputization by the county sheriff?

Paul: Well, we have talked to the county sheriff or his representative, his commander down here—Frank Andrews. Frank related to us orally that once we get a federal certification (in other words what Frank is saying is once the federal government recognizes you as a law enforcement entity), then we will [recognize you]; we'll share our resources with you. So, what we have to do is we have to motivate someone in the federal bureaucracy up there to say—look, we have a need and that need is a housing area with about 3,000 or 4,000 non-Indian people that are living on reservation land that have no law enforcement. So we are in a damned-if-you-do, damned-if-you-don't situation at this point. And, it behooves the Tribe, and it behooves me, to use every effort possible to get this federal certification. As a matter of fact, we have made some inroads; we have our second candidate who is graduating this next week, May 8th [1993], from the Federal Police Academy over in Artesia, New Mexico. I think that, in itself, is a victory of acceptance that they took one of our people over there to train. We are certainly going to pick his brain when he gets back. As it turns out, he is graduating at the top of his class. So we are sending some good people over there.

But, I don't understand. There is a question in my mind: Why in the heck they don't understand what we have? It's not as if we suddenly said, "Well, we've got 12 security guards that we want to make policemen." It's not that. We have the purpose and we have the mission, and we have the professional people. We are trying to be good neighbors.

COLMAC PLANT/INDUSTRIAL PARK

As Paul mentioned, on that part of the reservation developing into an industrial park, an energy-generating plant is now operating. Colmac is a clean, energy-producing plant that burns agricultural waste products and produces enough electricity to meet the needs of about 45,000 housing units. Like every other project the Cabazons have developed, it took seven years and a lot of battles with the local/state officials to bring this plant on line. The Colmac project began on the administrative watch of John Paul Nichols:

John Paul: In 1985 we approached a firm called Colmac Energy who was attempting to site a power plant in Coachella, California, and we suggested to them that there were some fee advantages to doing business with an Indian reservation.

Author: How did you come to approach them?

John Paul: There was a story in the newspaper. I can't remember if there was a rumor, that we heard that somebody named Sandy Walker—who was the Colmac person out of Los Angeles, California, who was really trying to put this thing together—that they had an option. I think that's how we heard [it]. I heard there was a large option for this large enterprise in the Coachella Industrial Park—45 acres. We suggested that—our hook [to Colmac] was—why pay option fees up the kazoo if you can go through this process on Indian land? With a local government you will have a governmental entity that will require "X" permits, as we will, but it [the government] is still going to be politically sensitive [in regard] to your project. We are going to look at this project at least as hard as they during the period before the permit phase, and, if it does not deserve it, we will say no, based on the facts, not on fears—not on whether someone is going to get elected.

That started the process that culminated in 1991—Colmac essentially powering up the plant. It was a very different change of pace in that we were attempting to diversify cash-and-carry business and retail-type businesses—commercial businesses to large-scale heavy industrial businesses—on a section of the reservation. We were doing that to diversify and not be so dependent on enterprises that were so, how can I call it, controversial in nature.

Again, I believe we underestimated the extent of controversy that business [Colmac] was going to generate. The controversy from my perspective had very little to do with the facts, and had much to do with jurisdictional power. Once again, a battle was joined with the County of Riverside (our nemesis, if you will), and the same Supervisor—"Corky" Larson—that we were fighting in the Supreme Court battle, and, in fact, who was embarrassed in the Supreme Court battle when they lost. I believe this caused them [the County of Riverside and Larson] to fight the Colmac project much harder than they would have otherwise . . . from a jurisdictional standpoint.

Basically, Colmac, in my view, ended up being reviewed far more closely and deeply than it would have been off the reservation, because of the fact that it was on the reservation with immediate assumptions totally unfounded, but nonetheless being "you Indians don't know what you're doing; you're a bunch of uneducated Indians, therefore nobody is looking at this project. It can't possibly be [being] regulated; and there must [certainly] be no impact statement—you can't be having any experts look at this sort of thing; you are just going to go out there and pollute." An immediate assumption was made, and the fight started. There was no attempt to really cooperate, no attempt to say, "well, let us be part of a panel." Nobody was willing to say "you've got a right to do this, but we would like to participate in the process." Instead it was "you guys are trying to make a pigsty out of the valley; you are trying to create a major pollutant out here," and all the rhetoric started.

Now we had learned some lessons, one of which was that sometimes just communicating, overly communicating, will sensitize the community to the fact that there are two sides to the story. We felt that public relations was critical. So, I guess we started playing the game a little differently. We also enlisted the help of the Bureau of Indian Affairs from the very, very beginning. From the "get go" we said that we would comply with all the local, state and federal environmental regulations, and we said to everybody that the EPA [Environmental Protection Agency] would either permit this project or not. If the EPA permits it on an air basis, we will then consider giving a conditional use permit, but, if it doesn't give it an air permit, then there isn't a chance in heck that it will get a tribal conditional use permit.

The BIA, not us, was going to run the environmental-impact-statement process, which ended up being far more cumbersome and expensive than if the County had run it. In fact (and we were not going to issue the conditional use permit unless the Bureau was satisfied), we wouldn't allow them to permit construction until the Bureau was satisfied. And the Tribe had to believe, specifically, that the project had merit. Last, but not least, even if those agencies permitted it, if the Tribe ultimately felt that it was not going to be in its own best interests, and if it was really going to damage the local pristine environment (which they and we have lived in for many, many more years than the people who had been complaining about this thing), the Tribe would have denied a conditional use permit.

Colmac now is opened and is operating, is not a blight on the environment, and is not—the greatest fears—burning garbage; in fact, it is a model plant. I believe anybody who would objectively look at the plant would say the same thing, and it's a much cleaner burn than what many other jurisdictions consider, including the County of Riverside, which are garbage burners—which we would not permit and did not want to permit on the reservation.

CHANGING OF THE GUARD

Within two years after the Supreme Court decision of 1987, the Cabazons would have another changing of the guard—of its Tribal Chairman and Administrator, the loss of both of which would be emotionally painful for the tribe's leadership and majority membership.

Art Welmas had been a strong force for progress in the tribe and part of its leadership for a dozen or more years. Even before being elected to any office, he had been appointed by the elected officers to represent the Tribe in state and national Indian organizations. He was known among the members as one who stood, and stood tall.

During the period of the Tribe's greatest triumphs and greatest trials, Welmas would always seem to meet the test. He and his non-Indian friend, Dr. Nichols, comprised a daring team. Neither was afraid to try new things, venturing out to expand the Tribe's horizons, with full knowledge that their enemies within and without would try anything to defeat them. As Elisa Welmas, Art's daughter, said, "We all owe where we are and what we have today to two people—my father, and Dr. John [Nichols]. None of this would exist without their early leadership."

Art, like his partner Dr. Nichols, also suffered the loss of his wife. And those who know him best say that he, too, reached out for self-destruction. He too seemed to have lost his rudder, and perhaps his center.

On May 3, 1989, the General Council met and one item on the agenda was election of officers. Instead of a re-election, the Tribe turned to long-time Secretary-Treasurer John James for Tribal Chairmanship. Elected with James were his daughter Brenda, as First Vice Chairman; Charles Welmas, Second Vice Chairman; Virginia Welmas-Nichols, Secretary-Treasurer; and Elisa Rosales Welmas, Art's daughter, as Liaison to the General Council.

One month earlier, in preparation for that momentous moment, the Business Committee approved a new officer position. It was that of Tribal Elder, and was designed to be a position of honor. It was the first provision the Tribe had made for retirement. The Tribal Elder had to be a retired person who had served 10 years as a tribal officer. The benefits included a lifetime annual salary of $45,000 with 5 percent annual increments, a new automobile with upkeep financed by the Tribe, and representation of the Tribe at Indian functions throughout the country. The Elder would be expected to share his wisdom and the Tribe's history with young tribal members. The position was a position of honor, and only two members qualified—Art Welmas and John James.

Nine days after his re-election defeat, the Business Committee met and approved Art as Tribal Elder, authorizing the start of his pension salary. But, tragically, Art's reach for self-destruction would end with his loss of his position of honor and being barred from tribal affairs and benefits for a 10-year period.

His son John was asked to relate what had happened to his father:

John: Well, it was a long time coming. It wasn't like it happened overnight and was a surprise to me, you know. Basically, he just started thinking for himself, and not for everybody else. He had everybody's trust through the whole Tribe—everybody, including myself, Virginia, and my sister, Lisa. Everybody followed him and looked up to him. Then, he went off! I guess he couldn't handle it; it went to his head or something. He just started doing for himself. I mean, you know, it seems like he was getting everything, and everybody else was left out. And when you would ask for something it was always a negative thing. When he didn't get re-elected, is that what you're asking about?

Author: Yes.

John: That didn't bug me at all, because at that time I was already set in my own mind because nobody was telling me what to think or anything like that, and I could see what he was doing. That's basically why I didn't vote for him.

Author: When did he change? I mean, was there any special event that took place that caused the change?

John: That caused the change in him? In my way of looking at it, I would say it was after my mother passed away—not very long after that.

It happened really quick. He took a downfall, you know, because he was married to her for almost 40 years, and then to be by himself—because all of us were grown. We had left the house, and he really didn't have anybody. Well, he really had everybody to turn to; you know what I mean? So, he met up with Vader, who is his wife now. In no more than five months she was already trying to snag him. I guess that's the word I want to use. After she did that . . . I mean Vader was his everything. Vader took him out of that little dark hole, what have you; you know—his hurt. Then he started putting everything towards her. That's when he started turning on the Tribe. Some things we didn't mind, but he was getting . . . a little bit carried away. I guess that's why everybody said it, and everybody got mad and really turned against him, and just said, "We're not going to put up with it anymore."

Author: In your view, after he was defeated, why did he join the opposition after he was declared the Elder with a handsome pension of $45,000 a year for life?

John: Well, there too, politics are politics. I know, he always told me to try to make up my mind with who to like and what have you. I never really listened. And one he was really concerned about was Linda Streeter[-Dukic]. "Don't listen to her. She'll get you in trouble. Don't listen to her"—this and that. I said, "Fine." So, I never did. I never liked her—you know, just because he told me not to like her, I guess.

After he retired, he was getting money. He got his car; everything was fine. He didn't have to work. He got more money than any of us ever made, you know, for the year, and he had it great. Then, I guess Linda Streeter[-Dukic] came along and started filling his head up . . . "I'll get you back in office. You'll be tribal leader again. You'll be this; you'll be that." Like I said before, Linda Streeter[-Dukic] has a way of talking to people and making them believe what she says. He believed her, and after all this time—with him telling me not to listen to her—he listened to her, and he's where he's at now. That's what I feel. I feel that if she didn't come around and talk to him, he would still be getting his retirement. He'd still have his car. He'd still have everything, and still have somewhat of the respect he had when he left—not much, but it was still some. But now, I don't think he's got any right now, you see.

Author: So you attribute it to Linda rather than Vader?

John: I think him not getting re-elected—it's kind of a two-sided thing: him not getting re-elected—I think that's attributable to Vader; him getting the sanctions and his money pulled away and all that—that's attributable to Linda. That's how I feel about it.

The future would present the Cabazon world with a strange sight indeed. Art Welmas would join the dissidents against whom he had fought for so many years, those whom he himself had called "turncoats" and worse. In happier times, he had proposed that a videotape recording should be made of them and their actions for the Tribe's posterity. In joining them, Art made war against his own children.

The other changing of the guard witnessed the resignation of John Paul Nichols. His decision to leave seemed like the second of a one-two punch to some of the tribal members. After a few days more than 10 years of running the tribal enterprises, it appeared to many that he, like Art, had always been there. And there was some truth to that since there was, in fact, no business entity here before he came—just an office being shared by the Tribe and his father's consultant businesses. With John Paul came Al Pearlman and the financing of the cigarette venture.

John Paul had arrived on June 1, 1979. As he describes, when he came "there were no buildings on the reservation whatsoever. There was, I think, a mobile home or a trailer on a section of the reservation owned by Joe Benitez, and an older home owned by Willie Callaway, the then Vice Chairman, on his piece of land—nothing on tribal land. No facilities, no water, no development whatsoever—just dry desert land."

Later, John Paul spoke of his decision to resign, the factors that led up to that decision and tribal reaction:

The last, but not least, catalytic event that occurred during my tenure was the progressive decline, I'll call it, of Art Welmas. Art—you have heard me speak of him as being creative, willing to try; had his eyes and ears open (although he was an alcoholic all his life; is still an alcoholic—I'm a recovering alcoholic, so I can speak with a little expertise). Art progressively, from 1984, got worse to the point that he used to binge on weekends, and we'd sober him, to the point where he was drinking every day. I spoke with him many times about getting help, especially after I personally experienced some help, but could not get him to. Some of his children—who went into treatment and are sober, recovering alcoholics today—attempted to get him into a system.

His wife of many years died and created sorrow and pain within him. He became associated with another woman, who he eventually married, who is also a relatively heavy consumer of alcohol. In fact, he was going in a downward spiral and became very egocentric—was not listening to his constituents, tribal members that voted for him every four years, including his own children. He was soliciting private bills to be paid with tribal funds, exhibiting basically threatening behavior—do it "my way or the highway"—was bringing white squatters on the reservation against the wishes of the majority, refusing to obey tribal ordinances that he, in fact, submitted years earlier (that he, in fact, made motions for and voted on) and now was saying, "well, I don't want any of that." When confronted by this—not by me—but, in fact, by the members of the Council, his reaction was basically "screw you."

The political mood of the Tribe was that Art was going to be out, and, in fact, that's exactly what happened. In May of 1989 there was a vote where Art lost 13 to 2. He only had two votes. In fact, the past dissidents for once joined as a whole with the remainder of the Tribe to vote Art out as the Tribal Chairman, and John James, who was the long-time Secretary-Treasurer, was elected Chairman. All of Art's children except Treasure voted against him because they could see the condition that their father was in. I had made a decision because of the fact that, during this whole period (the two months leading up to this) I was physically threatened and verbally threatened. My wife and my child were physically and verbally threatened. My job had changed dramatically . . . I was spending full time in trying to maintain tribal authority, because I realized that the Tribe—that all the economic gains that the Tribe had made over the years, were threatened; there wouldn't be any future left if, in fact, the Tribe would become fractious to a point where it would become 6 to 6, 6 to 7—it would be a dysfunctional Tribe.

What I really like doing is managing business, and I understand that every business has its own politics, so to speak, its own culture. But within a certain context, it's civil. The context that I was now managing the Tribe within was not civil, and in fact my wife said, "What do you need this for?" In retrospect, I had to agree with her. I didn't need it. I had a daughter and I had a wife, and I was bringing tension and stress home. I was a recovering alcoholic and had been sober for a few years, but on the other hand that's a fragile thing, and I didn't want to risk that.

I had to convince them (the Business Committee) that I wanted to leave, but I had to also convince them that Mark was the guy that should replace me, and there was not necessarily consensus in that. For one, Mark didn't know if he wanted to replace me, because he understood the political implications of the decision and he understood what the job did to you. You can see it, and he had his own concerns whether he would want it. So, that was number one—I had to see if Mark wanted the job. Ultimately he did, and has done an excellent job. Two, I had to convince six members of the Business Committee that Mark was qualified for the job. That was difficult, in all fairness. Whereas there was loyalty to the family and loyalty to the fact that "John Paul" has been with us for many years and worked it by hook or by crook. (Dad had lost his moral influence because of his problems of 1985. He wasn't disliked, but he didn't have influence. When I say influence, I mean the power to suggest to somebody something, without being rejected. He lost that; in fact that's the biggest thing he lost when he got out.)

Part of the deal that ended up being carved, if you will, was that I was to continue on a consulting basis for some indefinite period of time as Mark got established. That role has changed dramatically. I used to come out here [to the tribal offices] far more often. I would come up for four or five days at a time, and I was dealing more with what I would call business-sensitive issues, tribal political issues, and political-advice issues to the majority Council members. That's now changed to the point where I am now basically writing grants. The consulting role is now more of a technician, if you will, which is fine since Mark and the existing Business Committee have established themselves as the authority on the reservation and done so comfortably.

But, that was catalytic, in the sense that it required a lot of consensus-building on the part of those Committee members, because the initial inclination everybody had was—"Let's hire somebody else." There was initial anger towards me as some said, "Wait a second; we just went through this whole shift where we now have a new Chairman. We just went through all this and now you're leaving?" I had to say, "Guys, you have to understand that there's a time for somebody to leave."

In mid-June 1989, Mark became the Tribe's Chief Executive Officer. Twenty-one months later, he got his bath of fire from the dissidents. Linda Streeter-Dukic, during this period, came to the reservation seeking work, she said. A job was created for her. After a few weeks, and after failing to talk anyone into buying her a new white Cadillac, she left. In late March 1991, the dissidents launched their take-over attempt—what they themselves would call a "coup."

The "coup" attempt failed when they lost on every issue in a General Council meeting on April 30, 1991. During that meeting, resolutions were also passed to set up committees to investigate charges regarding Streeter-Dukic and Art Welmas.

On July 16, 1991, testimony was heard before the General Council on charges laid against Streeter-Dukic and Art Welmas. Each was represented by counsel. The decision of the General Council was that each should be fined $50,000, and that Welmas should be barred from all tribal activities and benefits for a period of 10 years with 20 years identical non-participation for Streeter-Dukic. What would be especially painful to the two of them was their inability to participate in a $35,000 per capita distribution of funds arranged by the Tribal Council.

In May 1991, the BIA approved the Tribe's sale and transfer to the Tribe of the purchase price of an easement to the State of California through tribal land. The Tribe voted each adult member a share of $35,000, with the remainder of the purchase price going to trust accounts for each non-adult member and a tribal-enterprise-development fund.

The dissidents appealed to the BIA and to the Board of Indian Appeals, the latter appeal from a February 19, 1992, letter from the Sacramento, California, Area Director, Bureau of Indian Affairs. That letter informed the dissidents that the sanctions imposed on them by their Tribe were . . . "purely internal Tribal matters that involve no BIA action and/or approval . . . and that their . . . appeal [did] not meet the test as an adverse enrollment action [under the law] since the BIA did not make the determination as to enrollment or disenrollment of the appellants, and, furthermore, the appellants have not been removed from Tribal membership rolls, only barred from Tribal affairs and benefits." The Board of Indian Appeals ruled in favor of the Tribe and against the dissidents in a October 20, 1993, final decision.

Mark Nichols was asked to talk about becoming CEO, what he has tried to do from that position, his views as to the strengths that have kept the leadership majority intact and what he saw as the future:

The chronology of my experience here, my participation out here, was that I became a [cardroom card] dealer, and after I became a dealer, I went to work in the cage as cashier for a short while. Then I was given an assignment as a foreman on the graveyard shift, and eventually I became the foreman on the graveyard shift.

After that, when the Bingo operation opened, I became the Bingo manager, and basically had the hands-on experience—the creation of forms, etc.—and really ran that business from the very start for the first couple of years there. Then I had a little hiatus, came back, and went to work as a Director of Operations, which is a little bit broader. Well, I was Director of Operations and comptroller, and I was given responsibility over the entire operation over there [at the cardroom/casino], in addition to the accounting and so forth, where John was the general manager and Tribal Administrator.

When my Dad went to prison, that created a big vacuum, so John Paul filled that vacuum and proceeded to get involved in the grant and political side of things and the development side of things—where I was left to run the operations because I was willing, ready and able. I mean, that was it. Nobody else was volunteering at that point. It was done with the understanding that I would be given a try. Eventually, after a period of time and after my father returned and Art Welmas started developing his own set of problems and losing his constituency, there were going to be some major changes that were going to take effect at that time. I would say that the environment was very uncertain. John Paul went to school while he was working, and completed his master's degree.

I had undergone a religious conversion at the time, and I was reassessing and reevaluating my ideology and my goals in life. I felt that I had abandoned something I used to have. I think earlier we talked about my belief that you couldn't really participate in society yet retain your idealism and your sanity, your separateness and your understanding of the insignificance of material—ultimate material gain. I felt that I had lost that and I had, in fact, gotten too involved with work which led to my experiencing some heart problems and so forth. So, I was at a point in my life where I told John Paul that I was going to discontinue working here.

John Paul . . . told me, "Gosh, I'm going to go too," because he didn't feel there was a certainty here. I didn't feel that [way], but he said, "Gosh, if you go, I won't go." Yet I didn't feel that was ultimately where it would go. So, I felt that I would be willing, and it was kind of funny because I prayed over this issue and felt that I needed to divest myself—the involvement in all the hatred and fighting and all the things that were going on. [And yet], lo and behold, the Creator was turning not half of it over to me—but *all* of it over to me.

There was this bridge, and I made this decision, as corny as this may sound, that I felt that I could make a difference in terms of making this be not something that was solely motivated by financial gain—but that it could once again become what it started out to be, which was in my view, a true revolutionary crusade. At that point, we had some discussion. John Paul and I talked about the fact that he wanted to go, that he had opportunities. I didn't have as many options in terms of where I might go, since my wife wanted to stay in the local area and look at different options here because I have several marketable skills, but not necessarily the educational credentials.

So we sat down and penciled out what would be potentially the reorganization where, at least during the transitional period, things could be maintained and then we would see where it would go from there. When I say "we"—I mean that *I* would have to see where it went from there and see how it all shakes out. So then, basically, John got employment elsewhere, and we presented it to the new Tribal Chairman which was John James. The deal was, "John, what do you have to lose? Give me a try; if I don't work out, I don't work out." That was the understanding I had.

There was a major shift at that point. We had a new Chairman and a new Business Committee, even though it was constituted in large part from some of the members that had previously been on it. Art Welmas really had exercised almost exclusive power as Chairman. One of the things that I had to decide on, in looking at what I was potentially confronted with prior to making the decision, were the roles and some of the models that John had operated under—and, frankly, created a culture, if you will—a corporate/organizational culture. I wasn't ready to accept it, and I didn't think it would be appropriate for some of the same style of management to continue, which tended to be more Machiavellian in nature. As part of this opportunity for change, I committed myself to making a much broader-based involvement on the part of the Committee members and those active Tribal members, and to generally what was going on. I think that that has come to pass anyway—at least as opposed to what had been going on, I think, for a few years.

There seemed to be a change when the Bingo operation got started. It was as if some of the social objectives had been somewhat downplayed and de-emphasized and lost for a period of time, which made what we did less fun. This is my own personal observation and perspective, and there could be lots of reasons for it; it could have been something that I was going through, but that's something that I felt needed to be recaptured, and I think that's the principal drive behind it.

I asked Mark, two questions: What is there about the people in this Tribe, in his point of view that led them through to this point? And related to the first question, what did he see in the future, both in terms of the Tribe and the revolution that has taken place?

What has brought the Tribe—I suppose what has allowed the Tribe to survive—has been that they have been doing it for a couple of hundred years under pretty oppressed conditions—particularly the last 150 years. That's a very collective thought. The tribal ethic is that which gives people a sense of belonging and a sense of purpose. Strip their religion, strip their livelihood, strip their dignity in various degrees and various ways, they somehow or another have maintained this group commitment. It transcends more of what you would think of as the Western or European concept of family value. It's a morphenogenic field which ties them together and which really has transcended all of the hard times. The U.S. Government recognized that and really attempted to destroy that—case in point by giving everybody 40-acre allotments and creating the spirit of private entrepreneurship, which culminated in people like Fred Alvarez or Linda Streeter [-Dukic] or LeRoy [their father]—perfectly functioning out there in the outer world, but really not thinking in terms of the group, and thinking in terms of themselves as isolated individuals.

On many reservations, the whole sense of organization and government was stripped away from them—from when everybody was given isolated pieces of property that they themselves possessed, and that they themselves could do with and manage in any way that they saw fit, without having to get the concurrence and wishes and feelings of the tribe. I was at a meeting yesterday in Torres Martinez and the Tribal Spokesperson was up there, and she said, "We, of course, cannot tell individual allottees what to do with their land." Well, that is 100 percent different from the old ethic—that communal, if you will, almost socialistic structure that tribes were really designed and emulated after—the pack, the group. Decisions had to be made in terms of being a group, and that's what the government was trying to destroy—not very successfully in many instances.

In this reservation, a lot of land was retained in common ownership, and I think that the common ownership of land created the impetus to keep this group together making these decisions. And, even if it got down to where you had a couple or one person who was taking advantage of the situation, you always had that common land that would bring the people back in order to make decisions.

Then there was something on the land, so they had to develop management skills. I think that the Tribe here (and this will sound a little self-serving) was very fortunate to have stumbled across a person who believed in a lot of the tribal ethics as they related to social organization, common goals, working together—and that was my dad, Dr. Nichols, with his basically socialistic philosophy bordering on being a communist, with this mixture of Judaic-Israeli philosophy mixed into it. It was something they could identify with, he could identify with, and it was just a real natural philosophical fit insofar as some of the members were concerned. The others were willing to ride along insofar as they were meeting their own objectives, which might have been personal wealth and so forth. There was a period when personal wealth became one of the motivating factors, and *is* to this day. But I think today, the way it is structured, it's a different structure—but that [the personal wealth motivation] created some of the impetus.

Where are we going? Where we are today is very successful. From a Tribe starting with a budget of probably $5,000 a year (something like that) and with grants of maybe $7,000, this year [1993] the tribal economy [businesses] will generate in gross cash receipts, the gross reservation product will be about $80 million. This past fiscal year we netted over $4 million, of which we distributed about $1.3 million—about $2 million went back into capitalization of tribal facilities and then nice cash reserves.

Not only is the Tribe now looking in terms of taking care of itself and its members, but it has broadened its perspective to the point to where it's taking care of its employees, and even beyond that there is a commitment to Indian people throughout the United States, and the willingness to be part of a national agenda. I predict that as the economics grow (and my guess is going to be by the year 2000) that we will have half a billion dollars worth of assets on the reservation—at least that is the rough goal. I would like to see the mission (and I've had some discussions with John James and some of the other folks in terms of taking the mission to an international scope) starting to look and protect and deal and get involved in the indigenous rights for tribal people throughout the world, particularly with a focus on places like South America and places here in the Western Hemisphere.

[I see] further development as a governmental entity, furthering of the Band's business interests, and making a difference. I see the young people having new levels of education, new levels of participation. I am guessing that by the year 2005 our membership will be closer to, or approaching, 70, and it could be well beyond that, depending on what they do with their blood-quantum [qualifications]. The bigger their enterprises and assets become, the more pressure there is going to be to open the membership and so forth—just naturally. And that, in itself, will not be as much of a pressure to change their membership structure as will be their offspring that don't meet those blood requirements. So they will open those up, and the population will broaden. That will create credibility from a standpoint of the outside. I think that there is a lot of credibility, but I think that there is animosity because you have a small group of people that can do so much. I don't know that that is a logical conclusion. I think that's just a matter of perception and jealousy. After all, 100 years ago this tribe numbered more than 500 members. It was decimated through theft of their land and water resources, the spread of smallpox and the use of bullets.

OFF TRACK BETTING

In the mid-1980s, the State of California decided to expand its horse-racing industry's offerings by licensing sites that would broadcast races by video feeds. As it had with so many other ventures, the Tribe recognized this as an opportunity to provide another service to its customers. And, as in every other venture that it decided to enter, the way was not clear for the inclusion of Off Track Betting (OTB) in its casino offerings. Tribal Attorney Glenn Feldman was asked about those early efforts and what followed:

Glenn: I can remember that John Paul and I met with the California Horse Racing Board, before there was an Indian Gaming Regulatory Act, to talk to them about the possibility of doing Off Track Betting on the reservation. This must have been between the time the Cabazon Decision came down, which affirmed the Tribe's right to have gambling, and the time that the Indian Gaming Regulatory Act (IGRA) was enacted—which would have been like an 18-month period. I remember we went up and met with them, and we met with some of the horse people, horse-track owners, and got nowhere. I mean, they basically didn't want to talk to us, but we started the discussions long before there was an IGRA.

Once the IGRA was passed—giving the Tribe the right to enter into these compacts, and basically requiring the State to negotiate with the tribes over certain forms of gaming—the Tribe then immediately filed a request with the Governor to negotiate, and it probably was an Off Track Betting compact, because that's what I think we were focusing on. So the Tribe then filed an immediate request to negotiate under the IGRA with the State over Off Track Betting. I don't remember very well exactly what the process was, although my recollections are very positive. Whereas they had been unwilling to even talk with us before the Act was passed, there was, I think, a dramatic change in their position after the Act was passed. They recognized right off the bat that they didn't have any choice; they needed to sit down with us and follow the dictates of the law. . . . It was a difference between night and day with regard to their response to our original request, and our request after the IGRA was passed. The negotiating process took a long time, and there were lots of questions.

This was literally the first compact that was negotiated after the IGRA was passed. There had been one before—the Fort Mojave Tribe had entered into an agreement with the State of Nevada before IGRA was passed—but the Cabazon Off Track Betting compact was the first one that was actually negotiated under the Indian Gaming Regulatory Act. To be honest with you, none of us knew exactly what we were doing. We were just sort of feeling our way through the dark, so the process took a long time to work through. I mean, today somebody says, "I want a compact," I've got 20 of them in my desk I can pull . . . do we want this one or this one? But there was nothing to work from; we were starting literally from scratch. It took a long time reaching agreement on issues, and a long time putting it on paper and getting it down in a way that both sides could agree with.

But, it was basically a pretty cooperative venture. The State took some very hard positions on certain issues, but their position was never, "we won't negotiate with you"; no way; no how. They were always willing to talk, and we got over some of the difficult issues. The one issue which we could never get over was the question of the state license fee and whether or not the Tribe's facilities are subject to this state license fee—which is a tax. It's called a license fee, but everybody agrees that it is a tax, and the only way we would resolve that issue was to agree to disagree. We said in the compact that we are going to file a lawsuit, and we will let the courts decide whether the State has a right to do that or not, which is of course the process that we are in now.

Author: Update me on where they are now. What are the legal issues?

Glenn: Well, the legal issue is whether—under either the IGRA or other principles of federal Indian law—the State can impose this so-called state license fee on the wagers that are placed at the Cabazon facility. It's a fee that's—it's a percentage; I think the answer is that it is a sliding scale. The percentage depends on whether it is day or night racing, thoroughbred or quarter-horse racing. There are a number of variables, so the actual percentage actually varies depending on the type of race and that sort of thing. But, it *is* a percentage based on the total amount of wagers placed at the facility.

Our position was that the State could not impose that, and that the Tribe was entitled to keep whatever that percentage was. It worked out, I think . . . it averaged 3.25 percent (just a ballpark figure seems to be 3.25 percent), and it was our position that the Tribe—under IGRA and under normal principles of federal Indian law—was entitled to keep that for themselves, and the State was not entitled to take it. The State's position was exactly the opposite—that nothing in IGRA or nothing in federal Indian law prevented them from imposing this tax.

The issues are real complicated because it has to do with the way in which the Off Track Betting actually operates, and who is responsible for what parts of it, and who actually collects the money, and how the checks are written. It is a very complicated issue; but basically the State's position is that it is not a tax on the Tribe or the Tribe's gaming at all, but that it's a tax on the racetrack where the race is being run. Our position is that it is a direct tax on the Tribe because for every dollar you take out of that pot of money, it is one less dollar that the Tribe would otherwise get.

We filed a lawsuit as the compact indicates we would. The Morongo Band then came along and got a similar compact sometime later with the same language in it, filed a separate suit. The two suits were consolidated in federal court in Sacramento. This was all argued with the Judge some time ago—I don't remember exactly when—and the Judge ruled against us. The Judge ruled in favor of the State. He said that the State was entitled to impose that tax; he basically bought their argument lock, stock, and barrel. We appealed that, and the case is now before the Ninth Circuit. All the briefs are in; we are just waiting for a hearing date from the Court, which we hope will be sometime soon. It has been many, many months since all the paperwork has been put in, so we are just waiting for the Court to give us a hearing date.

Author: Why is the OTB limited to Santa Anita?

Glenn: One of the issues that the State was adamant about when we negotiated the compact, is that the Tribe could only get [by video feed] the same races that all of the other State-sponsored OTB facilities in the State get. The State's position is that we are here to encourage and enhance and promote California racing—not racing in New York, Florida, or Chicago. So, the State only permits State-licensed OTB facilities to carry California races with a few exceptions. I mean, they make exceptions for the Kentucky Derby and the Preakness—the big national races that they are allowed to bring in—but 98 percent of the races that they carry have to be California races; and that was a position that the State required in the negotiations, and we could not get them to agree to anything other than that. So, we agreed to carry just the same races that everybody else in the State carries.

Mark Nichols recalls these negotiations somewhat differently. The second tribal negotiation team also included John James and Elisa Welmas as well as Glenn Feldman. "With IGRA in place," said Mark, "the negotiations could be characterized as civil, but with a clear "take it or leave it" attitude by the state on the three most significant issues—(1) state staffing and regulation; (2) state monopoly of signals; and (3) state taxation on the bets wagered—we elected to move ahead on the first two issues and got the state to agree to litigate the taxation issue in a "friendly suit."

On March 29, 1993, Glenn Feldman gave his written report on Current Legal Matters to the Cabazon General Council, comprised of all adult members of the Tribe:

1. Cabazon Band v. Wilson, No. 92-15751 (9th Circuit).

This is the case in which the Cabazon and Morongo Bands are challenging the right of the State of California to impose a "state license fee" on wagers placed at the tribal off track betting facilities. Last year, the Federal District Court in Sacramento upheld the State's right to impose this tax, and we have appealed that decision to the 9th Circuit Court of Appeals. The last brief was filed in this case in November 1992, and we are now awaiting a hearing date within the next 30 to 45 days.

2. Cabazon Band, et al., v. National Indian Gaming Commission, et al., No. 92-1103 RCL (District of Columbia).

In this case, the Cabazon Band and six other tribes from around the country have sued the National Indian Gaming Commission, Chairman Tony Hope, the Secretary of the Interior, and other federal officials. The suit contends that when the National Indian Gaming Commission issued its regulations last April, it acted improperly by classifying video pull-tab machines, like those operated by the Cabazon Band, as class III gaming devices instead of class II technologic aids. This difference is important because if the machines are class III devices, they can only be operated under a tribal-state compact, which the State of California has refused to negotiate. On the other hand, if the devices are class II, they can be operated without a compact.

At this time, the case has been fully briefed and we are waiting either for notice of a hearing date or a decision from the federal court in Washington, D.C. In the meantime, the authorities have not requested that the machines be removed. If such an effort was made, we would resist vigorously and seek an immediate hearing in federal court in Washington.

3. Rumsey Rancheria, et al v. Wilson, et al., No. CIV-S-92-812 GEB (Eastern Dis-

trict, California).

This case was brought by the Cabazon Band and seven other California tribes against the State and the Governor under the Indian Gaming Regulatory Act. In this case, the tribes have alleged that they are entitled to negotiate tribal-state compacts with the State for a broad range of class III gaming, including slot machines and blackjack. The State has taken a much narrower position, arguing that the tribes are only entitled to negotiate compacts for lottery games like those offered by the State.

Earlier this year, the tribes made a very generous settlement offer to the State in an effort to resolve this case. Unfortunately, the Governor rejected our proposal, and insisted that the federal court decide the issue. As a result, a hearing was held in Federal Court in Sacramento on this case on March 5, 1993. As you know from my memo after that hearing, the Judge did not issue a ruling at that time, but from his comments and from the tentative ruling that he issued the day before, it appears that he was generally sympathetic to the tribes' position. We are expecting a written decision from the court within the next two weeks. [Note: At mid-June 1993, the Judge had still not issued his written opinion.] At that time, there may be further settlement discussions between the parties, or the matter may be appealed by the losing side to the 9th Circuit. In the meantime, however, we are continuing to negotiate a compact with the State for keno and perhaps other games.

4. <u>Welmas and Dukic v. Sacramento Area Director, Bureau of Indian Affairs,</u> No. IBIA 92-141-A (Interior Board of Indian Appeals).

Arthur Welmas and Linda Streeter-Dukic have appealed with respect to the sanctions imposed on them by the Cabazon General Council on July 16, 1991. That appeal was rejected by the BIA Agency Superintendent in Riverside and the Area Director in Sacramento. Their appeal has now gone to the Interior Board of Indian Appeals in Washington, D.C. Welmas and Dukic are not directly appealing the actions taken by the Cabazon General Council. Instead, their appeal argues that the BIA needed to approve the sanctions imposed on them and failed to protect their interest when certain per capita payments were not distributed to them. The matter is now before the IBIA and we are waiting for a decision.

5. <u>Indian Sands Housing Project</u>.

After several efforts, all of the revisions to the Indian Sands lease requested by the BIA have now been made and the document should be in final form. At this time, we are working with the Planning Department on the development of CC&Rs for the development of the project. In addition, we are also providing assistance on possible bond financing of certain infrastructure improvement, such as sidewalks, sewers, and roads for the project.

6. <u>Ecology West Technologies Lease</u>.

A lease between the Cabazon Band and Ecology West Technologies has been negotiated and prepared. This lease would cover a 20 to 40 acre site for a soil recycling and composting facility, using bioremediation technology. The term of the lease would be five years, with a possible five year option. After review, the BIA requested a few minor revisions to the lease, which have been made, and the lease is now in final form.

John James, Tribal Chairman. Drawing by Ignacio Gomes, photograph by Jesse Alvarez.

Brenda Soulliere, Tribal First Vice Chairwoman. Drawing by Ignacio Gomes, photograph by Jesse Alvarez.

Virginia Welmas-Nichols, Tribal Secretary-Treasurer. Drawing by Ignacio Gomes, photograph by Ward P. Riggins III.

Charles Welmas, Tribal Second Vice Chairman. Drawing by Ignacio Gomes, photograph by Ward P. Riggins III.

Elisa Wildman, General Council Liaison. Drawing by Ignacio Gomes, photograph by Jesse Alvarez.

John Welmas, Member at Large. Drawing by Ignacio Gomes, photograph by Jesse Alvarez.

Chairman John James and U.S. Congressman Esteban Torres represented in a drawing presented to Congressman Torres on behalf of California Indians for his outstanding work for Indians nationwide. Drawing by Ignacio Gomes, photograph by Jesse Alvarez.

Bruce James, Tribal Code Enforcement Officer. Drawing by Ignacio Gomes, photograph by Jesse Alvarez.

Ribbon-cutting at the grand opening of the off-track betting facility, Indio Bingo Palace & Casino, 1991. Photograph by Jesse Alvarez.

Tribal Chairman John James at Little Big Horn, 1993. Photograph by Jesse Alvarez.

Hon. Brenda Soulliere, Judge of the Juvenile Court and
Hon. John James, Chief Judge of the Tribal Court.
Photograph by A. C. Patel.

Cabazon Band of Mission Indians Public Safety Department, 1994. Photograph by A. C. Patel.

Colmac Biomass Electric Generating Plant. Photograph by A. C. Patel.

Indian Sands planned residential community. Photograph by Jesse Alvarez.

Cahuilla Child Development Center, the first employer-sponsored child care center in the region, 1994. Photograph by Nancy Duteau

John Welmas and chef Jaime Angarita at the Tribe's Players Restaurant, 1993. Photograph by Taylor Sherrill.

Powwow sponsored by The Cabazon Band of Mission Indians, 1993. Photograph by Jesse Alvarez.

Mark Nichols, U.S. Senator Thomas Daschle, Virginia Welmas-Nichols, 1993.

Charles Welmas, Mark Nichols, U.S. Senator Barbara Boxer, John James, 1994.

Mark Nichols, Ambrose I. Lane, Sr., John James, U.S. Senator Dianne Feinstein, 1994.

U.S. Senator Dianne Feinstein and Virginia Welmas-Nichols, 1994. Photograph by Ward P. Riggins, III.

5

A Savage "Free Press"

A few weeks after arriving in Indio and setting up shop, Dr. Nichols received a visitor. After he and Joann welcomed this stranger, a portentous dialogue took place.

As Dr. Nichols remembers the conversation, the stranger opened his remarks with a question and the brief discussion went something like this:

> "Do you remember me?" the guest asked.
>
> "No, I'm afraid that I don't," replied Nichols.
>
> "Well, I remember you. My name is Lycette. I'm editor of the Indio *Daily News*. You led a strike against my company several years ago in Detroit and you almost put us out of business.
>
> "Well, I'm here to tell you that I'm going to do all I can to make sure you don't succeed here. We don't need your kind here stirring up our Aborigines."
>
> "Aborigines?" Nichols queried.
>
> "Yes, our Aborigines. They don't need a union organizer stirring them up and causing problems. Our Aborigines are hard-working, responsible citizens and we intend to keep things that way. So I just want to put you on notice that we'll be watching you and I promise you I will stop you."

So much for a free press and balanced, fair reporting. Eventually James Lycette became editor of *The Desert Sun*, today a Gannett daily. Among his protégés was Keith Carter, currently the editorial-page editor of *The Desert Sun,* from which he has repeatedly launched disinformation-filled attacks and smears on the Tribe and the Nichols family.

Lycette apparently tried to keep his word. But there is something inexorably powerful about an idea, when it is developed by courageous, determined human beings. Whomever the "Aborigines" were that Lycette thought he knew, they did not have a leadership that risked all to move their Tribe toward financial independence.

EARLY COMMENTS AND CRITICISM

But Lycette was not alone. He, at least, gave warning. Consider the words of a former Indio City Councilman who was interviewed for this book in May 1993. These comments came at the end of the interview:

Author: I appreciate your time. Is there anything you want to add?

Councilman: No, not really. I guess the only thing I would really say is, considering myself almost a native of the area, having lived here since 1960, there are many long-term residents here. The city has grown; we are over 40,000 now. It has quadrupled in size since I came here a little over 30 years ago. A great many people here are from somewhere else, obviously. They don't know anything of what's happened and probably don't give a damn, but there are a lot of residents here who remember things as they were, and see things as they are, and there are an awful lot of questions. . . . How did we get here today?

I think the Indian Tribe has only been seen in a positive way in the things they have done in recent years, but there's a dark, dark cloud over their early years, and there are many unanswered questions. But I really think this Tribe is involved locally, statewide, nationally, politically in the gaming industry; I mean it's a very complex situation. They haven't asked me for my opinion, so I'm not going to give it, but as far as the local issues go, I really think they should do something about dispelling rumor, innuendo, and some honest to God—not a press conference, but getting out in the community and telling their side of what happened and where they came from and where they started in the early years to now. I know they produced a videotape. I know that you are writing this book. I think that's wonderful. If the videotape does not address their issues, maybe the book will. If it does, I think it's a wonderful service. If it doesn't, there is still an area that needs to be addressed. I'm talking about the late—I'm talking about the '70s and '80s.

Author: In '81, the question was raised by the press about organized crime. Is there another one?

Councilman: When the Nichols family first came to the community, the Indio City Council was given in-depth police background checks. I had never experienced that kind of . . . being told things, given information about other people, in my life. I had never been in a position to receive it. At the time, I knew people, former chiefs of the tribe. I mean there wasn't a tribe, but they were the chiefs. I knew problems that existed, different factions within the Tribe. I was somewhat shocked to get these in-depth interviews. I mean, I felt like I'm just a small-town councilman, a small town; what the hell are we getting into here? That was my honest-to-God reaction. And I tended to be incredulous. I took a lot of it with a grain of salt. As I said, we were a five-member council. I'm speaking for myself. A couple of my colleagues were people who had—sometimes I thought they had great imaginations, and at other times I thought they had a lack of imagination. I really never knew where they were. I don't know how I affected them.

That's sort of one reason I personally wanted to get to know these people. I invited another colleague of mine and we came over to the casino shortly after they opened to see it. I met Dr. Nichols. As I mentioned earlier, we weren't bosom buddies; we didn't share Christmas cards, but we went out socially a few times, enjoyed each other's company. We'd talk on the phone occasionally. He was always very open. I treat people like they treat me. I take people at face value. If I find out that they're not what I feel they are, then prove to me different.

You know how it is, if you tell someone something and they tell someone something, six other people pass and add and subtract; you hear it; it didn't even happen on the same date, and it was night instead of daytime. That's all I'm saying. I mean, it's rare that you can't pick up an *Enterprise* or *Desert Sun* newspaper and see an article on gaming, and it's all relating basically to the current situation. I think that's a positive thing. They are not re-hashing 10 or 15 years ago where we came from. On the other hand, it's in their files, and you can rest assured it's going to be brought out again. I think the concerted effort on the part of the Tribe and a spokesman to put the whole situation in historically correct perspective would be a very big plus. I've never seen it done.

Author: In all your time with the Council, did you ever get such a briefing before or after? Was it right after they came in town or after some incident?

Councilman: If I recall correctly, I was elected to the Council in 1972, so I had been on the Council, and I think when we first got involved with the Indian situations, it became known. It was '78 or '79, and it basically started with the issue of the gaming, the liquor business, the cigarette business. I don't recall if the City ever had a problem . . . I mean, if they did, it was done at a level that I as a Council member wasn't aware of.

If I was aware of it, then I'll tell you flat out that I forgot about it. But in answer to your question, no, I don't think it was the first time we ever had this type of in-depth briefing, if you will. A couple of other incidences . . . had nothing to do with the tribe. One was basically the Teamsters' Cesar Chavez Movement. A couple of other background checks were actually done at the request of the Council or a Council member. Let me clarify that . . . over a development or developer's background, something of this nature. I never recall before or since having been called to the police station for an in-depth background briefing. As I recall, it was just not done on the local level. I can't say for sure that there was an FBI agent present. It seems to me there were a couple of unnamed people there that were just—I don't know if anyone asked who they were. I didn't. I was sort of in shock. I don't know if anybody asked. If they did, I don't know what the answer was. I don't recall. And I don't know if they were FBI, but a lot of the information would never have been able to have been arrived at by our local police department. Okay, I mean this was international. This had to do with South America, Florida, other countries. I mean I'm not so god-damned dumb that I knew—I thought we had a wonderful police department—but I knew they had limitations, and I was positive these guys in suits weren't there to apply for a job.

Earlier in the interview, the Councilman had estimated that it cost the City of Indio at least $250,000 in legal fees to fight the Tribe over gaming. I then asked him:

Author: Why did it cost the City of Indio so much money in legal fees? Did they have their own counsel, or did they hire outside counsel?

Councilman: No, we had a City attorney, but I believe he had some help. As I say, this is going way back. I was not an administrator; I was an elected official, a decision maker. I tried very hard never to get into the administration of day-to-day operations. I had great faith in our staff. We had talented, and I felt knowledgeable, staff and that included the City attorney, who I respected very highly.

Author: Why did the City spend so much money? I could never understand that.

Councilman: Well, first off, how could we afford to spend the money? The City was in great financial shape for many years. We had big surpluses. We had a well-managed City. I alluded earlier to a professional staff.

Author: You had a city manager situation?

Councilman: Yes—Council, city manager, active city manager; we had a financial director who seemed to make good investments; I'm speaking of the past. While I was involved, we had a very good, healthy financial situation. We were a growth-industry city government. We added employees every year. Rarely did the city employees not get raises. There was very little confrontation when it came to employee negotiations. As I say, I was not involved in the day-to-day or the administrative end of it. We would get reports on this case, that case. City government in California, at least as far as I know it, it's pretty much a formality because you're sued many times by many different people for many different reasons. It's basically a formality that your city attorney . . . staff, or outside contractor comes before your council and says, "This is a potential legal problem and may go to litigation. We are being sued for "X" amount of dollars; my recommendation is that you deny the lawsuit." So I say it was 99 percent of the time automatic. It would then go to the city's insurance carrier, and your insurance carrier and the litigant and your attorney and their attorney would solve the problems. It's rare that we ever heard anything more about any suit that was ever brought against the City.

Regarding the suit against the Tribe, we were [merely] updated. I don't know if we were ever voluntarily given the financial accounting of what the amount of money spent was. I probably upset people when I asked, "How much money have we spent?" And I think the first time I asked, I found out it was like $140,000. To say the look on the faces of my colleagues was one of shock would be an understatement. And, that's about the time I started pressing to end it.

But James Lycette's successors at *The Desert Sun* have not similarly "pressed" to end their war against the Tribe, nor the disinformation campaign they have waged in their newspapers for 15 years. As the Councilman suggested, they have repeatedly pulled their manufactured allegations out of their files to smear the Cabazons.

The press has, in fact, been savage in its attacks. They began with Lycette, but the lies, half-truths and sleazy innuendoes quickly bounced to the national level after court victories and the hatchet job done on the Tribe by Geraldo Rivera on *20/20*. And the disinformation grew as retellers of the lies became more creative.

In early 1992, the Tribe and its CEO began to talk about the importance of producing a book that would tell the truth about their climb out of poverty, as well as set the record straight. In a June 1992 Sunday spread, *The Desert Sun* rehashed every allegation, every smear. The heroine in the story, with picture, was Linda Streeter-Dukic, and the murdered hero, also with picture, was her brother Fred Alvarez. Mark Nichols was quoted as saying that the proposed book would "try and dismantle the myths" written about the tribe. In an anticipatory strike against the planned book, *The Desert Sun* editorialized that "it will take more than . . . a vanity-press book [meaning totally written and paid for by the Tribe] to chase away the dark clouds that still hang over the Cabazon tribe and its recent past."

After the Tribe let it be known they were going to write this book, another interesting thing happened. In the Spring of 1992 most records of the Indio Police Department, covering 30 years, were destroyed.

California has a state version of the Federal Freedom of Information Act, the California Public Records Act. In an effort to get documents regarding complaints and requests for police investigations of, for example, the drug-crazed threats including death threats made by Jimmy Hughes against tribal members and members of the Nichols family, as well as such records regarding an office break-in and theft of a safe and a large locked filing cabinet, requests for documents were made to the Indio Police Department for a period covering October 1980 through April 1984. The first response from Acting Chief of Police Roy T. Ramirez was puzzling. It said, in part, that "a search of our records reflects we no longer have the files you request. . . . I suggest you contact the law firm that represented the Cabazon Band of Mission Indians in the federal lawsuits during the time in question. They might still have access to copies of the police records you are interested in obtaining."

A follow-up letter was sent to Acting Chief Ramirez requesting clarification of his "no longer have" statement. Did it mean the department "no longer" had the specific records requested and/or no records of any kind on anybody? We then gave him a list of names of eight persons, members of the Tribe or associated with the Tribe, requesting copies of or access to their files.

The next response came from the Police Department's presumed representative, Attorney David J. Erwin of the law firm Best, Best & Krieger in Rancho Mirage, California. Erwin's letter simply said the records we sought had been destroyed.

On April 29, 1993, another letter on this matter was addressed to Erwin. Since his letter did not identify his or his firm's official role, copies of our letter were sent to Ramirez and the Tribe's attorney as well. In that letter, we again asked for specificity, "as the destruction of public documents is a potentially serious matter," and inquired as to the correctness of our interpretation of his earlier letter. We then requested that we be provided "any documents, reports, public records or writings (as these terms are defined under the above-cited Act) authorizing, suggesting, approving, ordering or confirming the destruction of these specific documents within the specified time period." We then repeated our listing of the eight files/persons to which we sought access.

On May 13, 1993, a response was received on the stationery of the same law firm, over the signature of Douglas S. Phillips, identified as Deputy City Attorney, City of Indio. Attached were two City Resolutions, numbers 3602, adopted March 3, 1982, and 3605, adopted April 7, 1982. Both resolutions authorized *"the Chief of Police to destroy the City Records"* (emphasis added), as described with great specificity in the body of the resolutions. Attached also to the letter from Deputy City Attorney Phillips was a memorandum, dated May 12, 1993, "Subject: Records Purge," from "Captain Carl Kennedy to Chief Tom Ramirez." That memo read, in full:

> On May 16, 1992, per Resolution No. 3602 adopted by the Indio City Council on April 7, 1982, I conducted a purge of Indio Police Department records. The purge included all reports dated 1955 through approximately 1985. The purge was conducted in accordance with guidelines as described in that resolution. All reports that were no more than seven years old were retained.

From April 1982, when the Chief of Police—and no one else—was authorized to destroy specific records because "the accumulation of these records is unduly cumbersome and counter-productive," until May 16, 1992, more than 10 years passed without the actual purge by any Indio Chief of Police, even by the Chief who requested the authorization, Chief Curtis R. Cross. Until May 16, 1992, the records were still intact. Truth is admittedly stranger than fiction, and often events that might appear related are just simply coincidences. But it seemed more than passing strange that Captain Kennedy would be the one Indio officer, not the Chief, who would conduct this purge, shortly after the Tribe began to tell people in the community it was considering having a book written to make the truth known to the world and to expose the lies, diplomatically called "myths" by Mark Nichols.

It seems also more than passing strange that it would be Captain Kennedy who conducted the purge, as he was identified by Dr. Nichols as one with whom he had cooperated. In his statement to the Court prior to being sentenced, it is stated that Dr. Nichols "advised that for approximately one year he has worked with Indio Police Department Chief Cross and Captain Kennedy, as well as Parole Agents and Probation Officers in attempting to stop the flow and use of Heroin in the local area." His statement also asserted that "just prior to going to the motel on the day of his arrest, he [Dr. Nichols] telephoned Sergeant Gilbert [Indio Police] and advised that he was going to go to the motel and attempt to recover his stolen property."

During a probation investigation, a deposition was taken from Captain Kennedy. But oddly enough, according to surviving records, he was not questioned regarding Nichols's statement that Nichols had been working with Kennedy for the previous year. The court report, prepared by Robert A. Logan, deputy probation officer, contained the following about the interview with Captain Kennedy in its entirety:

> Captain Kennedy advised that the defendant (Nichols) did not become involved in the instant offense with the intentions of gathering information for the Police Department. He was intent on doing what he set out to do. He intended to have the five subjects murdered. However, Captain Kennedy does not believe that he wanted the subjects murdered for the reasons that were given to Yolanda Duran. Regarding a recommendation, he advised that the instant offense is extremely serious and feels that the maximum penalty should be imposed.

Kennedy's statement without any evidence to support it—at least there were only naked allegations in the record—constituted a rather large nail in Nichols's coffin headed for prison. Although Dr. Nichols telephoned Indio Police—including Kennedy and Gilbert—from Miami on his way to and from Chile in December 1984, not one word appears in the entire record about these calls. Since all calls to the department were recorded, the probation investigation could have verified the truth or lack of truth in Nichols's assertions, and Kennedy and Cross and officers Gilbert and Sanchez could have been questioned about the content of all verified calls.

It is interesting that Council Resolution No. 3605 provided for the destruction of:

> tape recordings which are more than 100 days old and are made on a routine daily taping and recording of telephone communications to and from the City Police Department and all peculiar radio communications relating to the operation of such department.

Thus, not only were paper records subject to destruction, so were taped telephone communications.

The report also makes no mention—perhaps understandably since no hard questions were asked—of the fact of the deep animosity within the Police Department toward the Tribe and the White family "stirring them up." Someone is alleged, for example, to have had a picture of Dr. Nichols blown up to be used as a dart board in the police department, and that it was so used. A White freelance journalist who had lived in the area since the age of 7 suddenly found himself a victim of police harassment after being hired to do public relations work for the Tribe. When asked if it was true that he became targeted by the police because of his relationship with the Tribe, the journalist replied:

> Yes, kind of. I remember getting stopped for minor traffic things about six times in one month. I remember driving through Thermal, which is south of the Indio city limits, and being pulled over by an Indio squad car one night. One of the officers drew his gun and he pointed it in the window at me. Then, he looked at me and laughed and said, "No, this is the wrong guy." But, I figured it was just part of the treatment. It was nothing personal. He was just doing his job. . . . What I did was, I hung on to the steering wheel and almost pulled it right off. It was just part of the routine. I never reported it, not because I was afraid to report

it; it was just part of the routine. He didn't really, except for the gun, he didn't do anything else to intimidate me. That was enough! He didn't say anything that was harsh, or anything, it was just a laugh that they had the wrong guy. I took a lot of heat for a couple of years from a lot of people. I don't think that the Nichols family or the Tribal Council, or the Cabazon Band at large realized the amount of heat I took. I took a lot.

Not only does this palpable hostility of the Indio police toward the Tribe and the Nichols family not surface in any report, the local press has never reported any of this material, which was readily available. Why, one might ask, did not one single reporter interview Chief Cross, Captain Kennedy or officers Gilbert and Sanchez? If they did, it was never reported.

Why, one might logically ask, were no in-depth investigations or articles ever done on Fred Alvarez, Jimmy Hughes, Linda Alvarez Streeter-Dukic or Joe Benitez? And why, one might ask, has no local newspaper used the provisions of the California Public Records Act to try to get and publish the truth? Why, for example, has the public never been told of the police background briefings to the Indio City Council on Dr. Nichols and Cesar Chavez? In view of the close relationship of Chief Cross, Indio City Manager W. Philip Hawes, the press and the valley's power brokers, it is clear that all the "good ole boys" knew of these briefings. And therein might well lie the answers to these questions.

And now, we were told, Captain Kennedy had conducted a "purge" of critical records. Were it not for the extensive and meticulous record keeping of the Cabazons, only the lies or, in Mark's words "the myths" would survive. Let's examine some of those lies or "myths" we have not yet exposed.

In a *Desert Sun* article carrying the byline of John Hussar, dated March 27, 1985, the readers are told of a "security test" that took place "at the "*county*-owned police firing range" four years earlier on "September 10, 1981." One of the participants "*was rumored to be* Edén Pastora, otherwise known as Commander Zero, an Anti-Sandinista rebel who broke with the new Nicaraguan government after helping to overthrow dictator Anastasia Somoza in 1979." Accompanying the article was a picture, purporting to be Pastora, with a cutline reading "WAS HE HERE?—Nicaraguan rebel leader Edén Pastora may have witnessed security testing in the Coachella Valley in 1981." Seven years later, Hussar had turned his question mark into an exclamation mark. In a *Desert Sun* article dated June 14, 1992, under a subhead in bold print that read "*This is fact,*" Hussar wrote, "The now-defunct Cabazon Arms Co. conducted a demonstration of night-vision goggles and automatic weapons at Lake Cahuilla in 1981 *for Nicaraguan soldiers, including then Anti-Sandinista rebel leader Edén Pastora.*" (Emphasis added.)

However, no Nicaraguan soldiers or contras were ever involved in any of the activities of the Tribe and/or the Nichols family anywhere. And no Cabazon or Nichols family member and/or associate has ever been involved with Edén Pastora. This manufactured lie grew from a "rumor" in Hussar's columns to a "fact" in his later columns and in columns and articles in other publications that believe Hussar has been writing the truth.

In Hussar's articles, he smeared the Tribe and the Nichols family with clever literary tricks linking the two with the killing of Fred Alvarez. In his June 1992 article, after writing about what the Tribe's public relations video was designed to do—dispel "myths" and draw investors—Hussar then wrote that the video "doesn't mention controversies that have plagued the tribe." He then strings a list of "controversies" in such a way as to leave the impression that each is directly related to each other, feeling no constraints about using the Tribe's openness in talking with him to rehash all of the lies and half-truths and unproven allegations he has written about repeatedly.

Hussar starts with the murder of Fred Alvarez. Readers of this book now know more about Fred and his murder than all of the people who have read all of the articles appearing in *The Desert Sun* and the *Daily News* for the last dozen years, although everything appearing in this book about Fred and a great deal more is known or could have been researched by Hussar or any reporter. Yet not one word has ever been printed or broadcast by the electronic media.

Second in Hussar's string of controversies was the "bitter fight" being waged and led by Fred's sister to "oust Nichols." In his June 1992 article, Hussar writes that Linda "now lives out of the area." She has *always* lived out of the area. Interviews with people who know Linda and her "bitter fight," and what it really represents, could have revealed more of the truth about the situation than all of *The Desert Sun* articles on the subject for the past dozen years. The paper has told less than half truths over the years and has never done an investigative report on her or her father or her brother, but instead it has been content to libel the tribal leadership.

Third in Hussar's string is the conviction of Dr. Nichols, followed by the fourth, which repeats the drug-crazed allegations of one Jimmy Hughes, given the false title of "former tribal security chief," a title he never held. Hussar writes that Hughes had filed a statement in 1984 charging "there was profit skimming at the Cabazon Bingo Palace and that the Cabazons and the Nicholses family were involved in gun-running missions in Central and South America." By publishing this, Hussar was republishing two blatant lies: there have been no "gun-running missions" by the Cabazons or the Nichols anywhere in the world, and Hughes was never a Cabazon "security chief." In his repetition of these lies, he then added that Hughes claimed to be a "bagman" for Nichols in the Alvarez murder. At no time has Hussar written the truth about Hughes the "speed freak," although the truth was available, and Hughes was never a "bagman" for Nichols or the Cabazons for *any purpose*.

For example, one person who knew Hughes well told of his drug use and heavy use of "speed" in a March 1993 interview for this book:

anon: Jim Hughes basically sold drugs. He affiliated with bikers. He was always impeccably dressed.

Author: Was he also a drug user?

anon: Absolutely. Very, very much so. . . . Jim used to use a lot of amphetamines and his connection was through the bikers and through . . .

Author: Give me an example of his use.

anon: Oh, he would have half ounces, ounces—which are significant amounts. . . . You'd be having a conversation with him over a period of a couple of hours and he'd pull out the little vial—this is not cocaine mind you; this is methamphetamine. He might sniff or snort five, six times in a short period of time and every time he'd say "Here" and try to get you to [take a hit]. But there is a certain amount that you can tolerate. Jim frequently . . . you have to understand, this sort of progressed and it got to the point to where he would stay up two to three days. At times my guess would be . . . that . . . towards the end of his relationship here, [he was] staying up as much as seven days in a row. That's amazing.

But Jim, he started—in fact there was a little nickname for him; we call him "Skelton" and that was what we called the step after "Scullium-Mullium." Scullium-Mullium came when you got ragged. Skelton came when your eyes got totally black underneath and got recessed into your head, and you had paranoia starting to set in. Skelton meaning, of course, skeleton; near death was the inference.

But he pretty much kept to his own. He had a nickel-plated [revolver] that he was very proud of. And in fact he owned all kinds of paratrooper rifles.

I think he really wanted to be in the military. He wanted to be a policeman. He wanted to be all those things, but I don't think he really had the ultimate temperament to be patient, like I have no patience. And I think that really became amplified with the use of amphetamines.

Author: Did he exhibit paranoia or violent behavior . . . toward tribal members?

anon: Not that I know of. No, I can't say that I ever saw that. If anything, he would play very friendly with them because whatever he did was calculated.

After being fired as a security guard in early 1984, Hughes was banned from the reservation. In a resolution dated March 14, 1984, signed by all officers (Art Welmas, Brenda James, John James, and Charles Welmas), Hughes was "hereby and forever banned from the sacred land of the Cabazon Band of Mission Indians," and noted at the top of the resolution were the words "Hand Delivered." Two days later, according to a written security report by Security Guard Neil W. Pierce, Hughes was "observed . . . standing next to the Admissions Booth inside the Bingo Palace." According to the report, Pierce told Hughes to leave or the Sheriff would be called. After Hughes refused to leave, the Sheriff was called and Hughes was so informed. Wrote Pierce:

He [Hughes] became argumentative and belligerent, and invited me to step outside. I stepped outside with him, but he made no effort to strike me. We were joined by Charles Welmas (security guard), Treasure Welmas, Virginia Welmas, Carol Teagardin (all employees of the Bingo Palace) and Dr. John Nichols. Dr. Nichols tried to reason with him, to no avail. Jimmy Hughes directed his anger toward Dr. Nichols; told him *his days were numbered.* A minute or two later, just before entering his car, he told Dr. Nichols, quote, "You better leave the state," unquote. On his way out of the parking lot, three or four shots were fired. I can only assume they were fired by Jimmy Hughes.

Since Hughes, Gary Packham and John Patrick McGuire had earlier tried to "muscle" a takeover of the Bingo Palace, claiming they represented Wayne Reeder, who had entered into a joint venture to construct the Palace building, the Tribe informed Reeder in a March 19 memo of Hughes's banning from the reservation. In that memo the Tribe let Reeder know that "we are seriously considering, under advice of attorney, Cabazon Bingo, Inc.'s terminating their relationship with Bingo Pavilion, Inc." [Reeder's firm for the joint venture].

In a letter dated March 23, 1984, addressed to Art Welmas, Reeder wrote, "This is to certify that Jim Hughes is not an officer, shareholder or employee" of Reeder's firm.

But as later events would indicate, Reeder's letter was not the full truth. Hughes was on his payroll and would remain on his payroll until about July when his services were terminated. A reading of available documents and analysis of events could lead to the conclusion that Hughes, Reeder and Zokosky had cooked up a "scheme" to take over the Bingo Palace, using Hughes to cause trouble and using Zokosky's credibility, as a businessman whose wife was Indio's former mayor, to raise questions about the financial operation of the Bingo Palace. It could have been reasoned that if a public scandal became serious and explosive enough, revenues could fall sufficiently to cause the Tribe to be unable to meet the terms of its agreed-upon Reeder loan repayment schedule; at that point, a takeover could be possible. Hughes, regardless, was just a "pawn," but later events would prove Zokosky also a loser, if such a scheme was in fact what happened.

In September, seven months after Hughes was fired by the Tribe and banned from the reservation, Hughes, Reeder and Zokosky came to a parting of ways. According to court documents, the three had a meeting on September 13, 1984, to, according to Hughes's documented statement, "discuss my business arrangement with Mr. Reeder . . . and his future fulfillment of his promises to me. [Peter Zokosky, according to his own statement, attended this meeting at Wayne Reeder's request]."

According to Hughes's reconstruction of that discussion, he had soon found out that he had no future with Reeder. Reeder, according to Hughes's recollection, told him, "We've looked at a couple of things [proposed plans for a security company to be headed by Hughes and financed by Reeder] but things didn't look feasible."

Hughes said he then told Reeder, "You've made deals behind my back. You care more about you [sp] f—ing money than you do about people's lives. Don't you realize we're both in the same f—ing boats. You know there are contracts on both of us. If I die so will you."

Apparently, Reeder took Hughes's remarks and the tone of his remarks as a threat on Reeder's life. He thereafter filed legal action in the form of a petition for injunction prohibiting harassment. The false allegations made by Hughes against Dr. Nichols were made in Hughes's response to Reeder's petition. The record would seem to indicate that at some point Zokosky concluded that he, too, had no future with Reeder and joined Hughes in his response to Reeder's petition.

All of this background information was available to any enterprising reporter that had no anti-Indian, anti-Nichols agenda. This information has, however, never been published. And, the disinformation story on Hughes is always given one of two possible endings, either he is "reportedly living in Guatemala" or is in a "witness protection" program.

The sixth line in Hussar's string involves Michael Riconosciuto who, Hussar wrote, filed an affidavit which "said he modified the PROMIS software on the Cabazon reservation." Neither this assertion nor his claim to have been research director is true, yet these two lies continue to be printed. Riconosciuto was a patient of Dr. Nichols, not an employee of the Tribe or of any of the Tribe's businesses.

These are the basic allegations that have been made and used by a local press whose leaders began with an apparently hostile agenda to stop a former union organizer from "stirring up" the local "Aborigines." The repetition of the lies and disinformation has had a negative impact on the pace of tribal economic development and the public's view of the integrity of the tribe. Since tribal members were either dumb dupes of the White family, organized crime, the CIA or a combination of either, or were themselves crooks.

Finally, the litany of lies and misinformation revealed much about the sad state of journalism being practiced by many members of the press, in both print and broadcast journalism. The base of venomous, anti-Cabazon journalistic products laid by the now defunct *Daily News*, *The Desert Sun*, and some of their editorial staffs bore generations of misinformation, distortions and disinformation. It was as if the press came to believe that the greater and more outlandish the lies they published, the more they would be believed.

To one broadcast personality, Dave Emory of the Emory Radio Broadcast, for example, Fred Alvarez's death grew to become the "execution-style murder of three Indians" by "several ex-Green Berets then employed as firemen in the city of Chicago." It is unknown where Emory got the Chicago firemen angle (his is the only story we have found carrying this unique line) or where the two other murdered Indians came from. But, according to Emory, all three were executed for objecting to the manufacture by the Tribe of "weapons, chemical and biological warfare devices," as well as the "conversion of Inslaw's software."

The NAPA *Sentinel* newspaper created other and somewhat wilder scenarios for its readers. According to the *Sentinel*, a Cabazon security guard was the bagman who delivered $10,000 to a hitman to execute Alvarez. And the person who paid for Alvarez's murder, the *Sentinel* reported, had earlier been the triggerman who killed Chile's President Salvador Allende and was linked to assassination attempts on Fidel Castro and to the Mafia's Gambino Family and the CIA. In the delusionary mind of the Sentinel writers, this must have been the Godfather of all Godfathers. And no one at the Sentinel apparently asked the simple question: If this Godfather of all Godfathers killed Allende and tried to assassinate Castro and lived, why would he need to pay anyone ten grand to do a simple job like taking out Fred Alvarez? In the pages of the *Sentinel*, the number of Indians shot to death grew to a total of five, three of which killings "were authorized and backed by a government covert operation."

To Emory and the Sentinel, the Cabazons' relationship with Wackenhut was twofold. Its first purpose was to manufacture chemical and biological weapons. Its equally important purpose was to provide funding and supplies to the (Nicaraguan) Contras. And central to all of this, of course, was the White guy John P. Nichols, described by these "journalists" as a "old-time CIA operative."

The Emory and *Sentinel* "journalistic terrorism" just demonstrates two of the worst press actors in this drama. To the Cabazons, all of the press must have appeared to have taken LSD or Peyote or some other mind-bending drug, for the reality the press fed to the public was far from the reality being experienced by the tribe.

Hussar's base reality of lies, half-truths, innuendoes and seemingly purposeful disinformation was also picked up and used by "reporters" such as Jonathon Littman, formerly of the *San Francisco Chronicle*. In a three-part 1991 *Chronicle* series, Littman in effect portrays the Cabazons as a bunch of dumb Indians being fleeced by an evil mystery man, Dr. Nichols. He portrays the "Streeter-Dukic and Art Welmas" faction as the heroes, trying to take back control for the good of the Tribe. In a later freelance article for the *California Lawyer* magazine, he drags Fred Alvarez out of the grave and gives him the titles of "tribal vice-chairman and casino security chief." The Tribal Council minutes prove Alvarez had been defeated for re-election as Vice Chairman, and this self-admitted drug user was not and never would have been employed by the Tribe as security chief.

With Littman now in the picture, Hussar's disinformation gained heightened credibility. It now had convinced the *Chronicle* and *California Lawyer*. In between these two came *Spy* magazine and its writer, John Connolly. Although Connolly came to Indio, he lied by posing as a writer for *Forbes* magazine. After that Connolly, possibly prejudiced by an agenda, produced his *Spy* article, which was based on the Hussar-Littman false base reality.

The Cabazon Band of Mission Indians has expended hundreds of thousands of dollars over the years defending itself from attacks by several levels of government and to establish rights for itself and all Native Americans. In 1993 the Tribe reached the point where it no longer allows publications to libel its members. A great deal has been made by these "journalists" about the small size of the Tribe and its monumental achievements. What they need to understand is the Tribe's smallness may well allow it to sue for libel as a Tribe. And no publication in the nation will escape the Cabazons' reach if they decide to sue.

And sue they should. Every tribal member interviewed had stories of having to submit to painful questions asked of them by their neighbors and perfect strangers who have read the smears of *The Desert Sun,* the *San Francisco Chronicle* or *Spy* magazine, or heard the rantings of an obviously "sick jackass" like radio personality David Emory. As it is now affecting their children as well, members are determined to stop the libel and slander.

John Welmas was asked in an interview about how the press attacks had affected him personally:

I've lived here for a while, and I know a lot of the people who own stores and shops. I go in there, especially into the bank, and they always make little comments. It's kind of embarrassing when they ask me who was stealing what, or what have you—you know, stuff that they read in the papers. So yeah, personally, it did affect me for a while. I couldn't even go to the carwash for a while. Oh, I did go anyway, but I'd always get comments. "Do you really trust that man, Dr. Nichols?" "Do you think he's stealing any money?" and just negative stuff. You know, every place I went to, really, just little things: "Is he really doing that?" "Did you guys really sell guns?" "Were you really going to build a new germ-warfare plant and zonk everybody in the desert?" and stupid shit like that.

Although John has no children himself, he is concerned about the impact such attitudes will have on the children of other tribal members.

One important fact that has never been published in all of the column inches written about the Cabazons is the fact that the Tribe runs all of its own businesses. Since 1991 when the last management firm's contract was ended, the Tribe has managed its multi-million-dollar businesses itself, through the Business Committee. John Welmas was asked how he felt about the change:

It gives us a better feeling about ourselves doing it. A firm is good if you need it, and like I said, at the beginning we did need them because we did not know the business. I mean, we were not really dumb, but in certain areas we did not have the necessary technical knowledge. I mean, we couldn't go out there now and start putting wood and steel together and build a nuclear plant, because we're stupid at that. We don't know anything about it. Now that we do know a little bit about gaming we are doing it ourselves. It's a lot better because now everybody in the Tribe knows, although others assume that we still have people running it for us, but we don't. We run it ourselves. If you look at it now, from the Business Committee point of view, from way back when we got started, it was always the older tribal members, and now it's the younger members. The only older person still there I guess is John James. It's the younger ones now, the ones that we told years ago that, "Someday you'll be doing this." Now that it's happening, it's good.

When asked what he thought was the Tribe's most important decision, his response echoed what most members said:

We never really took the money out and distributed it out to everybody. You know, we just kind of held on to it and let them call us names and what have you. They're blind if they can't see what we've done so far. Especially, look at the room we're in right now [referring to the Tribal Chambers], the landscaping outside, and the plans that we have to grow, add the hotel, add a new restaurant, add a nightclub. I think we're going for a bigger and greater future. That's what I can see.

GOLAB ARTICLE

Fortunately for American journalism, some journalists and publications still research, write and publish balanced articles that reach for truth. Perhaps one of the most balanced articles about the "tribes" was a September 1983 *Los Angeles Times Magazine* close-up piece written by Jan Golab, titled "Indian Giver?"

Little things often mean a lot and are important in a professional journalist's search for truth. Golab's article contained many important little things. For example, the author revealed that Art Welmas "is a weapons expert." He is and so is John James. Golab described Dr. Nichols, in part, as "A Yankee blue blood who claims to be a direct descendant of Noah Webster," and "one of the founders in 1948 of Americans for Democratic Action (a left-of-center political action group that involved the labor movement and the left wing of the Democratic party) which also served as political forerunner of the '60s group Students for a Democratic Society. . . ."

Golab's article also revealed the hypocrisy of Linda Streeter. To Golab, Streeter posed as a defender of Joe Benitez. In reference to the $6,000 Benitez received from Naegele for the billboards contracts, Streeter told Golab, "What he really did was accept money for two billboards, which he had put on his own land instead of Indian land. I doubt there are any Cabazons who wouldn't have done the same thing in his position." She claimed, according to Golab, that the billboard controversy "was merely a ploy used by Welmas and Nichols to gain control of the tribe." The truth, however, is that Linda's brother, Fred, made the motion and her father Leroy seconded it to find Benitez guilty on that charge and Linda herself joined in a 14–0 vote to find him guilty.

Perhaps Golab's most important paragraphs were those that captured the essence of his interview with Regina Zokosky [Peter Zokosky's wife]. Although she was much more easily available to Coachella Valley reporters, it was left to a Los Angeles reporter to tell this story. This is what Golab wrote in the article about this former mayor of Indio:

> Regina Zokoski [sp], a former mayor of Indio, remembers [Fred] Alvarez as a bizarre individual "who had exotic notions of starting up gambling, prostitution and drug manufacturing operations of his own on Indian land." She also recalls that she first met Alvarez when he came to her office to express his concern over the way tribal funds were being handled—not by Art Welmas who later became Chairman, but by *Joseph Benitez.*
>
> Zokowski [sp], who still serves on the Indio City Council, describes herself as a moralist who is opposed to gambling. When Nichols instituted gambling on the reservation, she was one of many city officials who strongly opposed it and sought court action to close it down. Today, however, she admits she has been won over to the Nichols' camp. "In my opinion they've done nothing but help the Indians . . ," she says. "They had nothing, and now they have a lot of potential. I have far more faith in the current management of the tribe. Art Welmas is a gentleman with a real Indian code of ethics, and the Nichols family is far more honest and sophisticated than the average person." (Emphasis added.)

If the *Daily News* or *The Desert Sun* ever elicited such opinions from the mayor, our research for this book did not unearth them.

Yet things may be looking up in the desert, *The Desert Sun*, that is. On May 29, 1993, an unusual but positive thing happened. The newspaper reported that California's Attorney General Dan Lungren had taken campaign money from Nevada gambling interests. And a few days later, on June 2, 1993, the *Sun* editorially attacked Lungren's obvious hypocrisy.

In the earlier article, the *Sun* told its readers of Lungren's accepting "more than $10,000 from Nevada gaming interests," as reported in papers filed "with the (California) secretary of state."

Equally important, the *Sun* reported Lungren's unbelievably cynical assertion that "those were some of the cleanest contributions I had because they have no interest in California."

If Lungren thought Nevada gaming interests had no interest in California, the Reno attorney for the Nevada Resort Association thought differently. As reported by the *Sun*, the Association's attorney Brian McKay, former Nevada Attorney General, felt contributing to Lungren was in the Association's interest because Lungren "would fight to stop the expansion of Legalized gaming in California."

In its later editorial, the *Sun* took a principled position. It concluded that "Lungren should return the money" and stop "attempting to justify his acceptance" of it.

Another voice on this issue of the press search for truth, the May/June 1993 issue of the highly respected *Columbia Journalism Review* published a relevant and timely article, "Judgment Call: Big Stories, Spooky Sources" by Chip Berlet.

One of the stories review by Bertet was the death of journalist Danny Casolaro and the "spooky" source review was Michael Riconosciuto. Berlet writes that after Riconosciuto finished weaving his tale about the Cabazon reservation being a "supersecret" base for intelligence operatives, "Casolaro began to see the reservation as part of a globe-spanning entity of untold power, which he called The Octopus."

Berlet briefly referred to the San Francisco Chronicle series about the Cabazons written by Jonathan Littman, who also used Riconosciuto as a source. He quotes Michael Taylor—who wrote an article with Littman about the Cabazons using "Riconosciuto's claims,"—as saying "we had to throw out tons of stuff from Riconosciuto wholesale." Unfortunately, Littman did not throw out enough. But as he later told an associate, he almost got a Pulitzer Prize for his Cabazon series. Whether that was a Littman fantasy or reality, apparently even truth is to be sacrificed for a prize.

In describing "organizations that disseminate conspiracy theories," Bertlet concluded that they "tend to reinforce one another . . . (and) have started sort of a referral service: they all reinforce one another. So what you are doing is chasing a rumor around a closed circle." That closed circle, and the journalists running around in it, telling more and more outlandish tales, came close to destroying the rebirth of a people, the Cabazon nation.

GAMING AND CRIME

While state officials and Congresspersons and their "friends" in Nevada and Atlantic City still run the organized crime boogeyman flag up the flagpole, it is clear Indian gaming is the most scrutinized and regulated gaming in the country. In testimony before the U.S. Senate's Select Committee on Indian Affairs on March 18, 1992, the Department of Justice tried to make it clear that some folks were straining to make an organized-crime-infiltration mountain out of a molehill.

Paul L. Maloney, the Senior Counsel for Policy, Criminal Division of the Department of Justice, told members of the Select Committee of the Justice Department's vigilance in keeping Indian gaming clean and free of criminality. In his testimony, Maloney asserted that the "perception in the media and elsewhere that Indian gaming operations are rife with serious criminality does not stand up under close examination."

Maloney's testimony tells the true story:

Under analysis, the contention breaks down into three assertions—that the tribal games have been infiltrated by organized crime families; that they have been victimized by criminal elements not associated with the major crime families; or that the tribes are conducting illegal gaming.

Insofar as organized crime is concerned, the Department of Justice believes that to date there has not been a widespread or successful effort by organized crime to infiltrate Indian gaming operations. For several years the FBI has focused its efforts on monitoring those organizations and their associates to apprehend them as they engage in illegal activity or attempt to infiltrate legitimate enterprises. This kind of investigation revealed the attempt—which did not succeed—to infiltrate the gaming operation of the Rincon Band in California that I informed you last time resulted in the indictment of ten men on charges of racketeering, extortion, mail fraud and wire fraud. The FBI, moreover, informs me that there are at present fewer than five open investigations of organized crime family activity relating to gaming on Indian lands. As monitoring those families is one of the FBI's highest priorities, I am confident that should evidence of federal crime develop it will be fully investigated and referred to the United States Attorneys for appropriate action.

Furthermore, there has also been little evidence of criminal activity committed by criminal elements not associated with the major organized crime families. Again, on those occasions when such allegations have been brought to our attention, they have been investigated, and when sufficient evidence is developed for conviction, we have not hesitated to prosecute. One such case is that of the Indian official who skimmed the receipts of his tribe's bingo hall. I am informed that there are a handful of investigations into allegations of similar misconduct now being conducted.

Finally, we come to the assertion of "illegal gaming." This label also covers different kinds of regulatory violations. One set is gaming that is not operated under tribal auspices, and therefore cannot be legal under any circumstances. To my knowledge, all such operations have been shut down.

Although few stories were published about the truth of the relative "crime free" status of Indian gaming, the information has been easily obtainable.

In reviewing the multiplicity of disinformation and outright lies contained in a sea of stories about the Cabazons, it seemed probable that more was involved than total reliance on stories generated by *The Desert Sun*'s reporter John Hussar. The questions kept reverberating: How could reporters and editors keep repeating this material without other sources? What other source could give them a degree of confidence that what they were publishing contained facts and truth as well as protection from possible libel suits? Those questions created serious puzzlement, especially when two prestigious law firms, representing newspapers, declined to honor the Tribe's demand for retraction of libelous information. The puzzle began to unravel in mid-1993.

In footnote 222 of the U.S. House of Representatives Report 102-857, the Inslaw Affair Investigative Report by the Committee on the Judiciary, dated September 10, 1992, there appeared this reference:

> According to a law enforcement police report on file with committee, Dr. Brian together with Michael Riconosciuto, among others, attended a weapons demonstration at Lake Cauchilla [Cahuilla] gun range in Indio, CA during the evening of September 10, 1981. See Riverside County District Attorney's Office Special Operations Report, October 10, 1991, pp. 2-4 (on file with the committee).

The footnote concluded:

> The continuing intersection of the names of Michael Riconosciuto, Dr. Earl Brian, Robert Booth Nichols and the Cabazon Indian Reservation are certainly intriguing and curious "associations" but without the requisite degree of causation and factual convergence necessary to draw conclusions at this time into potential wrongdoing in the INSLAW matter.

In a March 16, 1993, letter to Riverside County District Attorney Grover Trask, a request was made by Tribal Chairman John James for a copy of that Special Operations Report and for "any other 'public records' as that term is defined under the 'California Public Records Act.'" In a response dated seven days later, the Tribe was informed by Assistant Chief Investigator Allan W. Lynch of Trask's office that the District Attorney's Office was "declining to release any report and or records." Cited as the basis for declination were provisions of California Codes. In a follow-up letter, the Tribe requested clarification as to the specific provisions on which reliance was placed for their declination.

(California law requires that each of its agencies "shall determine within 10 days after the receipt of such request [for a copy of records] whether to comply . . . and shall immediately notify the person making the request of such determination and the reasons therefore." In "unusual circumstances" the response time "may be extended by written notice by the head of the agency to the person making the request. . . . No such notice shall specify a date that would result in an extension for more than 10 working days.")

After receiving the Tribe's follow-up letter, District Attorney Trask, himself, called tribal offices and asked the Assistant to the Tribe's Chief Executive Officer who it was in the DA's office that had responded to the Tribe's first letter. Although he was given the answer he sought, and was sent one other letter from the Tribe's attorney requesting a response, only silence has emanated from the DA's office.

In a related search for documents, the Tribe sent another letter, dated May 6, 1993, to the Riverside County Sheriff Cois Byrd under the same California Public Records Act. That letter requested copies of documents related to:

1. Raids conducted against gambling facilities on the Cabazon Indian Reservation on or about October 18, 1980 and in May 1981, and the execution of a search warrant on the Reservation on or about 8/5/81;
2. Complaints filed between October 1980 and April 1984, with the Sheriff's Department by tribal members and/or staff (namely, John P. Nichols, John Paul Nichols, Philip Nichols, Mark Nichols, Robert Nichols) regarding acts against the tribe, its members and/or staff and its property(ies), including, but not limited to Sheriff's Department Case No. VC181182009, initially investigated by Detective John T. Swearingen;
3. Report(s) filed by either of the following members of the Sheriff's Department regarding the death of Alfred M. Alvarez on and/or subsequent to the date of the finding of Alfred M. Alvarez on 7/1/81, namely, Deputy Vaughn, Det. Mapula, Swearingen, Det. Lasiter, Lt. Landy, Lt. Conroy, Inv. Burge and Garcia, Sgt. Carlson, I.D. Technician Reyes, Evelyn Raygor, Jerry Hopf, and Robert L. Drake;
4. Accessible records and/or reports regarding the life style, drug use and/or sales of drugs by Alvarez, Patricia R. Castro, Ralph Arthur Boger, and/or the husband of Castro and investigative reports;
5. Complaints filed regarding threats made against members of the Nichols family by a Mr. Jimmy Hughes, the theft of finger printing equipment and filing cabinets and files subsequent to his being fired, as well as complaints and investigative reports of damage done by Hughes to the homes of Brenda James and Charles Welmas during the period of January through May 1984;
6. Information given to any member of the press regarding items 1–5, above, including the identity of the person(s) to whom such information was transmitted.

To date, there has been no response by the Sheriff's office. On June 8, 1993, the Tribe's attorney wrote the Sheriff reminding him of "the clear time requirements specified in the law." Still, no response. Why would officials sworn to uphold the law violate the law by withholding documents?

A partial answer may have been provided in the Report of Special Counsel Nicholas J. Bua to the Attorney General of the United States regarding "The Allegations of Inslaw, Inc." The report, dated March 1993, was transmitted to the Congress by Associate Attorney General Webster L. Hubbell on June 17, 1993, requesting their comments by August 1, 1993. One section of Bua's report is of special interest. It deals with the varied allegations of Michael Riconosciuto and the Riverside County District Attorney's Office Special Operations Report, referred to earlier. That section reads:

(ii) The September 10, 1991 Weapons Demonstration

The House Committee Report said that it was aware of a Riverside, California police report that indicated that Earl Brian was present at a shooting demonstration at the Lake Cahuilla gun range in Indio, California on September 10, 1981. According to the police report, the purpose of the demonstration was to test a new night vision device (of the type that the joint venture was trying to market). The report identifies by name 16 people who were present at the gun range (and four police officers who were in the surrounding hills conducting surveillance), including Peter Zokosky, Michael Riconosciuto, John Nichols, Art Welmas, Sam Cross and Earl Brian. (Brian's presence at this demonstration would be significant because he has steadfastly denied ever having been to the Cabazon reservation, or ever having met Riconosciuto or any one affiliated with the Cabazons.)

We located the report to which the Committee referred. It is a singularly unusual document. It is a four page report on a "Special Operations Report" form. Under the heading "Subject" it lists "Cabazon Indians." The title of the report is "Nicaraguans and Earl Brian at Lake Cahuilla-9/10/81." The typing date of the report, however, is ten years later, on "10/10/91." Although the word "intelligence" appears at the top of the first page, from a quick reading of the report one is given the impression that it is a surveillance report. This results, in part, from the fact that the report lists no informants or sources, or in any other way indicates that the information in the report is something other than a law enforcement officer's observations. Also, the report contains various license plate numbers and automobile registrations for the cars that were observed at the demonstration, just as one would expect to find in a regular police surveillance report.

We were intrigued by this report, and thought it might be the key to our finding evidence that would corroborate Riconosciuto. Such was not the case. What we found was that all the information in that report, save for the license plate numbers and the registrations, came from Riconosciuto.

The report was prepared by Gene Gilbert, an investigator for the Riverside, California District Attorney's Office. We interviewed Gilbert. He told us that he prepared the report in 1991 after interviewing Riconosciuto in jail. He said that the purpose of the interview was to find out if Riconosciuto could provide any information about an unsolved murder that happened in Indio in 1981. He said that he had obtained the license plate and registration information from Dave Baird, a former Indio police officer who was present at the demonstration, and who had saved this information over the years.

The Riverside County District Attorney's Office was not pleased with all the attention this report had brought to them. The problem was that *the report had been leaked, and virtually every reporter interested in the Inslaw case had a copy of it, as did many private citizens.*[38] ([38] Material Omitted Pursuant to Fed. R. Crim. P. 6 (e) which states that matters occurring before the grand jury, which are described in several places in this report, cannot be disclosed without leave of the Chief Judge of the district court.) When we met with Gilbert he told us words to the effect of "if I had known what a stir it would cause I would have left Earl Brian's name out, because he has nothing to do with the murder investigation." We found it difficult to believe that the mention of Earl Brian's name was coincidental. For example, we asked Gilbert why he put Earl Brian's name in the title of the report. He said it was because Brian was a new name to the investigation. When we pointed out that there were a lot of names in the report that were new to his investigation, Gilbert had no explanation as to why their names were not in the title. We also never received an explanation as to why *Gilbert did not mention Riconosciuto in the report as the source of the information*, or why Gilbert created a separate report concerning everything else Riconosciuto told him in the interview. (Emphasis added.)

Gilbert told us that after he began to get numerous inquiries from the press about the report, it became apparent to him that the name in the report that everybody was most interested in was Earl Brian. He said at that point he decided to see if anybody besides Riconosciuto would say Earl Brian was there. Gilbert then went to see Dave Baird, the officer from whom he had obtained the license plate numbers. After meeting with Baird, Gilbert prepared another report saying that he had shown Baird a photograph of Brian, and that Baird had identified Brian as being one of the individuals at the gun range on September 10, 1981. We went to see Dave Baird. That is not what he told us.

Dave Baird is now a Riverside County Deputy Sheriff. During 1981 he was an officer with the Indio Police Department. He told us that shortly before September 10, 1981, he was told by Police Chief Sam Cross that City Manager Phil Hawes had arranged for a demonstration by the Cabazons to take place at the Lake Cahuilla gun range. Baird said that Hawes and Cross asked him to be present at the demonstration to determine if the Cabazons engaged in any illegal activities involving automatic weapons. He said that when he went to the demonstration he was suspicious about what was going on, and so he memorized the license plates of some of the cars that were there. When the demonstration was over he checked the registrations of the plates he had memorized. He obtained a copy of the registration printouts he ran.

One of the cars at the demonstration was a Rolls Royce that belonged to a real estate developer named Wayne Reeder. According to Riconosciuto (as reported in Gilbert's first report), Wayne Reeder arrived with Earl Brian. Baird said that he remembered that Reeder did arrive with someone, but that he didn't know who it was. Baird's handwritten notes that he made when he originally ran the registrations, however, refer only to Wayne Reeder in the Rolls Royce. (The absence of such an indication in his notes is significant, because his notes for other cars indicate that they had multiple occupants in them.)

We then asked Baird if he had previously told investigator Gilbert that the other occupant was Earl Brian. Baird said he had not. Baird told us that Gilbert showed him a poor quality photocopy of a picture in a magazine, which Gilbert said was Earl Brian. Baird told us that the most he could say was that the person in the magazine photograph had the same general physical characteristics as the person who was with Reeder. (Given the nature of the identification attempted by Gilbert—a one person photo "show-up" ten years after the witness saw the subject on one occasion, at dusk—we suspect that even a positive identification by Baird would be inadmissible in court.) When asked what those physical characteristics were, Baird said, "large, middle-aged, white, male." We then asked Baird if he thought he could identify Brian if we showed him a clear photograph of Brian taken in 1981. He said that the most he ever would be able to say was whether the person had the same general physical characteristics as the occupant of the car. This hardly constitutes an identification of Brian.

We also spoke with Peter Zokosky (Material Omitted Pursuant to Fed. R. Crim. P 6, [e]), Wayne Reeder, John Nichols, and Art Welmas, all of whom were at the September 10, 1981 demonstration. While they have somewhat conflicting recollections of the event (For example, Reeder recalls that he had a date that night, and for that reason believes he came alone. Zokosky also recalls Reeder having to get to a date that night, but says that he thinks he drove Reeder there, and that's why Reeder couldn't get to his date until the demonstration was done. It seems more likely that Zokosky is mistaken, given that Baird is quite certain he saw Reeder's car there, and in fact "ran" Reeder's license plates), they all agree on one point: Earl Brian was not there. When asked if there were any people at the shooting they did not know, they mentioned only some unidentified Spanish speaking men that Nichols had invited, all of whom were Hispanic and do not fit Brian's description. We also talked to Scott Westley of the Pickitinny Arsenal, who Riconosciuto identified as being there. He absolutely denies being at the demonstration. Given that Westley makes no attempt to hide the fact that he met on occasion with the people from the joint venture, it seems he would have little motive to lie about whether he was at this demonstration.

In summary, Riconosciuto's allegation that Earl Brian was at the demonstration at the Lake Cahuilla gun range does not withstand scrutiny. The credible evidence is overwhelming that Brian was not there. Moreover, we obtained considerable evidence tending to show that Brian was in his New York office on September 10, 1981. We obtained a copy of Brian's personal calendar from 1981. In it is the handwriting of Brian's former personal assistant. The personal assistant's writing, (Material Omitted Pursuant to Fed. R. Crim. P. 6 [e]) indicates that Brian flew from Washington to New York on the afternoon of September 9, and that she (the personal assistant) ordered a limousine to take Brian between his New York office and his home on September 10. Brian's expense records, including an airline receipt for the trip from Washington to New York, indicate that the calendar is accurate for that week.

(iii) **Riconosciuto's March 29, 1981 Arrest**

Riconosciuto and others have suggested that the timing of his 1991 arrest on drug charges, coming as it did only eight days after he executed his affidavit in the Inslaw case, demonstrates that the government was retaliating against him for his testimony. As already noted above, Riconosciuto's defense at this drug trial was that he was being framed by the government.

We reviewed the entire transcript of Riconosciuto's trial, along with many of the DEA [Drug Enforcement Agency] reports, and spoke with the Assistant United States Attorneys who prosecuted the case against Riconosciuto. We are convinced beyond all doubt that there was absolutely no connection between Riconosciuto's prosecution and his allegations in the Inslaw matter. The fact of the matter is that the case that resulted in Riconosciuto's arrest and prosecution began as a local drug investigation by Washington State authorities. As part of that investigation a small time methamphetamine dealer began to cooperate with the police. It was only after the local authorities determined that the supplier of the cooperating drug dealer was distributing on a large scale, that they decided to call in the Seattle office of the DEA to assist in the investigation. There is no evidence that anybody from Washington, D.C., either from DOJ [Department of Justice] or elsewhere, had anything to do with the prosecution of Riconosciuto in Tacoma [Washington].

In addition, the evidence against Riconosciuto at trial was overwhelming. The DEA in that case captured Riconosciuto delivering methamphetamine on videotape on more than one occasion. The testimony also established that Riconosciuto was running a large methamphetamine lab at the property where he was living. Riconosciuto testified that the case was a set up, that the DEA had altered the videotapes to make it appear that he was where he wasn't, that the government had altered telephone records, and that his lab was only for mining metals, not for making drugs. It is not surprising that the jury rejected this testimony. It was as unbelievable then as it is now. (Claiming that he is the victim of a frame-up is nothing new to Riconosciuto. When he was arrested, tried and convicted on PCP charges in the early 1970s, Riconosciuto's defense was that someone had planted the PCP on him.) Even the judge commented at sentencing that he was not sure whether Riconosciuto could tell fact from fiction. (Material Omitted Pursuant to Fed R. Crim. P. 6 [e].)

Riconosciuto (along with two local gadflies) filed a lawsuit purporting to challenge the authority of this investigation. Included within the bizarre allegations of the lawsuit were claims that I was involved in various organized crime murders and that one of the FBI agents assigned to the case had murdered the journalist Danny Casolaro. Riconosciuto also claimed that my staff had threatened to kill him, and that he and his family were in danger. (Riconosciuto's lawsuit was subsequently dismissed by the district court as patently frivolous. Riconosciuto v. Bua, No. 92 C 6217 [U.S.D.C. N.D. Ill.].) (Material Omitted Pursuant to Fed. R. Crim. P. 6[e].)

In analyzing Riconosciuto's allegations we have attempted to focus on the substance of his claims and whether they are supported or contradicted by other evidence. We cannot entirely ignore certain general credibility issues, however. Riconosciuto was involved with hallucinogenic drugs at least as far back as 1972, when he was convicted on a PCP charge. In addition to that charge (Material Omitted . . .) and his 1992 drug conviction, NCIC [records indicate he also has burglary and bail jumping convictions from the early 1970s.]

Most people who know Riconosciuto told us that he displays a high degree of familiarity with scientific and technical concepts. None of the people we talked to, however, could confirm the extraordinary claims Riconosciuto makes about his past exploits. He claims, for example, to have worked with the CIA, to have developed a radio detonator device used to overthrow the Allende government in Chile, to have patented various revolutionary devices, to have recovered computer data from computers damaged during the overthrow of the Shah, to have personally been involved in handling the so-called "October Surprise" payments, and to have convinced certain organized crime members associated with Tony Accardo (a now deceased head of the Chicago mob) not to commit a murder. We came across no credible witness who could confirm any of this.

In conclusion, we found Riconosciuto to be a totally unreliable witness in connection with the allegations he has made about the alleged theft of PROMIS software. Riconosciuto's story about PROMIS reminds us of a historical novel; a tale of total fiction woven against the background of accurate historical facts. For example, it is true that there was a Wackenhut-Cabazon joint venture, and that there was a demonstration in September 1981 at a gun range in Indio. The overwhelming weight of the evidence, however, is that Earl Brian had nothing to do with either of these events. Riconosciuto's efforts to place Brian at the Cabazon reservation and at the center of a conspiracy to steal PROMIS do not withstand any level of scrutiny. (Emphasis added.)

As valuable as is the Bua report, it does not provide comprehensive answers to the questions that are still puzzling. It is to be hoped that the Tribe's continuing search for truth will provide those answers. If official records are made available and not destroyed, the truth will emerge. And, it will emerge sooner if non-Indian leaders can divorce their mind-sets from an anti-human past, and look toward the creation of a new century really devoted to the well-being of all humankind.

What the Bua report does, it is hoped, is to alert journalists to the continuing truth that "leaked" documents from law enforcement agencies too often serve only the narrow interests of some actors in law enforcement and not the search for truth. Although, at this writing, we cannot identify how many of the journalists who wrote disinformation and even the "insane" articles about the Cabazons based their articles on Gilbert's so-called Special Operations Report, it would not be surprising to find that most or even all did. We also do not know how many other such bogus reports have been "leaked" to journalists. How many "Gilberts" and "Special Reports" have been floated? Unfortunately, even at this writing only the tip of a potential iceberg of lies and other distortions of truth is exposed to public view, which is a tragedy for the Cabazons, other Indian tribes and non-Indians alike.

What have been the critical issues that have driven the conflicts between the Cabazons and non-Indian officialdom for a decade and a half? Although there were many, two have been central and overriding: (1) The right of non-Whites to access capital and wealth, and (2) the definition of patriotism.

ACCESS TO CAPITAL AND WEALTH

Let's return briefly to the mid-1800s, to the discovery of Sutter's Mill gold, to the organization of California as a new state, to the insistence of its new leadership that the Treaty of Guadalupe Hidalgo be dishonored, that the Indians be driven from this new state, and to the dishonorable actions of an unelected U.S. Senate in refusing to ratify 18 treaties with California Indian tribes. The issue then and now is the same.

The invading Europeans believed that only they, the then-aliens, had the God-given as well as legal right to the land and the minerals under the land; in short, the right to capital and to whatever of value that could be converted to capital. Even in the dishonored treaty negotiated by Indian Agent O. M. Wozencraft, and signed by "the Chiefs, Captains and Head Men of the San Louis Rey, Kah-we-as [sp] and the Co-com-cah-ras tribes of Indians" on January 5, 1852, the reservation lands reserved "to the government of the United States all minerals found thereon."

In this regard, little has changed in America. Too many of the philosophical descendants of those "invading" Californians of a century and a half ago still occupy positions of power and influence in California and America. They are true believers that only they should have the right to access to and possession of capital, capital equivalent and wealth. And they become confused and upset when others—especially non-White others—assert their right to access.

A few decades ago, for example, what is now legal in many states—the lottery—was illegal. Then it was called the "numbers game" or the "numbers racket," depending on who was making the characterization. Thousands of people served jail time for being "numbers runners" or "numbers bankers." To many poor people the numbers game meant jobs or, to the lucky few, extra income to buy things their low salaries would not afford. To others, it meant a loan from the "numbers banker," a loan that "legitimate" bankers would not make, to open a small business.

Then two decades or so ago the "numbers racket" became legal and respectable. Why? Well, it was believed that Black Americans, as had Italians, Jewish and other minority Americans, were getting access to capital, opening businesses, sending children to colleges and forcing an end to Black-only apartheid. The solution devised for this "problem" was to legalize the "numbers racket" and funnel these billions of dollars through the hands of representatives of the only Americans who—in their minds—should have access to capital and wealth.

What happened to the "numbers game" is now being devised for Indian gaming. Reading the disinformation and propaganda from spokespersons and politicians defending Nevada and Atlantic City gaming interests can be a nauseating experience. One of their favorite ploys, for example, is to spread fear that Indian gaming will result in widespread prostitution. They never couple that propaganda with the fact that prostitution is legal in Nevada. To them the bottom line is the same: Indians have no right to access to capital and wealth, especially potential wealth and capital of this magnitude; thus, Indian gaming must end.

PATRIOTISM

Those Americans who remain committed to a republican form of government define patriotism differently than other Americans. They are patriotic to the concept of a country that serves the best interests of the privileged few, not the many. They question the wisdom and efficacy of America, the democracy.

The Cabazons and the Nichols family and many Indian tribes define patriotism another way. They are patriotic to a country that serves the best interests of the many, as expressed in the Bill of Rights and other Constitutional Amendments, not the few. They would question the wisdom and efficacy of America the republic. Art Welmas, John James and Gene Welmas, among many other American Indians, served the country they believed adhered to the Bill of Rights, not one that served only the few. Dr. Nichols believed so passionately in the concept of democracy he spent most of his life, often at great danger to that life, trying to bring its benefits to working people and desperately poor people in and out of his own country.

It was and is inevitable that whenever forces with such diametrically opposed definitions of America and patriotism meet, there will be conflict. It may also be inevitable that until America's leadership changes, the powers of law enforcement will continue to be misused to undermine America's majority and the forces moving America towards greater democracy and greater sharing of capital and wealth.

Perhaps Thomas Jefferson said it best:

I am convinced that those societies (as the Indians) which live without government enjoy in their general mass an infinitely greater degree of happiness than those who live under the European governments. Among the former, public opinion is in the place of law, and restrains morals as powerfully as laws ever did anywhere. Among the latter, under pretense of governing, they have divided their nations into two classes, wolves and sheep. I do not exaggerate.

This is a true picture of Europe. Cherish, therefore, the spirit of our people, and keep alive their intention. Do not be too severe upon their errors, but reclaim them by enlightening them. *If once they become inattentive to the public affairs, you and I, and Congress and assemblies, judges and governors shall all become wolves.* It seems to be the law of our general nature, in spite of individual exceptions: and experience declares that man is the only animal which devours his own kind; for I can apply no milder term to the governments of Europe, and *to the general prey of the rich on the poor.* (Emphasis added.)

On June 12, 1993 *The Desert Sun* reported:

The Cabazon Band of Mission Indians chose to stay with the same leaders in an election participated in by 20 of the tribe's 21 eligible voters [a 95% rate of participation].

Tribal Chairman John James was re-elected for another four-year term.

Also re-elected Wednesday were Tribal Business Committee members Brenda Soulliere, first vice chairman; Charles Welmas, second vice chairman; Virginia Nichols, secretary-treasurer; Elisa Welmas, general liaison; and John Welmas, member at large.

Postscript

Towards a New Century

From the early days, when development was only "a hope and a determination," according to John James, Art, Gene and Sammy Welmas in the Tribal Council minutes, as the Tribe worked and brainstormed with Pro Plan to develop the Ten Year Plan, it was never intended that gaming would be all there is. That is why they took risks and supported the Nichols "tribe" in taking risks and pursuing any legal opportunity that seemed possible and appropriate. That spirit now lives in the young turks who followed and currently run the tribal entities.

Among other tribal projects, Colmac, a 48-megawatt biomass power plant that burns agricultural wastes, municipal wood residues and tree prunings, and waste from mills such as sawmills and pallet-making mills, is currently the only occupant of the Tribe's Mecca Heights Industrial Park. Colmac produces and sells to Southern California Edison enough electricity for 45,000 housing units.

Colmac will soon be joined by three additional environmentally safe operations. One will utilize what is known as a bioremediation process to reprocess and clean petroleum contaminated soil. Another operation, a thermal desorber process, will remove hydrocarbon molecules from the soil. And a third operation will convert biosolids into usable soil amendments for use by the agriculture industry.

When all operations are on line, the Tribe will be able to share with the nation one of the few—if not the only—industrial parks fully devoted to industries solely created to clean the nation's environment.

A major expansion of the Bingo Palace and Casino is now under way, its size to be tripled to 116,000 square feet. In addition to enlarging its current operational space, the expansion will add another restaurant, a lounge for live entertainment, and banquet and meeting facilities.

Adjoining the Casino in an attractive setting will be two man-made lakes, a shell-amphitheater in a park-like setting, and a family entertainment complex that will include miniature golf, batting cages, a Ferris wheel, food shops and other amenities for family enjoyment. Close by will be a 40-acre RV Resort with 300 spaces for vehicles. The Tribe plans to invest upwards of $20 million for this expansion and the family entertainment center. And while this expansion is being completed, a study will be undertaken to determine if a 300-bed motel should be added. All of these additions will complement the existing Swap Meet, Players Restaurant and day care facilities already in place. The Tribe, in truth, is making the desert bloom.

A question often asked is: What are the benefits to tribal members? In addition to having equal ownership of the entire development, the tribe enjoys these benefits:

Employment—Every member who wants a job and can and will work is guaranteed employment, including whatever special training is required. But nobody is paid who refuses to work within his/her capacity. If special distributions are voted on and approved, every adult member gets an equal share, and special shares are placed in trust for non-adult members.

Education—The Tribe will pay all expenses for public and/or private education, including day care through graduate education, as long as grades are in an acceptable range. When appropriate, living and transportation expenses are paid by the tribe. The Tribe has even paid the educational expenses for members' children that do not meet the tribe's blood-quantum requirements. For example, although Linda Alvarez Streeter-Dukic's daughter does not meet the Tribe's blood-quantum requirement, the tribe has always helped pay for her college education.

Day Care—Day care services are paid for any tribal member needing day care.

Health Care—Every tribal member is covered by complete, top quality, independent health insurance. All members are fully covered for medical, dental and vision care.

Housing—The planned Indian Sands Housing Project is a planned community to cover 220 acres, with a projected 944 units for sale. Seventeen custom homes have already been reserved for tribal members on oversized sites.

What a departure from the scene that greeted John Paul Nichols when he first set foot on Cabazon land more than a year after his father arrived. As he said, "there were no buildings on the reservation whatsoever. There was, I think, a mobile home, or a trailer rather, on a section of the reservation owned by Joe Benitez, and an older home owned by Willie Callaway, the then Vice-Chairman, on his piece of land, *nothing on tribal land. No facilities, no water*, especially *no development whatsoever, just dry desert land.* The tribal office at that point in time was a rented, two-room office on Miles Avenue in downtown Indio. . . . It wasn't even close to Indio at the time. . . . We had to think of some way to attract people out here. There was no conceivable business that could have succeeded other than one that didn't already exist closer to town." (Emphasis added.)

The Cabazon Band of Mission Indians has traversed the bridge that leads from nothingness to victory, from addiction to sobriety, and from hope to realization of dreams. Every member interviewed said the secret ingredient was unity at the core, the center, the moral center that demanded honor, and that always produced unity at the core. It was often painful and family-rending to fight off what Art Welmas always called "the turn-coats." But even when some were in the grip of addiction, the honor-demanding moral center produced both individual and group unity sufficient to be victorious.

As the Tribe moves with the rest of the world inexorably toward the new century, it will only be that unity, that moral center, that honor, that will sustain them and preserve their successes for their children. And that can only happen if their children are grounded in the truth of how the bridges were traversed in a hostile environment, among government officials whose philosophical ancestors go back at least to those first California officials who demanded their removal, or their deaths.

The State is simply more sophisticated now in its Indian "hunts," its Indian targets now being those who have dared to risk all to create tribal wealth. And, of course, one way to defeat Indian gaming is to make it universally available.

From this author's point of view, in addition to retaining their moral center, maintaining inter-generational understanding and a grounding in the truth of their history, the Cabazons must continue the diversification of their enterprises, focusing on industries of the future, and the Tribe must move to protect itself from yellow journalism in the hands of its enemies. Tribal ownership and control of a means of mass communication is the key to insuring that its story—its truth—can always be told when and as many times as it wants or needs to tell it. In an age wherein fewer and fewer alternative sources of information are available, any minority group that can afford it should purchase control of radio or television entities to preserve its precious First Amendment rights.

Two "tribes" met in Indio, California, and the desert bloomed. As long as wise investment, guided by integrity, is made for future generations, and the two tribes' moral centers remain intact, there is no reason the land of their peoples should not go on blooming.

Selected Bibliography

BOOKS

Abourezk, James G. *Advise and Dissent: Memoirs of South Dakota and the U.S. Senate*. Chicago: Lawrence Hill, 1989.

The Annals of America, Vols. 18 20. Chicago: Encyclopedia Britannica, 1977.

Commager, Henry Steele and Elmo Giordanetti, eds. Was America a Mistake? New York: Harper & Row, 1967.

Garrow, David. *Bearing The Cross: Martin Luther King, Jr. and the Southern Christian Leadership Conference.* New York: Vantage Books, 1986.

Terrell, John Tipton. *Land Grab: The Truth About the Winning of the West.* New York: Dial Press, 1972.

SELECTED CABAZON TRIBAL MINUTES

February 10, 1963; January 1966; May 6, 1967; September 21, 1967; March 25, 1973; September 6, 1975; September 25, 1976; October 23, 1976; May 14, 1977; September 10, 1977; December 10, 1977; April 29, 1978; September 16, 1978; September 30, 1978; October 28, 1978; November 4, 1978; November 25, 1978; January 6, 1979; January 27, 1979; March 10, 1979; June 2, 1979; June 27, 1979; September 8, 1979; September 21, 1979; November 1, 1979; January 3, 1980; January 31, 1980; February 9, 1980; May 24, 1980; July 22, 1980; September 11, 1980; November 12, 1980; November 15, 1980; January 7, 1981; March 5, 1981; April 29, 1981; June 6, 1981; October 21, 1981; August 24, 1982; March 7, 1985; May 2, 1982; April 30, 1991; July 16, 1991; March 29, 1993

SELECTED CABAZON TRIBAL LETTERS

June 8, 1966 to BIA

November 14, 1966, BIA to Tribe regarding membership roll

November 29, 1967 to John James from Leroy Alvarez regarding lowering blood quantum

October 15, 1978, Joseph Benitez to General Council regarding Dr. Nichols

June 1, 1980, Benitez to General Council

September 23, 1980, Tribe to Benitez

May 11, 1981, Arthur Welmas to local Congresspersons and California's Senators

SELECTED OTHER LETTERS

September 11, 1978, Gordon Law, Assistant and Science Advisor to U.S. Department of Interior Secretary, to Dr. Randolph T. Blackwell, Director, U.S. Department of Commerce, Office of Minority Business Enterprise (OMBE)

November 19, 1979, to Tribe from Chief Enforcement Agent, Connecticut Department of Revenue Services, regarding Jenkins Act

April 9, 1981, from Intersect Vice President and Director R. Barry Asby, regarding authorization for conveyance and use of night vision equipment

April 14, 1982, Defense Investigative Service to Tribe re: eligibility determination for security clearance

December 18, 1982, DIS regarding progress report

July 29, 1983, DIS regarding granting of security clearance

October 27, 1982, Appeal by Glenn Feldman, Tribal Attorney, to SBA finding that the Tribal Joint Venture with Wackenhut was "not an eligible small business concern..."

June 6, 1984, WSI to CIS-WSI Joint Venture terminating Joint Venture

SELECTED MEMORANDA, REPORTS AND RESOLUTIONS

May 25, 1981, Wackenhut Inter-office Memo regarding WSI-CSI Joint Venture Activities

July 1&2, 1981, Reports by Coroner and Investigator of the Riverside County Coroner's Office regarding murder of Fred Alvarez and companions

June 29, 1983, to Tribe from SBA Attorney Advisor regarding Tribe's appeal to SBA Size Appeals Board

"Inslaw Affair Investigative Report, Committee on the Judiciary," U.S. House of Representatives, Report 102-857, September 10, 1992.

"The Allegations of Inslaw, Inc.," Report of Special Counsel Nicholas J. Bua to the Attorney General of the United States, March 1993, submitted June 17, 1993.

Resolutions: RIV-67-34; RIV-67-35; RIV-67-37; RIV-67-63; RIV-18-79

ARTICLES

"Anti-gambling Lungren takes Casino Funding." *The Desert Sun*, No. 298 (May 29, 1993): A1.

"Attorney General Should Avoid Even Appearance of Conflict in Dealing With Gambling Issues." *The Desert Sun,* Number 302, June 2, 1993, A10.

"Business Roundtable: New Lobbying Force." *Congressional Quarterly*, (September, 1977): 1964-1968.

"Casino Okay Given to Dresser." *Daily News*, no. 257 (January 3, 1979): 1, 2.

"Carter Pardon." *Congressional Quarterly*, (January 29, 1977): 177.

"Casino Permit Winners to Hedge Bets." *Press Enterprise*, (January 4, 1979): 1, 2.

"Characteristics of Members of 95th Congress." *Congressional Quarterly*, (January 1, 1977): 19.

Chip Berlet, "Judgment Call: Big Stories, Spooky Sources." *Columbia Journalism Review*, (May/June 1993): 67-71.

Daedalus, The Journal of the American Academy of Arts & Science, Fall, 1965.

Golab, Jan. "Indian Giver." *Los Angeles Times* (September 1983).

"Indian Claims Settlement Proposed to Carter," *Congressional Quarterly* (July 23, 1977): 1531, 1532.

"Indians: No Participation." *Congressional Quarterly* (April 30, 1977): 809.

"Jojaba, Its Future is Limitless." *New Directions in Santa Barbara Business*, vol. 1, no. 2 (February 1979): 6-8.

New Spirit Magazine (July-September): 1979.

"Political Notes: Abourezk Retirement." *Congressional Quarterly*, (January 29, 1977): 179.

"The State of Civil Rights, 1976." *U.S. Commission on Civil Rights*, (February 15, 1977).

"Tribal Goal: 'Dismantle the Myths'." *The Desert Sun*, no. 301 (June 14, 1992): A5, A14.

Index

About the Author

A prolific writer, Reverend Lane has been published in such dailies as *The Washington Post* and has received lead editorial treatment by *The Wall Street Journal.* He has authored books, pamphlets and written hundreds of editorials on the major issues of his time.

Reverend Lane also has been a Washington, D.C. radio talk show personality and a political and religious commentator for more than 15 years on Berkeley, California-based Pacifica Foundation's WPFW-FM, a 50,000-watt station in the nation's capitol. He co-anchored Pacifica's national gavel-to-gavel broadcasts of the U.S. Senate confirmation hearings on the nominations of David Souter and Clarence Thomas to the U.S. Supreme Court. He also co-anchored "America: Never Again For White Males Only" on Pacifica's Los Angeles station KPFK; the program will be published as a book in 1995. He currently serves on Pacifica's board of directors and is a member of its executive committee.

In 1977, Reverend Lane was a founder and incorporator of the Martin Luther King Jr. Community Church Inc., headquartered in Columbia, Maryland. He also was that body's first ordained minister. Envisioning a new century of interfaith worship, he subsequently founded the Martin Luther King Ecumenical Interfaith Congregation Inc. in 1991, headquartered in Ellicott City, Maryland.